THE ARTS ~
WORLD THEMES

THE ARTS~
WORLD THEMES

GERALDINE NAGLE

Wayne County Community College

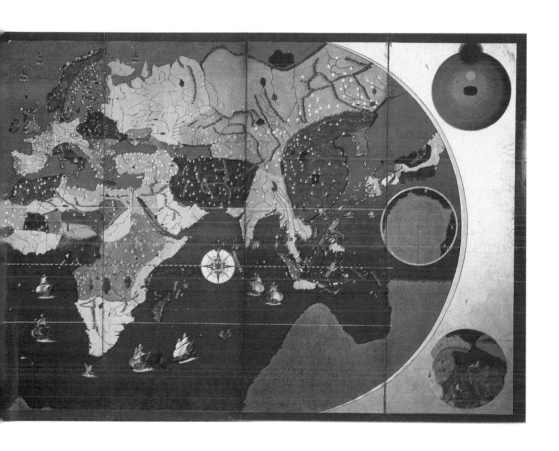

Boston, Massachusetts   Burr Ridge, Illinios   Dubuque, Iowa
Madison, Wisconsin   New York, New York   San Francisco, California   St. Louis, Missouri

McGraw-Hill

A Division of The McGraw·Hill Companies

Book Team

Editor *Kathleen Nietzke Wolkoff*
Developmental Editor *Deborah Daniel Reinbold*
Production Editor *Suzanne M. Guinn*
Photo Editor *Robin Storm*
Permissions Editor *Vicki Krug*
Art Processor *Brenda A. Ernzen*
Visuals/Design Developmental Consultant *Marilyn A. Phelps*
Visuals/Design Freelance Specialist *Mary L. Christianson*
Publishing Services Specialist *Sherry Padden*
Marketing Manager *Steven Yetter*
Advertising Manager *Jodi Rymer*

Vice President and General Manager *Thomas E. Doran*
Editor in Chief *Edgar J. Laube*
Executive Editor *Ed Bartell*
Executive Editor *Stan Stoga*
National Sales Manager *Eric Ziegler*
Director of CourseResource *Kathy Law Laube*
Director of CourseSystems *Chris Rogers*

Director of Marketing *Sue Simon*
Director of Production *Vickie Putman Caughron*
Imaging Group Manager *Chuck Carpenter*
Manager of Visuals and Design *Faye M. Schilling*
Design Manager *Jac Tilton*
Art Manager *Janice Roerig*
Permissions/Records Manager *Connie Allendorf*

President and Chief Executive Officer *G. Franklin Lewis*
Corporate Vice President, President of WCB Manufacturing *Roger Meyer*
Vice President and Chief Financial Officer *Robert Chesterman*

Interior and cover design by Tara Bazata

Customized paging by Denis Dale

Cover Image: Bankoku Sozu Map of the World, 1645. Courtesy of the Kobe City Museum, Kobe, Japan

Inside back cover map: From Arthur Getis, et al., *Introduction to Geography*, 4th ed. Copyright © 1994 Wm. C. Brown Communications, Inc., Dubuque, Iowa. All Rights Reserved. Reprinted by permission (in press)

The following illustrations are by Rolin Graphics, Inc.: Figure 2.1 and text art 4.2, 4.4, 4.6, 4.8, 4.10, 4.12 a and b, 4.14, 4.16, 4.18, 4.20 and 4.22

Photo Research by Kathy Husemann

Table of Contents
p. v top: © Barry Herem; **p. v bottom:** Alisa Mellon Bruce Fund. National Gallery of Art, Washington, D.C.; **p. vi top:** © 1990 Warner Bros. Inc./Nelson Entertainment Film/Icon Distribution Co. All rights reserved; **p. vi bottom:** © Lucas/The Image Works, Inc.; **p. vii top:** HOA-QUI Agency, Paris; **p. vii bottom:** © Jack Vartoogian

Chapter Openers
Opener 1 (left to right): Hirmer Fotoarchiv, Courtesy of Jesus Moroles Studio; **2 (left to right):** Albright-Knox Art Gallery, Buffalo New York. Gift of Seymour H. Knox, 1956. © 1992 ARS, NY/SPADEM, Paris, Philadelphia Museum of Art: Purchased: The Lola Bowin Peck Fund. 70-190-8, © Barry Herem; **3:** Paul Higdon/New York Times Pictures; **4 (clockwise):** Hirmer Fotoarchiv, Hirmer Fotoarchiv, © Wayne Source, © Bathazar Korab, Ltd., © Wayne Source; **5 (clockwise):** CBS Masterworks/Sony Classical Archive, © Eugene Gordon/Photo Researchers, Inc., Wide World Photos, Inc.; **6 (left to right):** © Jack Mitchell, Courtesy of the Glyndebourne Festival Opera © Guy Gravett

Library of Congress Catalog Card Number: 91–78159

ISBN 0–697–12048–1

Printed in the United States of America

20   19   18   17   16   15   14   13   12   11

Contents

CHAPTER THREE
CAMERA ARTS

CHAPTER FOUR
ARCHITECTURE

CHAPTER FIVE

MUSIC

CHAPTER SIX

DRAMA AND DANCE

PREFACE

One influence more than any other helped determine this book's focus and framework: the National Endowment for the Art's most recent Report to the Congress summarizing the status of arts education. NEA statistics reveal that 81 percent of U.S. adults over the age of twenty-four have never had a course in the study of art; 80 percent have never had a course in the study of music; 68 percent were never taken by parents or teachers to a professional performance.

What this means—and what arts and humanities professors understand only too well—is that the arts constitute a neglected and often misunderstood subject. Since for many students, a painting by Rembrandt may be as "foreign" as one by Kuan Tao-Sheng, any division between Western and Non-Western cultures is moot. This book is intended to help make all art less "foreign" by demonstrating its connection with students' own lives.

THEMES AS GLOBAL CONNECTIONS

The Arts: A World Journey is based on themes because these universal human experiences are able to bridge distances of culture, geography, and time. Romantic love, for example, is a theme connecting the recent film *Out of Africa* (page 132) with the nineteenth century opera *La Traviata* (page 314) and the seventeenth century Kabuki drama *A Messenger of Love in Yamato* (page 312). Parental love is another timeless theme evident in Mary Cassatt's nineteenth century painting *The Bath* (page 59) and in Yang Hsien-chih's fourteenth century play *Rain on the Hsiao-Hsiang* (page 308).

As these themes connect, they also reveal certain cultural and historical differences. For this reason, I make frequent use of analogies, comparisons, and contrasts, while encouraging the reader to do the same.

THEMES AS HISTORY

When selecting themes, I adopted precepts of The New Historicism, which emphasizes history as context rather than chronicle. Even a theme as seemingly innocuous as "Portraits" cannot be isolated from its background. Consider, for example, John Singleton Copley's portrait of Paul Revere (page 51). Here is Copley the artist, a Boston bred British sympathizer who cannot wait to get to England, and Revere, a name that jumps off the pages of American history and literature; but the portrait reveals more. Its subtext communicates both men's pride in their respective crafts. Revere chose to pose with his silversmith's tools and holding one example of his work, and Copley used his skill as a painter to capture Revere's self-esteem. This kind of pictorial definition of the work ethic culminates a hundred years later in the Occupational Portraits that followed the advent of photography.

HISTORY, PARALLEL EDITING, AND FLASH-BACKS

Emphasizing context rather than chronicle is not a new idea. In 1903, filmmaker Edwin S. Porter pioneered parallel editing over the strong objections of producers who believed the public could only understand events if they were presented in rigidly ordered time. Today's students—and television viewers generally—are accustomed to the scene shifts resulting from parallel editing. I employ it to establish a greater sense of immediacy. For example in the architecture chapter, scene shifts direct students' attention to two events occuring simultaneously in 1871: the construction of the Paris Opéra as part of Napoleon III's grand plan for the city, and the devastating Chicago fire with its resultant changes in city planning and building safety.

Creative minds rarely follow clock-calendar time, and I believe the study of artists' achievements should be similarly unfettered. Twentieth century architect Frank Lloyd Wright devised his concept of space with the help of a 2500 year flash-back to Lao-Tzu, the founder of Taoism. The twentieth century plays of David Mamet owe much to Molière's eighteenth century comedies of character and manners. In some instances, flash-forwards can provide the definitive framework for comparison. Studying D. W. Griffith's 1915 film *The Birth of A Nation* together with Ken Burn's 1990 television epic *The Civil War* gives students two quite different perspectives on a single historical event.

APPLYING ARTS' LANGUAGE

Because so few students in introductory arts and humanities courses have studied the basic elements, these are introduced, explained, and reviewed in every chapter. First, the elements are introduced by application in much the same way words are introduced conversationally in a foreign language class. Later, the elements are defined and reviewed in a section titled *Language* at the end of every chapter.

The music chapter has a slightly different organization, with the *Language* section ahead of a section titled *Musical Compositions*. What is most noticeable in this chapter is the absence of musical notations: no clefs, notes, or keyboard drawings. I gave much thought to these deletions, and based my decision on the realities of teaching facilities that can lack a tuned piano or a keyboard.

The music chapter is unique in two additional ways. It spreads over into the film chapter and into the drama chapter, where you will find discussions of opera, musical theater, and dance. The chapter also includes, in a brief biography of Glenn Gould (page 263), an explanation of recording methods that are so like film editing. This inclusion highlights two controversial issues: the first a question of authenticity between live performances and recordings; the second, the technology that has changed the way we listen to all music.

OPTIONS AND ANCILLARY MATERIALS

This book does not require a long list of additional materials; neither does it require special tapes. Films are available on standard, commercially distributed videotape. Most dramas are available on videotape and all of them are available in print. Music examples are available on commercially distributed CD and cassette recordings. The following resource materials are available through your Brown & Benchmark representative. A set of 71 **Humanities Transparencies** provides examples of art concepts and media; architectural styles; maps; and musical notation, style, and elements. The **Humanities Slide Bank** allows instructors to order reasonably priced customized slide sets through SANDAK, Inc. **Culture 1.0** © is a 7-disk software program developed by Cultural Resources, Inc., for the interdisciplinary humanities course and is available in IBM PC or Macintosh format. The text includes pronunciation keys, a suggested reading list, and a glossary.

An accompanying Instructor's Manual/Test Item File includes a number of optional aids. One aid is *Suggestions for Students Writing about the Arts.* This aid lists and explains the six most common forms of writing assignments given in introductory arts and humanities classes. It is intended to enrich students' grasp of composition by demonstrating ways they can tap into their own creativity.

Another aid consists of chapter summaries that highlight central ideas. A third aid consists of a set of discussion/essay questions for each chapter. These are of three types: questions pertaining directly to the chapter under study; questions pertaining to two or more chapters; questions requiring outside reading, research, or projects related to information in the chapter. The last aid is the Test Item File that consists of a set of objective test questions with answers for every chapter. The Test Item File is also available on **TestPak 3.0,** Brown & Benchmark's computerized testing service that provides instructors with either a mail-in/call-in testing program or the complete test item file on diskette in IBM PC, Apple, or Macintosh format. **GradePak** is part of TestPak and provides a computerized grade management system for instructors.

ACKNOWLEDGMENTS

Many people helped make this book possible by generously sharing their knowledge and insight and offering support in countless ways. My thanks to: Brown & Benchmark editors Meredith Morgan and Deborah Reinbold and to members of the WCB book team: Suzanne Guinn, Mary Christianson, Robin Storm, and Vicki Krug. Additional thanks to Kathy Husemann and Marilyn Phelps, and to colleagues, associates, and friends: Edwin DeWindt, University of Detroit Mercy; Anne DeWindt, Wayne County Community College; David Nagle, The University of Michigan; Robert Nagle, Schoolcraft College; Barry Herem; Steve Brown; and Carol King. I also wish to thank the following reviewers:

Larry L. Brock
Brevard Community College
Bill Bryant
Northwestern State University–Louisiana
Donna Karber
Mississippi County Community College
Anne K. LeCroy
East Tennessee State University
Alice Gates Schwehm
Pensacola Jr. College
Richard Sietsema
Warren Wilson College
Sydney Sonneborn
Miles Community College
Stephen A. Wallace
Pima Community College–East
Sylvia White
Florida Community College–Jacksonville

Geraldine Nagle

THE ARTS~
WORLD THEMES

Chapter One

OVERTURE

This is a book about people and their achievements. Some are adventurers: men like William Henry Jackson, a soldier during the American Civil War and afterwards a photographer who traversed the deserts and mountains of the West, sometimes with only mules for company. Others led lives more staid: women like the painter Kuan Tao-Sheng who succeeded despite the demands of family and the social restrictions of thirteenth century China. In the twentieth century, photographer Ansel Adams contended that artists illuminate the world. If this is true, then you are about to meet people whose achievements outlast corporations, nations, societies, and entire civilizations.

IDEAS

Side by side are two works of art with a common bond (fig. 1.1 and fig. 1.2). The first is a gold coffin made by an anonymous Egyptian artist more than three thousand years ago. The second is a granite sculpture made only recently by the American artist Jesús Bautista Moroles. The Egyptian created a work of art intended to honor and protect the mummified body of King Tutankhamen; subsequently he knew that what he created would be hidden inside the king's tomb. His was an art for the dead. In contrast, Moroles created a work of art because sculpture is the way he communicates his ideas and feelings. His is an art for the living.

What is the bond between the two sculptures? Both are ideas in beautiful forms. Beauty—contrary to the cliché—is not in the eye of the beholder but in the form of an object or a performance. Beauty results from the manipulation of materials into the form you see or hear. To create the portrait of King Tutankhamen, the artist molded, hammered, soldered, and incised sheets of gold. He used lapis lazuli to paint eyebrows and eye lines, and accented other details with inlays of quartz, carnelian, and glass. Above Tut's brow he placed a gold vulture and cobra to signify the king's sovereignty over Upper and Lower Egypt, and in Tut's hands he placed the crook and flail, emblems of the God Osiris and carried by Egyptian kings for ceremonial occasions. An inscription dedicated to the Sky Goddess Nut appears just below the hands, and covering the coffin are spells and incantations from the Egyptian *Book of the Dead*.

FIGURE 1.1 • Coffin of King Tutankhamen, ca. 1340 B.C., Gold, 6'1" (185.5 cm) high. Egyptian Museum, Cairo.
© Hirmer Fotoarchiv.

FIGURE 1.2 • *Spirit inner column #1*, 1985. Jesús Bautista Moroles. Dakota Granite 77 × 8 × 6 1/2".
Courtesy of the Jesús Bautista Moroles Studio.

The artist designed and crafted these and other details with an eye to the form as a whole. Notice the sculpture's symmetry: the crossed arms holding the crossed crook and flail; the curves repeated by the crossed pieces just beneath the arms, and the crossed wings of the goddess sweeping upward. Shapes are balanced and repeated. The form, in its entirety, is a composition of lines and shapes, colors, and textures. It is also a composition of ideas. Symbols, emblems, spells, incantations—all were a means of bringing back the spirit that had escaped at death and then safeguarding the spirit and the mummified body.

Moroles' sculpture reveals another kind of spirit. Whether called *soul, self, essence, psyche,* or *spirit,* it is the concept of this invisible force that Moroles makes visible. Then he imprisons it behind forty rigid stone slabs.

If you were able to see *Spirit Inner Column #1* in Houston, you could walk around it, stand near it, and you might find yourself looking up to it. The sculpture is taller than the photograph suggests, over six feet. Yet it is incredibly slender, only six by eight inches thick. Standing in the same room with it, you sense its precariousness. If you touch its base, your fingers will feel the rough texture of natural granite that your eyes may have missed. The top portion of the sculpture is, of course, smooth, mathematical, precise: a series of repetitive rigid shapes that confine the single, very different shape inside. Or is it confined? Notice how it curves, coils, writhes, thrusting upward as if attempting to break free of its bonds.

LITERACY

Most of the visual images people encounter are designed for instant communication. Art is not. To read a work of art takes time: considerably more time than the standard thirty seconds it takes to grasp the visual images in television, magazines, and newspapers. You have just *read* two works of art, so you may agree that a certain amount of effort is required to perceive the shapes, textures, and other visual elements that reveal both a form's ideas and beauty. Some readers may find this a new experience, since in the United States, reading art—visual literacy—is not a priority of the educational system.

When you consider the time and effort spent teaching children to read print, is it not surprising how little time is spent teaching children to read pictures? This gap is something of a paradox because, in a single year, the average television viewer is exposed to more than thirty-two thousand commercials—all visual images—and this number does not include pictures in magazines and newspapers.[1] Little or nothing prepares children and adults for such a barrage of visual images, so they are left unaware of these images' tremendous power and subjectivity. When visual images can disperse information and plant suggestions inside of thirty seconds, they are powerful. They are also simple and direct because they are made for quick consumption.

A work of art does not release ideas quickly, and it does not plant suggestions. To the contrary, a work of art encourages visual literacy by inviting viewers to spend time with it, to look and look again, to enjoy or question or puzzle over what they see. A work of art never tells viewers *what* to think. Doing so would be the very antithesis of everything art stands for.

POWER AND PARADOX

For centuries, the arts were bound by a system of patronage and censorship. When Johann Sebastian Bach, one of the great performer-composers of all time, asked permission to leave the service of his patron, he was thrown in jail. Bach lived at a time when professional performances of music were private affairs held in royal courts, residences, and churches. During Bach's lifetime public music concerts made their first feeble start in England, but they did not become established elsewhere for another hundred years. Art museums took still another hundred years.

Why, during all these centuries, were the arts controlled by societies' upper classes? Since most professional artists and musicians came from the middle classes, what was behind the widely held assumption that the public had little interest, use, or need for art? This attitude was pervasive, extending over Europe, China, Japan, India, Indonesia, and most of Africa. Only in the last two centuries have the arts become accessible to the public. Ironically, public attitudes have not always kept pace and censorship remains.

The twentieth century's most notorious example of censorship took place in Germany during the 1930s. Under Adolph Hitler's Nazi regime hundreds of artists and their works were labeled "degenerate." Books were censored and all so-called "degenerate" examples—including Ernest Hemingway's novels— were destroyed. Paintings were torn off museum walls and either burned or sold at auction in Switzerland. Abstract painting and sculpture and jazz music were singled out for the worst abuse. Any painting or sculpture that did not look "real" was called "monstrous," or worse if the artist happened to be Jewish. Jazz, which had become very popular in Germany, was labeled "primitive" and designated "inferior." Filmmakers, museum directors, architects, and orchestra conductors were constantly under fire, and newspaper articles invariably began with the caption: "Taxpayers, you should know how your money was spent."[2] While this became an official party line for the masses, members of the old German aristocracy and government officials, including Hitler's second in command, Hermann Goering, were amassing huge art collections for themselves (fig. 1.3).

FIGURE 1.3 • An American soldier at a church used to store objects confiscated by the Nazis in Ellingen, Germany, in 1945.

Courtesy of the National Archives.

Why are the visual and performing arts so feared? Again, there is a paradox. On one hand, the arts are considered an educational elective rather than a basic; on the other hand, the arts are still being censored. If the arts are merely education's "frills" and society's decorations and entertainments, why police them?

WORLD JOURNEYS IN TIME

The arts build long and strong bridges to understanding. Consider "Treasures of Tutankhamen," an art exhibit that broke attendance records worldwide. The exhibit arrived in the United States in 1976 and toured for three years with stops in Los Angeles, Seattle, Chicago, New Orleans, and New York. It drew enormous crowds in every city, yet every work of art displayed represented a culture totally different from anything experienced by the people attending the exhibit. Is this what fascinated them?

The arts are interesting in ways that facts and figures are not. The arts are human images, human endeavors, human stories. Civilizations are, after all, made of people, not facts. Although all sorts of information about Tutankhamen and his treasures was readily available, evidently it was not enough for people who wanted to come face-to-face with objects that had been part of the young pharaoh's life and death.

Timelessness is as much a part of art as cultural diversity. People who saw the "Treasures of Tutankhamen" exhibit walked through an open doorway and into a three-thousand year flashback. Scientists tell us that time bends. Seneca, the Roman philosopher and playwright who lived in the first century, tells us that "Life is short, art is long."

Open the door.

NOTES

[1]Stuart Ewen interviewed on Bill Moyers "The Public Mind," Program I, "Image and Reality in America: Consuming Images." PBS, Winter 1988.

[2]For a report of this and other aspects of Nazi censorship see Barron, Stephanie, "Degenerate Art" The Fate of the Avant-Garde in Nazi Germany. (Los Angeles: Los Angeles County Museum of Art, 1991).

Chapter Two

PAINTING, PRINTMAKING, AND SCULPTURE

FIGURE 2.1 •
FTD Logo: Courtesy of Florists' Transworld Delivery Association, Southfield, MI.

O‌urs is a world of visual images, where billboards and neon signs fight for attention and where highway and traffic signs give directions with symbols (fig. 2.1). **Icon,** once a term more familiar to logicians and historians, is now a buzzword of the computer age. In the consumer marketplace, logos replace slogans. In the media, pictures catch attention before words.

Try to imagine a world without visual images: a world without computers, fax machines, television, or cameras; a world where the only images are drawings, paintings, and sculptures. Here, life is less frenzied, but it is also less colorful. Books are rare and extremely valuable because they must be written and illustrated by hand. Photograph albums, those treasure stores of family memories, do not exist. You own no pictures of yourself—none, unless you can afford to commission one from a painter who probably has a waiting list of wealthier and more prominent patrons.

Photography is 150 years old, the printing press 550, but painting and sculpture existed for thousands of years before the printing press was invented. Painting and sculpture are civilization's most ancient forms of image making. Seeing those images now, displayed in museums or pictured in books, far removed from the context of their own time and place, can you grasp their initial significance? Can you imagine their power in a world where images were rare and precious?

ART OF THE CAVES

The time is 1940, the place southwestern France in an area of the Dordogne Valley. The day is sunny, and a small group of children are playing in a field. Suddenly one of the children sees his dog run behind a clump of bushes at the edge of the field, where it disappears: swallowed up, or so it seems, by the earth. Quickly, the children run after the dog, following his path until it leads them through a small opening in the ground, then underground and into a series of narrow cave chambers. Like a storybook Alice falling down a rabbit hole or little Max sailing away from his bedroom, the children become adventuresome wanderers in a strange, unknown world. When their eyes finally adjust to the darkness, they see monstrous painted animals encircling them (fig. 2.2). Many beasts are as large as sixteen feet. Some follow each other in solemn parades, but others swirl about, sideways and upside down. Strangely solemn, these beasts are not Alice's Mad Hatter or Max's Wild Things, fantasies read and seen in the safety of a child's bedroom. These are real.

The animals are bulls, wild horses, reindeer, bison, and mammoths outlined with charcoal and painted mostly in reds, yellows, and browns. Scientific analysis reveals colors were derived from ocher and other iron oxides ground to a fine powder. Methods of applying color varied: some colors were brushed or smeared on rock surfaces and others were blown or sprayed. It is possible that tubes made from animal bones were used for spraying because hollow bones, some stained with pigment, have been found nearby.

FIGURE 2.2 • General view of cave chamber at Lascaux, ca. 15,000–10,000 B.C. Dordogne, France.
Courtesy of the French Government Tourist Office.

One of the most puzzling aspects of the paintings is their location. Other rock paintings—for example, those of Bushmen in South Africa—are either located near cave entrances or completely in the open. Cave paintings in France and Spain, however, are in recesses and caverns far removed from original cave entrances. This means that artists were forced to work in cramped spaces and without sources of natural light. It also implies that whoever made them did not want them easily found. Since cave dwellers normally lived close to entrances there must have been a reason why so many generations of Lascaux cave dwellers hid their art.

Scholars offer three different but related opinions about this puzzle. One opinion is that the paintings were a record of the seasonal migrations made by herds. Because some paintings were made directly over others, obliterating them, it is probable that a painting's value ended with the migration it pictured. Unfortunately, this explanation fails to explain the hidden locations, unless the migrations were celebrated with certain secretive rituals.

Another opinion is that the paintings were directly related to hunting and were an essential part of a ritual to prepare hunters. This opinion holds that the pictures and whatever ritual they accompanied were an ancient method of psychological motivation or *imaging*. Considerable support exists for this opinion because several animals are wounded by arrows and spears. This opinion also attempts to solve the overpainting problem by explaining that an animal's picture had no further use after the hunt.

A third opinion takes psychological motivation much further into the realm of tribal rites and mystery. It is the totem theory: a belief that certain animals assumed mythical significance as primal ancestors or protectors of a given tribe or clan. Two types of images substantiate this theory: the strange, indecipherable geometric shapes that appear near some animals, and the few drawings of men. Wherever men appear they are crudely drawn and their bodies are elongated and rigid (fig. 2.3). Some men are in a prone position and some have bird or animal heads. Advocates for this third opinion point to reports from people who have experienced a trance state. Uniformly, these people experienced weightlessness and the sensation that their bodies were being stretched lengthwise. Advocates also point to practitioners of animism worldwide, particularly shamen who believe an animal's spirit and energy is transferred to them while in trance. Figure 2.3, showing the man with his birdlike head and the wounded bison with exposed entrails, would seem to lend credence to this third opinion, but there is still much that remains unexplained. For example, where is the proof that the man in figure 2.3 is a shaman? He could as easily be a hunter wearing a headmask. Many tribal hunters, including Native Americans in the Plains areas, camouflaged themselves by wearing animal heads and hides. Another unexplained image is the bird on the rod. Is it a shaman's wand or simply a decoy attached to a stick?

FIGURE 2.3 • Well Scene, Lascaux, ca. 15,000–10,000 B.C. Dordogne, France. Courtesy of the French Government Tourist Office.

Perhaps time's erasure is so complete there never will be satisfactory answers to the cave images, but their mystique only adds to their importance. Certainly a great art exists, and by its existence reveals that the most ancient and primitive human beings were not without intelligence, skill, and sensitivity. The animals of Lascaux were a tremendous discovery, but sadly, the large number of visitors to the caves brought an unforeseeable change to the fragile underground environment. In a relatively short time the paintings began to discolor from calcification. To prevent any further damage the caves were closed to the public, and the animals returned to solitude and darkness.

Art of the Dead

When the hunter/gatherer society of cave dwellers evolved into an agricultural society, the needs and reasons for creating art also changed. Seasonal cycles of planting and harvesting brought a new stability and a different attitude toward life and death. From the death of a plant came the seeds of new life; from the death of winter came the resurrection of spring. If these cycles, year after year, were eternal, then was it not possible for human beings to have similar everlasting cycles? Surely there must also be a continuance, a life after death for humans.

From these questions came rituals and practices involving art. In Jordan fleshless skulls were covered with plaster and bone and shaped into portrait sculptures. Halfway around the world in Peru, bodies were wrapped in beautifully woven shawls and blankets. In societies everywhere, people attempted to give the dead whatever was needed to assure a good afterlife and, in most instances, paintings and sculpture were another assurance of immortality.

Egyptian Tomb Sculpture and Painting

Belief in a life after death became the foundation for religious practices that touched everyone in ancient Egypt. Pharaohs spent lifetimes planning and overseeing the construction of their tombs and mortuary temples. Ordinary citizens scrupulously saved to pay for the cost of their embalming and funeral rites, and the first duty of children was to see that their parents were given proper burial. If there was enough money the mummies were interred in private family tombs; if not they were stacked in mass communal graves.

These practices originated with the religious belief that every person had three "selves." First, the *akh* or personality; second, the *ba*, which is a kind of spirit or ghost that lives after death and moves with ease between "heaven" and earth; and third, the *ka*, the most important aspect of self. The *ka* is a life force and a human being's greatest potential, but it is fulfilled only after death. Before this fulfillment can take place, the body must be preserved, specific rites performed, and the *ka* furnished with food, drink, and protective prayers.

This is the reason for the pyramids and for the cliff tombs that eventually replaced them. A tomb's size and richness signified the deceased's nobility and wealth; its design ostensibly protected the mummy from grave robbers and enemies. Tomb statues, ranging from a few inches to life-size, served the same dual purpose. If the mummy was destroyed, the *ka* could use a statue as substitute. The tomb statue of Zoser (Djoser), a pharaoh of the Old Kingdom (2780–2180 B.C.) was carved for that purpose (fig. 2.4). Zoser's architect Imhotep built an elaborate mortuary temple for the use of priests and relatives who would continue to bring the necessary prayers and offerings (see fig. 4.4 and fig. 4.5). The temple, although adjacent to the pyramid, was too far from Zoser's underground tomb chamber for his *ka* to receive the offerings it needed. Imhotep solved the problem by placing the tomb statue of Zoser inside the mortuary temple. He enclosed the statue behind one wall but left a narrow slit that let the *ka* peer into the offering chamber.

Because tomb statues served an important function, their sculptors were careful to create as close a portrait of the deceased as stone would allow. Zoser's statue, carved more than 4,600 years ago, is made from the same white limestone used for his pyramid. The statue is not quite life-size and depicts him seated on his throne, a pose uniformly used for Egypt's rulers. Originally the sculpture was painted and its eye sockets held precious stones. Despite their loss and some damage to his nose and cheek, his face retains a remarkable degree of naturalism and character. Zoser's statue was found still inside its walled up chamber and relatively unscathed considering the damage done to the pyramid. There, every chamber had been plundered, Zoser's sarcophagus opened, and his mummy torn apart.[1]

Besides free-standing tomb statues, many Egyptian tombs included **relief sculptures** (fig. 2.5). Typically these covered walls and pillars and invariably pictured pharaohs in the company of gods. The relief sculpture of Sesostris I and the God Horus (fig. 2.6) is from a small temple at Karnak (now destroyed). This particular scene is from one pillar and shows the pharaoh embraced by the Hawk God Horus. According to the beliefs of Egyptian religion, all pharaohs were direct descendants of Horus, so the god's presence here is a reminder of the pharaoh's divine origins. Sesostris wears the crown of Upper and Lower Egypt and, at the base of the crown, in the center, is the Uraeus, the cobra protector of the sun gods and their earthly descendants. Inside this temple dedicated to Horus—but actually built to honor Sesostris I—every pillar displays a scene showing the pharaoh with a different god. These little narratives reinforced the concept of a ruler's divine origins and provided visible proof that a pharaoh would take his rightful place among the gods through eternity.

Because the pyramids had failed to thwart grave robbers, later tombs were built into the sides of cliffs. In many instances their rock-hewn walls were too rough for relief sculptures; consequently painted walls were substituted. Painted

FIGURE 2.4 • (Opposite) Portrait statue of King Zoser, ca. 2667–2648 B.C., White Limestone: 4'7", from the tomb of the King at Saqqara.
The Egyptian Museum.

FIGURE 2.5 • Antonio Beato, *Interior of Temple of Horus, Edfu*, ca. 1862. Albumin Print.
National Gallery of Canada, Ottawa.

walls were also less expensive and were widely used in the tombs of lesser nobles and ordinary citizens. The vaulted tomb in figure 2.7 belonged to man named Sennedjem, an artisan of considerable prestige who probably worked in the royal tombs at Thebes. His tomb chamber contains painted scenes of the comforts and luxuries of life and is similar to hundreds of tombs belonging to well-to-do citizens. For these people, pictures were a substitute for reality and an assurance that all that was good from their earthly lives would remain with them always.

In Sennedjem's tomb, the far wall combines religious scenes of the afterlife with scenes of a prosperous earthly life (fig. 2.8). At the top, in the arched space beneath the vaulted ceiling, the great god Amon-Re sits in his bark, flanked on either side by sacred baboons. Beneath this scene a wavelike chevron pattern signifying the Nile River forms a border for five horizontal panels. The top panel shows Sennedjem and his wife Iyneferti kneeling before five gods. The three largest gods are Re, followed by Osiris, God of the Dead, and Ptah, Creator of the Universe. Next to the small bark, a priest stands in front of a mummy and holds a hooked tool used to perform a ceremony of the dead called "Opening the Mouth." This ceremony was one of the last rites performed after embalming, and it returned to the dead their ability to speak, eat, and drink. The next two panels show Sennedjem and Iyneferti working in the

FIGURE 2.6 • *Sesostris I and the God Horus,* ca. 1971–1928 B.C. Limestone; width 3'6". From a destroyed temple at Karnak.
The Egyptian Museum

FIGURE 2.7 • Tomb of Sennedjem, ca. 1150 B.C., Deir el Medineh.
Photograph by Egyptian Expedition, The Metropolitan Museum of Art.

FIGURE 2.8 • (Opposite) Detail from tomb of Sennedjem.
© Hirmer Fotoarchiv.

heavenly fields of their afterlife. These were, of course, magical fields where work was always pleasant and harvests always bountiful. The two lower panels contain fruit-bearing trees and plants.

CHINESE TOMB SCULPTURE

Unlike Egyptians, the Chinese did not have any clear picture of an afterlife or any specific guidelines for getting there. Their early religions were pantheistic, and their greatest spirit was Shang Ti, the First Ancestor. The single most important aspect of life to the Chinese was maintaining the fragile harmony between human beings and the universe; consequently the death of a ruler was considered a break in that harmony. Asian scholar John D. La Plante described how this fear influenced royal burials: "The death of a Shang ruler was a catastrophe upsetting the balance between man and universe. In the hope that he would continue to exercise his influence in the realm of the ancestors, the ruler was provided with everything he had known in life: useful and ceremonial objects, chariots and horses, servants, and possibly even members of his immediate family."[2]

One of the world's most elaborate and fantastic tombs was described by the Chinese historian Ssu-ma Ch'ien in the second century B.C. He wrote about a "Spirit City" built by the Emperor Ch'in Shih Huang-ti, who had ruled a century earlier. According to Ssu-ma Ch'ien, the mortuary complex took thirty-six years to complete and involved more than 700,000 workers. This gigantic

underground tomb consisted of palaces, pavilions, and a domed sky of bronze. Buildings were filled with precious stones, and the sky was covered with constellations of pearls. Gold and silver birds were everywhere. Models of the Yangtze and Yellow rivers were filled with mercury flowing through a complex mechanical system that continuously cycled the silvery liquid. Ssu-ma Ch'ien wrote that everything the emperor could possibly need or desire was buried with him, including his childless wives, certain household members, and high officials.

Until 1974 there was no proof of the ancient historian's report considered by many as too imaginative to be true. Then, a mile from the tomb complex and beyond its double walls, an enormous army of life-size clay figures was discovered accidently (fig. 2.9, fig. 2.10, and fig. 2.11). Archaeologists estimate the army's size at 7,000 men: officers, infantrymen, crossbowmen, and

FIGURE 2.9 • Warriors from the tomb of Ch'in Shih Huang-ti. Ch'in Dynasty (221–207 B.C.). Terra-cotta warriors then life size.

Photo: Shaansi (Shensi) Provincial Studio, courtesy of Museum of Qin (Ch'in) Dynasty.

FIGURE 2.10 • Kneeling Crossbowman. Terra-cotta.

Photo: Shaansi (Shensi) Provincial Studio, courtesy of Museum of Qin (Ch'in) Dynasty.

charioteers with their chariots and horses. The men's weapons are authentic and their uniforms, still showing traces of the original paint, identify different regiments. No two men are alike (fig. 2.12). Historians and archaeologists generally agree that the men who belonged to the Imperial Palace Guard more than 2,000 years ago were the models for these clay images. Several satellite tombs have also been unearthed. These tombs, displaying royal seals, held the bodies of five men and two women whose ages were between twenty and thirty. All had been killed either by hanging, beheading, or dismemberment.

The emperor's own tomb complex is an enormous mound of earth, not as high as Egyptian pyramids but three times larger in area than the great pyramid of Cheops. The emperor's tomb complex has not been opened, and the Chinese government has not revealed any plans for its excavation in the near future. Considerably more is known of the emperor and his reign. He chose his own name, Ch'in Shih Huang-ti, which means "The August First Emperor of Ch'in" because he believed the Ch'in Dynasty would last 10,000 generations. Actually it lasted only fourteen years. Ch'in Shih Huang-ti was a tyrannical ruler and an enemy of Confucian scholars, but he managed to weld China's warring factions into a unified nation and to complete the Great Wall. An egomaniac, he was obsessed with delusions of immortality. He once sent doctors and officials abroad to search for an elixir of life and when they failed to find any such miracle drug he had them burned alive. Ch'in Shih Huang-ti died unexpectedly while on an expedition, and historians believe court intrigue brought about the murder of all his heirs except one son. If this is true, the bodies in the satellite tombs may be the murdered heirs.

FIGURE 2.11 • Head of Horse, terracotta, with original bronze fittings reassembled on leather bridle.
Photo: Shaansi (Shensi) Provincial Studio, courtesy of Museum of Qin (Ch'in) Dynasty.

FIGURE 2.12 • Heads of warriors, terra-cotta, with traces of pigment. Life size.
Photo: Shaansi (Shensi) Provincial Studio, courtesy of Museum of Qin (Ch'in) Dynasty.

RELIGIOUS ART

Art in Egyptian tombs and mortuary temples is one example of how sculpture and painting transform ideologies into visible images. For this very reason Islam and certain Protestant religions forbid the display of human images in mosques and churches. Other religions traditionally display human images and symbols to provide their followers with concrete associative objects. Religious followers can see or perhaps touch the images with reverence; they can place votive offerings in front of them, attach flowers or pieces of cloth on them, and direct their prayers through them. Such images are, in essence, both receptacles and personifications of faith.

Historically, religious images were also an effective means for educating illiterate populations. Religious stories could be described in paintings and sculpture. Religious personages could be identified by certain physical characteristics or by accompanying symbols like halos and wings. Sometimes icons took the place of human figures. Buddhists, for example, allowed no human representation of the Buddha for several centuries; instead, they devised a set of icons as substitutes. To Buddha's followers a parasol, throne, lotus, wheel, footprints, or the Bodhi Tree signified his presence. To nonbelievers and the uninitiated, these were simply objects in a picture or sculpture. Buddhist art, like Christian art, can be read with dual meanings.

BUDDHIST SCULPTURE IN INDIA

Buddha means "Enlightened One" and is the name given to Siddhartha Gautama, a prince born in India in the sixth century B.C. Buddha, like Christ, was a great preacher who, together with his disciples, wandered the countryside. He taught that salvation is attained by following an Eightfold Noble Path and that meditation is a way of achieving **nirvana,** the final, ultimate state in which all desires and passions are finally extinguished, leaving the soul totally free.

The religion based on Buddha's teachings was not organized until several centuries after his death. Gradually two different forms or schools of the religion developed. One is *Hinayana,* which means "Lesser Vehicle" and is found in India, Sri Lanka, Burma, and other areas of southeastern Asia. The second is *Mahayana,* which means "Greater Vehicle" and is found in Tibet, China, Korea, Japan, and also India. The *Hinayana* consider Buddha a great prophet; the *Mahayana* consider him a true god without beginning or end. Within these two schools are several different sects, however the two most familiar to Westerners are the Zen Buddhists in Japan and the Tantric Buddhists in Tibet.

East *Torana* of the Great Stupa at Sanchi, India

Stupas were originally burial mounds containing ashes, but to Buddhists they became spiritual centers for worship (fig. 2.13). Stupas are reminders that Buddha's ashes were taken to the great centers of India. Every stupa is considered a cosmic center and its **toranas** (gates) are located at the four cardinal points. The faithful worship by walking through one of the four toranas, step-

FIGURE 2.13 • The Great Stupa, Sanchi, India, completed first century B.C. Shown are the west and south *toranas*. Scala/Art Resource, NY.

ping onto a narrow fenced path, and circling the stupa clockwise. The toranas perform two functions: their positions mark off holy ground and space, and their carvings remind visitors of Buddha's life and teachings

On the east gate, scenes from Buddha's life are carved on the vertical supports and on center sections of the three cross bars (fig. 2.14). Carved between these scenes and on the ends of crossbars are important human and animal images and symbols. The most noticeable symbols are the spirals on the ends of the crossbars. The spirals are snake symbols and relate to one of Buddha's temptations when a snake coiled itself around his body seven times (fig. 2.15). The peacocks are a heraldic emblem belonging to the dynasty of rulers who built these particular gates. The lions to the left of the peacocks are symbols of royalty and emblems of the Sakya family to which Buddha belonged. Elephants figure prominently in Indian art as manifestations of the animal world.

Next to the large elephant and just below the peacocks and spiral, a **yakshi** wraps her arm around the limb of a mango tree while reaching up with her other arm to pluck a fruit. Yakshis are female fertility figures from an earlier Dravidian religion. Although they played no part in Buddhist theology or

FIGURE 2.14 • East *torana*, Great Stupa, Sanchi, India, first century B.C.
Courtesy of The British Library.

mythology, they were included in Buddhist art and in later Hindu and Jain art, mainly because the people became attached to them. Unabashedly erotic, yakshis stand in dancers' poses that accentuate their voluptuous breasts and hips. Always their deep-set eyes are half-closed and their lips, slightly parted, hint at a smile. Although yakshis are intentionally seductive, they are never considered offensive. To Buddhists the senses are a natural part of being human, and the enjoyment of the senses is but one step in overcoming sensuality on the long path toward spiritual ascent.

FIGURE 2.15 • Yakshi, east *torana*, Great Stupa, Sanchi, first century B.C.
© Giraudon, Paris.

A narrative scene from the life of Buddha appears in figure 2.16. The scene, carved on a vertical pillar, describes the miraculous story of Buddha walking on water. Buddha performed this supernatural feat to convert unbelievers, represented here by men in the boat and other men on shore. Included in this little scene is an entire world of nature. Flowering plants and trees with birds and monkeys on their branches rise from the panel's base and sides. Shells float among lotus buds, and swans and ducks swim in full view of a crocodile with his snout perilously close to one duck's tail. A snake hangs from the limb of a tree while a monkey, hanging upside-down two limbs higher, watches the snake. All aspects of nature, including wind rippling the water, are represented in the panel. Only the figure of Buddha is missing. Instead, his presence is signified by the icon of a plank floating on the water, just above the group of standing men.

FIGURE 2.16 • Sculptured panel showing Buddhist miracle, on east *torana* pillar, Great Stupa, Sanchi, first century B.C.
Courtesy of The British Library.

Sculpture of Buddha at Mathura, India

Nearly 300 years separate the relief sculptures on the gates at Sanchi from the sculpture of Buddha shown in figure 2.17. During this time Buddha's followers felt the need for a more representative image, something human in form yet godlike in appearance. In their quest for a suitable image, they demanded what the Indian scholar Benjamin Rowland calls ". . . signs of superhuman perfection distinguishing the body of Buddha from those of ordinary mortals."

What are the signs? The seated Buddha must be shown in a yoga position to signify his final nirvana. His head must have the perfect shape of an egg. His eyes must resemble lotus petals. His body must taper like that of a lion, with shoulders rounded like an elephant's head. Buddha must always be shown with the **ushnisha,** the protuberance on top of his head that signifies wisdom, and with the **urna,** a small tuft of hair, often depicted as a dot in the center of his forehead. Buddha's earlobes must be elongated to signify his royal birth, and magic wheels must appear on the soles of his feet. Buddha's hands must be as graceful as flowers and must form the proper gestures called **mudras.**

The stone statue from Mathura, India, incorporates every sign (fig. 2.17). Holy wheels appear on Buddha's hand raised in a blessing and on the sole of each foot. Three small lions, the royal family emblem, guard Buddha's throne, and royal attendants, one holding a fly whisk, stand on either side. Celestial beings, similar to Christian angels, appear to float in the space above Buddha's head, and a sun disk forms the back of Buddha's throne. The Bodhi Tree, symbol of the Tree of Wisdom, branches out from behind the throne. On the statue's base, an inscription tells the faithful that this work of art was carved as a tribute to Sakayamuni, Buddha's family name.

CHRISTIAN ART IN EUROPE

Christianity spread quickly from Asia across the Roman Empire into Europe. When Roman Emperor Constantine proclaimed freedom of religion throughout the empire in the fourth century, Christians were at last able to worship openly. Constantine initiated another historic event by moving the capital from the city of Rome to the ancient Greek city of Byzantium and renaming it Constantinople (now Istanbul, Turkey).

The centuries that followed these two events witnessed an ongoing dichotomy between Eastern and Western Catholicism, a split reflected in religious art. Although Eastern emperors built elaborate churches, conservative Byzantine churchmen banned the use of sculpture, considering it a form of idolatry. They did, however, permit **mosaics** and paintings. Church canons (rules) of art were strictly enforced and resulted in a Byzantine Style that, with few changes, became a lasting influence on Balkan and Russian religious art. Prior to the twelfth century, Western European monarchs and churchmen built monasteries and abbey churches with plain fortresslike exteriors that gave no hint of the valuable sculpture and objects inside. During the twelfth century, this changed. In France alone, 600 cathedrals were built between the twelfth and thirteenth centuries, all of them in the Gothic Style (see figs. 4.21–4.26). One characteristic of this architectual style is the inclusion of art, particularly sculpture and stained glass windows.

Mother of God Mosaic from Hagia Sophia, Istanbul (Constantinople), ca. 537

The Mother of God mosaic (fig. 2.18) is in the south vestibule of Hagia Sophia, an enormous domed church built by the Emperor Justinian (see fig. 4.17a). Like all Byzantine art, the mosaic portrays Mary and the Infant Jesus as divine royalty. Mary's throne is architectural in design; her position in the scene is central and dominant. The Emperor Justinian stands on the left, holding a model of Hagia Sophia. The Emperor Constantine stands on the right, holding a model of his city.

Byzantine style is evident in the shapes of the four figures and their poses. Bodies are flat and linear. Mary and Jesus have aristocratically narrow and expressionless faces and rigid poses. Bodies and hands are elongated, stretched to visually emphasize the important religious concept that these are not merely human beings but divine and saintly human beings standing beside deities. Realism is not a consideration.

FIGURE 2.17 • (Opposite) Seated Buddha, second century. H. Sandstone 27 1/4″.
Archaelogical Museum, Mathura, India.

FIGURE 2.18 • *Mother of God* mosaic, south vestibule, Hagia Sophia; Constantinople (Istanbul, Turkey), ninth century A.D.
Byzantine Visual Resources, © 1992 Dumbarton Oaks, Washington, D.C.

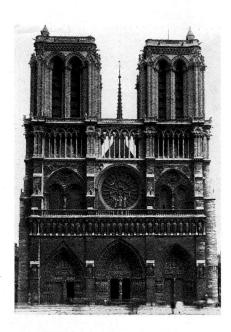

FIGURE 2.19a • West facade, Notre-Dame, Paris, begun 1163.
Photo © Museum of Notre-Dame de Paris.

FIGURE 2.19b • (Opposite) Portal of *The Last Judgment*, Notre-Dame, Paris.
Bildarchiv Foto Marburg/Art Resource, NY

FIGURE 2.20 • Portal of *The Last Judgment*, Notre-Dame, Paris (Detail).
Bildarchiv Foto Marburg/Art Resource, NY.

The Last Judgment Portal, Cathedral Notre-Dame, Paris, 1225–1230

The sculpture and stained glass of Notre-Dame, Paris and other cathedrals built during the Middle Ages heralded the beginning of an art that would become more and more realistic: more natural in style and more human-centered in concept. This trend can be seen in the portal carvings of Notre-Dame (fig. 2.19a–b). Here, despite formal repetitive patterns, the human images are far less rigid than their Byzantine counterparts. Christ, shown in the upper panel above the doors, is more human than godlike in appearance (fig. 2.20). He raises his hands not in blessing or judgment but to reveal his wounds. Angels at his side hold the instruments of his crucifixion; his mother Mary kneels on the left and St. John kneels on the right. These poses are more relaxed than those found in Byzantine mosaics. Garments are more lifelike—notice how realistically Christ's mantle hangs from his shoulders and drapes across his knees. Faces are rounder and have slightly more expression.

As natural as the panel is, it still suggests royalty. Christ is a centrally enthroned figure backed by a richly detailed halo. Mary and St. John kneel to symbolize their homage and the angels serve as Christ's attendants. More angels, much smaller in size, fill the nearest arch as if to embellish St. Matthew's description of the Last Judgment (25:31), "When the Son of Man comes in his glory, and all the angels with him, then shall he sit upon the throne in his glory."

Directly beneath the enthroned Christ are two panels, each containing a scene of the Last Judgment. In the lower panel, the dead rise from their graves to meet their reward. In the middle panel, St. Michael holds a scale to weigh their deeds. On his left stand the good souls wearing rich robes and crowns. On his right, chained together and facing away from him, the evil souls stumble toward hell.

Creatures already in hell are carved in lower arches on the right (fig. 2.19b). Some are the devil's demons and others are wretched souls undergoing the tortures of the damned. Filling the arches above and to the left are the angels already mentioned with Biblical prophets and saints. The twelve apostles flank the doors; and between the doors stands a second sculpture of Christ, this one representing Christ as Teacher.

A cathedral portal has a significance that far exceeds its function as a doorway. As a designated entry into a sacred building it is demarcation between secular and religious activity. Just as a *torana* marks the sacred area around a stupa, a cathedral portal marks off a sacred enclosure.

The Last Judgment, Sistine Chapel, Rome, Michelangelo Buonarroti (1475–1564)

Three hundred years separate the Last Judgment portal of Notre-Dame, Paris, from Michelangelo's (me kell AHN djay lo) fresco painting of the Last Judgment in the Sistine Chapel (fig. 2.21). Those three centuries saw the flowering of a great period in history called the Renaissance. The word *renaissance* means rebirth, and while explorers crossed oceans in search of new worlds, scholars discovered the ancient worlds of Greece and Rome in archaeological excavations and in revised translations of old manuscripts. For Renaissance artists, the ancient sculptures that were unearthed exhibited a radically different approach to the human body and to the very concept of what constitutes being human. The mostly male sculpture of the Greeks and the Roman copies of Greek art displayed an idealized physical beauty and a spirit that revealed no frailty. For Renaissance scholars, the ancient literature and philosophy opened entirely new channels of inquiry and gave birth to two new philosophies: Humanism and Neo-Platonism. **Humanism** is based on the belief that people are free to make their own choices and chart their own destinies within the guidelines of religion. **Neo-Platonism,** leaning toward mysticism, holds that talent or genius is a gift from God and that people born with this gift are destined to create something that has never before been in the mind of any other person. That "something" consists of the idea of perfection as described by the ancient Greek philosopher Plato.

Michelangelo was an avowed Neo-Platonist whose interpretation of the Last Judgment was totally different from anything painted before. The Sistine Chapel Christ is a God of muscle and bone, a man commanding and powerful, but human enough to reveal the wounds inflicted by his crucifixion and the sword that pierced his side (fig. 2.22). Michelangelo's images are very human. His angels are wingless, and few people have clothes to hide their frailties or to indicate their social class. Because Michelangelo considered the human body a manifestation of the soul, his people come to their judgment nude, as they were born.

The top of the painting shows the Kingdom of Heaven with Christ as its center. Mary, his mother, stands slightly behind him on his left, and around him are apostles and saints. The saints who were martyred hold the instruments of their deaths: St. Catherine the wheel; St. Andrew the cross; and St. Sebastian the arrows. St. Bartholomew holds his skin and the knife used to

FIGURE 2.21 • (Opposite) Michelangelo, *The Last Judgment.* 1534–41, Sistine Chapel, The Vatican, Rome. Fresco, 48 × 44'. Vatican Museum Photograph Archive.

flay him, but the distorted, pathetic face on that skin is Michelangelo's own self-portrait. Just above St. Bartholomew stands St. Peter holding two large keys that symbolize the Papacy. Above these groups, in swirling spaces, angels hold the instruments of Christ's death. On the left is the cross, and on the right, the pillar at which he was scourged.

In the center of the painting, beneath Christ, are the seven angels described by St. John in the Apocalypse. Two angels hold open the Book of Judgment with its pages containing the name and life story of every mortal being; other angels summon the dead with trumpets. The lower left corner shows the newly risen dead (fig. 2.23). Some are still in their winding cloths and others, older in death, are mere bones and skulls. The demon Charon, to the right, stands in the boat used to ferry lost souls. Michelangelo gave a literal interpretation to the words of the fourteenth century poet Dante, who described Charon with eyes "glowering like coal" (fig. 2.24).

FIGURE 2.22 • (Opposite) Michelangelo, *The Last Judgment* (Detail). Sistine Chapel, The Vatican, Rome.
Vatican Museum Photograph Archive.

FIGURE 2.23 • Michelangelo, *The Last Judgment* (Detail). Sistine Chapel, The Vatican, Rome.
Vatican Museum Photograph Archive.

Twenty-four years before beginning *The Last Judgment*, Michelangelo painted the Sistine Chapel ceiling, another masterpiece and one that required four years of almost superhuman effort. When Pope Paul III commissioned *The Last Judgment* for the wall above the altar in the Sistine Chapel, Michelangelo was already in his sixties, tired and well past the average life expectancy for a sixteenth century man. Nevertheless he accepted the commission. He spent the next three years planning and making preliminary drawings for the painting and another six years completing it. The mural brought him praise and recognition, but it brought criticism and censorship as well. He was vociferously attacked for the nudity in this painting and in other works. One critic remarked that his art was better suited to a bath house. Ultimately censorship won. The veils and loin cloths you see in *The Last Judgment* were painted over Michelangelo's original work by order of Pope Pious IV. The over-painting took place in 1564, the year of the artist's death.

The Virgin with the Monkey, Albrecht Dürer (1471–1528)

This picture is only four by seven inches, but it exemplifies the Renaissance's social and philosophical shift toward the importance and dignity of the indi-

FIGURE 2.24 • Michelangelo, *The Last Judgment* (Detail). Sistine Chapel, The Vatican, Rome.

Vatican Museum Photograph Archive.

FIGURE 2.25 • Albrecht Dürer, *The Virgin with the Monkey*, ca. 1498–1499. Engraving, 7 1/2" × 4 13/16".
University Art Collections, Arizona State University, Tempe. Gift of Mr. and Mrs. Mullen.

vidual (fig. 2.25). Byzantine artists depicted Mary as the Queen of Heaven enthroned, but Renaissance artists depicted her as the Mother of God and were likely to place her inside a palace or a house or, as Dürer (DOO er) did, in a landscape setting. Several Renaissance artists, Dürer among them, took the humanization of saintly figures one step further by personalizing them. In Dürer's *The Virgin with the Monkey* there is little Biblical authenticity. Only the bird in Jesus' hand and Mary's missal and halo identify this as something more than a picture of mother and child. The little house in the background is a typical sixteenth century northern European half-timber structure that never stood in Nazareth. Actually it is a fisherman's hut, drawn from life and featured in an earlier watercolor painting by the artist (see fig. 2.58). Dürer's Mary, with blonde hair and plain dress, could be any young mother living in the artist's city of Nurenburg, and her child any energetic infant pushing and straining against its mother. These are changes the public favored. Relating to a religious image was easier when it looked like other common folk— especially since the Biblical Mary and Joseph were plain and humble people.

FIGURE 2.26 • Peter Paul Rubens, *Prometheus Bound*, 1611–12. Oil on canvas, 95 7/8 X 82 1/2 inches

Philadelphia Museum of Art: The W. P. Wilstach Collection. W50-3-1.

Favorable public response was important to Dürer because *The Virgin with the Monkey* was not a commissioned painting but a print—one of many made for sale to the general public. Prints, unlike paintings, are multiple works of art made in numbered editions, and although they involve challenging techniques, they are not one-of-a-kind art, hence they are more affordable. The fact that this picture was printed to be sold may account for the monkey—which certainly did not belong in either Nazareth or Nuremburg. Occasionally, monkeys did appear in Christian art as symbols of lewdness and greed, but in this instance the symbolism does not not seem to apply. Dürer's biographers mention his great love for animals, especially exotic ones. His travel notebooks are filled with sketches of animals, birds, and fish that he observed with studious attention and drew with great detail, often adding notations. Since in this picture he drew the rare animal tethered like a pet, he probably included it as much for the sake of attention as for his own personal satisfaction.

MYTHICAL ART

For countless centuries, myths have provided artists with a treasure-trove of subjects. Myths are stories that attempt to explain the mysteries of the universe and human behavior. How did the world begin? Why are there seasons, tides, cataclysms of nature? What causes greed, jealousy, love, heroism? Since prehistoric times, human beings have asked these questions in their search for order and harmony. Myths give them answers with plots and archetypal characters that cover the entire spectrum of the natural phenomena of human behavior. In his book *The Power of Myth,* Joseph Campbell writes that myths are "clues to our deepest spiritual potential, able to lead us to delight, illumination, and even rapture."

PROMETHEUS: THE MYTH AND THE PAINTING,
Peter Paul Rubens (1577–1640)

The Flemish (Belgian) artist Peter Paul Rubens liked to have an apprentice read aloud to him as he worked. Rubens was particulary fond of ancient Greek and Roman literature, so it is not surprising that he gave this painting the same title as the play *Prometheus Bound,* written by the Greek dramatist Aeschylus in the fifth century B.C. (fig 2.26). Who was Prometheus? A mythical Greek god, a Titan who fought courageously alongside Zeus. He was also a hero compassionate enough to risk his life by bringing fire to earth. With this feat Prometheus saved the human race from certain death—but incurred Zeus' wrath. Thus Prometheus became the archetypal hero who performed a morally just act, was found guilty of disobedience, and was sentenced accordingly (see p. 286).

Rubens' painting is an interpretation of the sentence with all its horror. The painting shows Prometheus chained to a rock and attacked by an eagle who comes each day to tear at his flesh, "feasting in fury" on his liver. Because Prometheus is a god, his body heals at night, and the torture continues day after day. To emphasize the extreme cruelty of Zeus' punishment, the artist gave the Titan a physically perfect body—then contorted and convulsed it. What you see is a body writhing in pain but refusing to die. You can almost feel Prometheus' feet strain and push against the rocks and his arms pull against the chains. His struggle is futile. His strong face, bleeding from the eagle's claws, is agonized, but the bird continues to feed at the gaping wound while beating its wings triumphantly. Adding to the tumult, a ferocious wind rolls black clouds across the gray sky and batters the solitary stalwart tree.

DANAË: THE MYTH AND THE PAINTING,
Rembrandt van Rijn (1606–1669)

The myth of Danaë concerns the futility of attempting to circumvent fate. This concept, with its origins in Greek polytheism, is a recurring theme in ancient Greek literature, drama, and art. The Greeks believed a person's fate was based on character rather than circumstance. Fate was *moira:* a pattern determined largely by a person's actions in a given set of circumstances. In essence this meant that behavior was the result of inherent traits of character. The worst possible character flaw to the ancient Greeks was *hubris:* the excessive pride and arrogance that could prompt a mortal to make decisions or take actions better left to the gods. Such actions shape the plot of Danaë.

Danaë was the only child of King Acrisius of Argos. She was a beautiful girl with a kind and generous character, but her father wanted a son. He sought the advice of an oracle and was told that he would never have a son. Worse—the prophet told him that his daughter would bear a son who would one day kill him. The king was terrified. Returning home he looked at his daughter with the realization that her beauty would bring many suiters. He could not bring himself to kill her, but he vowed that she would never know a man. To safeguard her virginity he had a tower built of bronze and there he imprisoned the girl. He allowed her a servant but forbade her to have contact with any other human being or with the world outside the tower. Acrisius forgot, however, that Danaë could never be hidden from the gods, and that Zeus had an insatiable appetite for beautiful mortal women. In a very short time, the ruler of all gods seduced Danaë in a shower of gold that rained in through an opening in the roof. Later, when the king learned that his daughter had given birth to a son, he decided to kill them both, but again he was afraid to anger the gods. He decided instead to let the sea bring about their deaths. Accordingly, Acrisius gave orders for Danaë and her young son Perseus to be put inside a large wooden chest that was tossed into deep water. Like the plots of so many myths, this one winds and turns and develops sub-plots. Mother and child were saved from the sea, and Perseus grew into a semi-divine mortal who had many adventures of his own. Ultimately, the oracle's prophesy came true, but only by accident, for Perseus had a noble character and by then was a hero in his own right.

Inevitably, when this myth became a subject for art its moral was lost in the dramatic impact of the seduction scene. Zeus' deviousness and the fantasy of a seduction by a shower of gold ignited artists' imaginations. The seventeenth century Dutch painter Rembrandt was no exception, but his treatment of the subject was masterfully unique in several ways.

The shower of gold is missing in Rembrandt's painting of the seduction (fig. 2.27). In its place is a light that originates somewhere outside the picture and enters from above, behind the curtain. The light touches the face of the servant, who stands next to the bed holding a ring of keys, and softly illumi-

Figure 2.27 • Rembrandt, *Danaë*. Oil on canvas, 72¾ × 80 inches.
Scala/Art Resource, NY.

nates the center of the room, highlighting the ornate gold bed post and gold cherub. The light accents Danaë. Its brilliant reflections impart a luminous quality to her skin and its shadows model the soft fleshiness that was considered so beautiful in a woman. Rembrandt's Danaë is as voluptuous and sensuous as a yakshi. Her hair is arranged and ornamented; she wears bracelets on both arms, a ring on her left hand—and nothing else—yet she is without embarrassment or temerity. Quite the opposite: her smile, her glance, her raised hand are provocative. Her surroundings are opulant and luxurious, but they are not Greek. Instead they exemplify seventeenth century Dutch extravagance, and their every surface is a visual, tactile cue inviting the viewer's own associations. Pillows are soft and their delicate linen coverings are decorated with lace and tassels. The bedcover is heavy silk brocade, and the tablecover is rich red velvet crusted with embroidery. Underneath Danaë's jeweled slippers, thick pile rugs cover the floor, and silk drapes wrap around the bed so loosely they hint at closing with a single touch.

Rembrandt made an ancient myth part of his own time and place, and as a way of explaining the naturalness of human sexuality he portrayed human sensuality as open and without shame. Then he gave the picture one moral fillip by adding an ornamental bronze Cupid. As if to signify that the painting illustrates that moment of anticipation just before the seduction, he shows the little god of love crying because his hands are still bound like a prisoner's.

GONA'X'DEIT: THE MYTH AND THE SCULPTURE, *Kadjis-du-axtc (ca. 1750)*

Native Americans living along the Northwest Pacific coast adopted certain animals, birds, and fish as clan totems, personifying them in myth and believing them to be the ancestors of humans. *The Man who Killed Gona'x'deit* (gahn ah ka det) is sometimes called "The Mother-in-Law Story," and it is a wonderful mix of totems, fearlessness, and human foibles. The story begins with a young man who could not support his high-caste wife in a style suitable enough to satisfy his mother-in-law. One day he caught and killed a sea monster called Gona'x'deit (Wasco in some versions). After killing the monster, the young man discovered that by wearing its skin he could miraculously swim beneath the sea and catch all kinds of fish. He told his wife about this wonderful feat, but swore her to secrecy, warning her that he must always return to his human form each morning before the raven's first cry. That winter famine came to their village, but the husband was able to provide food for his own household, and every morning before dawn he generously left a fish at his mother-in-law's door. Now, the old lady was not only a mean-tempered greedy nag but a social-climber as well. To improve her status she began to invite some of the villagers to eat with her, telling them the food came from her magical powers. When she kept inviting more and more dinner guests, her son-in-law was forced to bring her larger and larger fish. Finally he brought her a seal, then a sea lion. When even that was not large enough, he struggled with a whale—which, of course, was his undoing because that morning he was unable to climb out of the monster skin before hearing the raven's call. When the villagers found his body, together with the monster skin and the whale, they guessed what had happened to this brave but foolish man who died trying to please a thankless relative. His mother-in-law eventually died of shame, and his wife who loved him mourned for many months. One evening as she walked along the beach, an unusual pattern of ripples caught her attention. She knew then that her husband's spirit had returned to her, and that he had become Gona'x'deit. She went beneath the sea to live with him, and they had two daughters who are called Women of the Creek. They are the spirits who bring the salmon, and seeing their spirits or the spirit of Gona'x'deit brings good luck.[3]

The Gona'x'deit myth appears on several totem poles and house posts belonging to different tribes along the Pacific Northwest Coast (fig. 2.28 a–c). The myth, however, is not easily identified. The unique style of this art makes positive identification a challenge and all the more difficult when totems represent family legends or variations of mythic themes. The Gona'x'deit housepost shown here is one of the oldest in existence and belongs to the descendants of a dynasty of great Tlingit chiefs of the Nanya'ayi clan from Wrangell, Alaska.[4]

The human figure is the young husband of the story who stands on the head of Gona'x'deit. On his own head is a very old type of war helmet worn by the Tlingit. This one is carved as a dogfish, a totem belonging to Nanya'ayi. The helmet has neck flaps which also serve as Gona'x'deit's tail fins. The small creature held by the husband has not been identified, but the round human face on its tail is an image signifying a strong spirit, usually a supernatural one. The man's tongue turns into the creature's back fin, and this signifies that an exchange of power is taking place (see fig. 2.28c). The creature's own tongue becomes the tongue of a bird, probably the raven in the story. Notice that the raven's wings bend upwards, along the man's legs, but its talons are at the very bottom of the post, extending from Gona'x'deit's mouth. Its wings also double as Gona'x'deit's lateral fin.

This is an art that does not separate images: husband, bird, creature, and Gona'x'deit are all linked as closely as the characters who make up the story. They are also powerful images meant to instill fortitude and courage in future generations whose very survival would depend on their knowledge and skill as fishermen and hunters.

Children of the Nanya'ayi grew up with these images because two houseposts stood like portals just inside the entrance to their house and two more stood near the entrance to the chief's private quarters. During long winter nights when their familiar world was hidden by fog and mist, children were told the stories of the totems, and during times of potlatch (a great feast), they witnessed the reinactment of these same stories through dance and music. Children of the Nanya'ayi and other great clans grew up with a rich, imaginative mythic art to help shape their lives.

Houseposts were considered especially valuable and were the only totem poles not allowed to "die." Totem poles that stood outdoors inevitably decayed, but this was expected since wooden poles in coastal Alaska's damp climate had about the same life span as humans. When poles fell to the ground they were left to rot like a dead tree. Houseposts were the only exception. The Gona'x'deit post is one of four that were moved at great expense some years after the old village of Wrangell moved to the town's present location. That move occurred in 1834 during the Russian occupation, and the Nanya'ayi posts were already old at the time. This means they were carved sometime in the mid or late 1700s, a date that makes them the oldest totem poles in existence.

FIGURE 2.28a • Kadjis-du-axtc,
Gona'x'deit Housepost, ca. 1750,
Wrangell, Alaska. Cedar, height
approximately 9'.
© Barry Herem.

FIGURE 2.28b • Kadjis-du-axtc, Gona'x'deit Housepost, ca. 1750, Wrangell, Alaska. Cedar, height approximately 9'. (Detail)
© Barry Herem.

FIGURE 2.28c • Kadjis-du-axtc, Companion Houseposts, ca. 1750, Wrangell, Alaska.
© Barry Herem.

PORTRAITS

The Renaissance biographer Vasari wrote that Leonardo da Vinci was so fascinated by faces he would follow a stranger, all day if necessary, until he could draw the face "as well by memory as though they stood before him." Portraiture as an art form has been scattered worldwide. For every society that needed some tangible long-lasting evidence of human existence, there were others that considered any self-image meaningless—nothing more than marks on paper or scratchings on stone. Sometimes, when self-images were introduced to societies, they were met with incomprehension and even fear.

BRONZE PORTRAIT HEAD FROM ILE-IFE, NIGERIA, ca. 1100–1600

With the exception of Egypt, portrait art is rarely found in Africa because African cultures generally stressed tribal importance over self-importance. For this reason the African portraits that do exist have more generalized—and very often abstract—features. Faces show no flaws or defects and no signs of age. Depicting physical imperfections would have been a sign of disrespect. Similarly, portraits were never intended to reveal individual personalities, hence they display little or no emotion. They were created solely as ritualistic objects and they were used for functions that varied with their tribal origins.

The life-size bronze head of an Oni (king) from Ile-Ife is an idealized portrait with classic features and a regal, serene countenance (fig. 2.29). Unfortunately it is a great work of art about which very little is known. What it originally signified, what purpose it originally served are questions that can be answered only in part and only by matching recent archeological evidence with ancient myth.

The portrait head comes from the city of Ile-Ife in a region of Nigeria inhabited by the Yoruba people. According to myth, the Yoruba culture began in that sacred city when gods descended to earth on an iron chain. The god who founded Ile-Ife and became its first king was named Odudusa, and his descendants, like Egyptian pharoahs, were considered semi-divine.

Only about thirty bronze portrait heads have ever been found, but all are similar in style. This raises the question as to whether their rarity and their similarity connect them somehow to the myth of semi-divine rulers. Tests reveal that the portraits were made sometime between the eleventh and fourteenth centuries—a three hundred year time difference! The fact that they are bronze raises another question, namely the metal's source. Metal is not indigenous to this region, and it would have been necessary to transport it by camel from the southern Sahara or perhaps from Morocco. Could the importation of metal be the true significance of the mythical god's iron chain? A curious feature about this and other portrait heads are the small holes along the forehead, face and chin and the larger holes at the base of the neck. The holes over the lips and chin show evidence of having once held beads, and it is possible that the beads simulated a moustache and beard.[5]

An ancient tradition of the nearby Benin tribe may furnish a few answers to these questions. When a king of the Benin died, his head was severed and

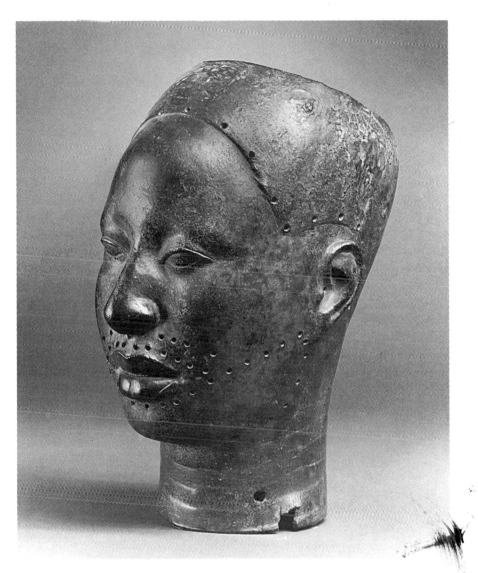

FIGURE 2.29 • Head of an Oni, ca. twelfth-fifteenth century. Zinc brass; 11 5/8".

From Wunmonije Compound, Ife. Museum of Ife Antiquities, 12. © Dirk Bakker.

sent to Ile-Ife. The head was buried there and a memorial head was cast in bronze and sent back to the Benin to be used for a ceremonial burial. Ethnologists William Fagg and Frank Willett, who have worked extensively in Ile-Ife, believe that the Ife portrait heads served a similar purpose. This region's extreme heat necessitates immediate burials, so there would not have been time enough to prepare the kind of elaborate funeral required for a king. Fagg and Willett believe that in the past a second funeral was held for the kings of Ile-Ife. In the interim, enough time was allowed to cast a portrait head in bronze and to make other arrangements for the ceremony. It would have been possible to attach a portrait head to a wooden body through the neck holes, and a crown could have been attached using the holes along the hairline. This would have made it possible to remove the crown and present it to the next king when the ceremonial funeral ended. This theory, of course, is merely a supposition, but it is based on the fact that other portrait heads found in the region are considerably smaller in size and are made entirely of clay with crowns attached.

GINEVRA DE'BENCI,
Leonardo da Vinci (1447–1522)

The only painting by Leonardo da Vinci in the United States is the portrait of Ginevra de'Benci in the National Gallery in Washington, D.C. (fig. 2.30). John Walker, former director of the National Gallery, purchased the picture in 1966 from Franz Josef II of Liechtenstein. The painting had been in the prince's family since 1733, and for twenty years had hung in the family's medieval castle in Vaduz. Few people knew of its existence. Fewer saw it. Now it is a national treasure.

Who was Ginevra? Thanks to John Walker's vigorous and scholarly research, there is a considerable amount of information about the Renaissance lady.[6] She was born in 1457 to a family of wealthy Florentine bankers. Her father was a supporter of the ruling Medici family and her brother was a personal friend of Leonardo's. She knew prominent politicians, artists, and literary figures, and she wrote poetry, although no examples of her work remain. Ginevra was married to Luigi Niccolini, a widower considerably older than herself. A few years after the marriage, when she may have been eighteen, she fell in love. The man was Bernardo Bembo, newly appointed Venetian ambassador to the court of the Medicis in Florence. Bernardo Bembo was, from all accounts, both handsome and charming. He was also married. When, at the end of five years, he was recalled to Venice, he returned to his wife and son. Ginevra was shattered. Sensitive and impressionable, she had not taken the love affair lightly. This is alluded to in correspondence between Lorenzo de' Medici to Ginevra mentioning her grief and her long illness.

Art historians do not know exactly when da Vinci painted her portrait. Sir Kenneth Clark thought it might have been a marriage portrait, but John Walker believed it was painted later, after the affair with Bembo. The fact that Ginevra is dressed in somber brown and black lends credence to Walker's opinion. Conservators found that the painting had once been damaged and about six inches cut from the bottom. Possibly the missing section showed her hands resting just below the lacing of her bodice. A drawing by Leonardo—a study of hands—at Windsor Castle seems to fit this particular portrait.

Looking at the portrait reproduced here and reading some of the details of Ginevra's life, do you form impressions of your own? Do you feel something of the human spirit in the face? John Walker thought her a "cold, melancholy Florentine lady." Certainly she is pale, her gaze reflective. Nothing in her demeanor suggests gaity or spontenaity. Her eyes are without luster and her mouth, though soft, is downturned. Her hair is worn in the style of Renaissance women and her eyebrows plucked thin in the fashion of the time. Around her neck is the narrow black scarf worn by certain Renaissance women as a reminder of religious faith and their own mortality.

Like his portrait *Mona Lisa*, Leonardo's painting of Ginevra has a certain sense of mystery, yet the artist hints at mood. He shows Ginevra in the sunless light of evening and in an autumnal landscape. The leaves on the trees are brown and dead and the more distant trees cast brown shadows over the grey water. Beyond those trees, a more distant landscape, vague and grey, is barely

FIGURE 2.30 • (Opposite) Leonardo da Vinci, *Ginevra de'Benci*, ca. 1474. Oil and tempera on panel, 15 1/4" × 14 1/2". (Detail)
Ailsa Mellon Bruce Fund. National Gallery of Art, Washington, D.C.

FIGURE 2.31 • Emblem painted on back of Leonardo da Vinci portrait, *Ginevra de'Benci*. (Detail)

Reverse of *Ginevra de' Benci*, Leonardo Da Vinci, National Gallery of Art, Washington, D.C.

suggested. The barbed juniper tree directly behind her is a visual clue to her name since Ginevra is derived from *ginepro*, the Italian word for juniper. The back of the painting holds another clue: an emblem made from laurel, palm, and juniper sprigs (fig. 2.31). The palm is a symbol of prosperity and laurel was the tree of Apollo, god of poetry. Part of the emblem is a narrow scroll with the Latin inscription *Virtutem Forma Decorat*, which means "Beauty Adorns Virtue." In the past, "virtue" had a different connotation than it does today. *Virtu* as interpreted by Renaissance humanists implied great strength of character.

PAUL REVERE,
John Singleton Copley (1738–1815)

John Singleton Copley was the son of Irish immigrants who settled in Boston. He was a self-taught painter whose only exposure to masterpieces was a collection brought to Boston by a British portrait painter who took up residence there. The collection consisted largely of paintings by relatively obscure artists plus a number of black and white prints that were copies of original works, and some plaster casts of Greek and Roman sculpture. Copley's initial art training came from his stepfather, a part-time painter and engraver, but the young man's skills quickly surpassed his teacher's. By the time he was twenty he was considered one of Boston's major portrait painters.

Copley was an indefatigable worker, but he was also a perfectionist who could require his subjects to pose for as many as fifteen separate sittings, some of them lasting as long as six hours. His attention to detail and his skill in rendering textures and colors gave his paintings an authentically lifelike quality, but equally important was his ability to capture his subjects' personalities. To achieve as truthful a portrait as possible he liked to include some object belonging to a sitter that "spoke" of the person's interests. He considered the pose itself vitally important, because he knew how much is revealed by a certain stance or turn of the head or a small gesture.

His eye for exactness and detail is apparent in the portrait of Paul Revere (fig. 2.32). Revere was a silversmith, and this is how Copley portrayed him: as a craftsman displaying his work. Copley posed him behind his work bench

FIGURE 2.32 • John Singleton Copley, *Paul Revere*, ca. 1768–1770. Oil on canvas, 35 × 28 1/2 in.
Gift of Joseph W., William B. and Edward H. R. Revere. Courtesy, Museum of Fine Arts, Boston.

and in shirt sleeves holding a silver teapot balanced on a leather hammering pillow. Evidently the teapot needed only its artist's signature for completion because the tools lying on the bench are engraving tools. Copley painted Revere's face partly in shadow and partly in strong light. To intensify this effect, he painted a reflection of Revere's white shirt on the smooth benchtop and a reflection of his fingers on the teapot's highly polished surface. By posing Revere with his chin resting on his right hand Copley chose an unusual gesture, one rarely seen in portraits. Evidently to the artist's discerning eye, the pose was as characteristic of Revere as his straightforward, determined gaze.

This portrait painted just prior to the American Revolution has an element of irony. Politically Copley and Revere were exact opposites. Copley, who had always wanted to travel in Europe, left the Colonies in 1774 and the following year, just before war was declared, sent for his wife and children. He took up residence in London with his family and never returned to the States. Revere, on the other hand, was one of America's great patriots. He was a leader of the Boston Tea Party, a courier for the Massachusetts Assembly, and an officer in the Massachusetts Militia. His warning to fellow patriots was the inspiration for Henry Wadsworth Longfellow's famous poem "Paul Revere's Ride."

ARASHI-KITSUSABURO I AS GOFUNKUYA JUBEI,
Shibakuni (ca. 1803)

In the city of Osaka, Japan, where the artist known as Shibakuni lived, kabuki theater and book publishing flourished during the nineteenth century. Before the advent of photography, book illustrations were printed from wood blocks. In Osaka and other large cities, booksellers sold the illustrations and other prints in their shops and stalls. Prints of kabuki actors were especially popular, and artists strove for authenticity by portraying actors in full make-up and costume.

Shibakuni's portrait of kabuki actor Kitsusaburo is somewhat unusual because it shows him in the privacy of his dressing room and reflected in a mirror (fig. 2.33). By posing Kitsusaburo at a dressing table and including such personal items as his make-up bowl, brushes, and the cloth used to remove make-up, the artist created a true behind-the-scenes picture. This was something that the actor's fans, waiting eagerly outside for a glimpse of him, would never have an opportunity to see—unless, of course, they bought the picture.

FIGURE 2.33 • Shibakuni, "Kabuki Actor" Arashi-Kitsusaburo I as Gotunkuya Jubei, ca. 1818, published 1821. Color Woodblock.
Philadelphia Museum of Art: Purchased: The Lola Dowin Peck Fund. 70-190-8.

If they did, they would recognize certain crests and names unfamiliar to today's viewers. They would know that the orange blossoms on the mirror frame were Kitsusaburo's personal emblem and that the characters on the mirror stand spelled "Oka." Oka is an abbreviated version of the actor's special theater name Okajimaya. "Oka" is what his fans yelled loudly when he made his first appearance on stage during a play. Shibakuni expressed his own enthusiasm when he included all five volumes of the play script and described his opinion of the actor's performance with a poem written across the top of the print.[7]

TWENTY-FIVE COLORED MARILYNS,
Andy Warhol (1925–1987)

Unlike nineteenth century Kabuki fans who sought some small glimpse into the offstage lives of favorite actors, Marilyn Monroe's twentieth century fans knew practically everything about her. Gossip columnists and the news media seldom let her out of the public eye. Even today, more than thirty years after her death, a new generation recognizes her name and face from a proliferation of old movies and hype. All the Marilyn Monroe images the public could ever want are readily available—and this is why Andy Warhol's portraits are so different.

Warhol created numerous portraits of Marilyn Monroe: all variations on a theme; all based on the same studio publicity still from a 1953 film *Niagra*. To Warhol this was the prototype image, and he proceeded to portray Monroe not as a person but as a media-blitzed sex goddess, complete with overbleached hair and blue, blue-shadowed eyes (fig. 2.34). He turned the lipstick-red smile into a logo and froze it for all time on a face three times larger than life—a screensize face. For this particular portrait he repeated that larger-than-life face twenty-five times, literally bombarding the viewer with the same icon, the same cliché, the same movie image, frame after frame after frame.

Warhol's techniques originated with a commercial printing process called photographic silkscreen. This same process is used to print T-shirts and souvenirs, and cheap production runs of these items can result in off-register colors. Warhol wanted a blurred effect and achieved it by intentionally changing the print register while he silk-screened sections of the photo onto a large piece of canvas. As a result, some faces have black streaks and smudges, others have faded areas, and what viewers see as painfully obvious, mismatched blue, blue eyelids and red lips. Warhol made his "plastic" goddess from the same gaudy pinks, reds, yellows, and blues used for cartoons and souvenirs.

FIGURE 2.34 • Andy Warhol, *Twenty-Five Colored Marilyns*, 1962. Acrylic on canvas. 89 × 57 in.

Collection of the Modern Art Museum of Fort Worth, The Benjamin J. Tillar Memorial Trust, acquired from the Collection of Vernon Nikkel, Clovis, New Mexico, 1983. Photo: Lee Clockman.

FIGURE 2.35 • (Above left) Pieter Bruegel, the Elder, *The Wedding Dance*, ca. 1566. Oil on panel: 47 × 62": 119.38 × 157.48 cm.
The Detroit Institute of Arts. City of Detroit Purchase.

FIGURE 2.36 • (Above right) José Clemente Orozco, *Barricade*, 1931; oil on canvas, 55 × 45".
Collection, The Museum of Modern Art, New York. Given anonymously. Photograph © 1992 The Museum of Modern Art, New York.

SOCIETY AND CULTURE

If it is true that artists hold a mirror to their societies, than there was no better purveyor of the 1960s and 1970s than Andy Warhol. As one of the first artists to recognize the impact of commercial media on human lives, Warhol successfully used a part of that media as the basis for his art. He was, in effect, a social commentator. Historically many artists have assumed that role. Sixteenth century Flemish artist Pieter Bruegel painted scenes of ordinary peasant life, and, viewed together, his pictures are an extraordinary chronicle of the times. The *Wedding Dance* and his other paintings and drawings provide traces of a society for which there is little written information (fig. 2.35). Other artists have chosen to communicate their committment to social change. Early in the twentieth century, a dynamic political group emerged in Mexico during its twenty-year revolutionary upheaval. Three painters of that group—Diego Rivera, José Clemente Orozco, and David Alfaro Siqueiros—spearheaded a movement known as the Mexican Renaissance. The movement resulted in displays of public art, mostly murals, describing Mexico's history with forceful, expressive imagery (fig. 2.36).

WORLDS WITHIN WORLDS:
Mary Cassatt (1844–1926) and Emily Carr (1871–1945)

Mary Cassatt (cah sat) painted only one small part of nineteenth century society; it was a little world, but the one she knew best. Cassatt created drawings, paintings, and prints of upper-middle class women and children, but to this rather narrow subject she brought a personal style that transformed it into universal themes of "Womanhood" and "Mother and Child."

Cassatt was an American artist who lived most of her adult life in France. She began her formal art training in Philadelphia at the Pennsylvania Academy of Fine Arts where, at the end of four years, she became thoroughly frustrated by the school's double standards. Among other restrictions, women were not allowed to attend nude life drawing classes but were given their own "special" classes in anatomy (fig. 2.37). Cassatt moved permanently to France when she was twenty-two and was almost immediately introduced to the work of the French Impressionists. The Impressionists were a group of nineteenth century painters who changed the course of art by emphasizing the effects of light on color and by presenting informal, candid views of their subjects. Cassatt shared many of the Impressionists' professional goals and exhibited with them on a regular basis.

Her pictures are mostly of women in surroundings of gentility and comfort, lovely images of women who never smile. They wear beautiful gowns, feathered and ribboned hats and proper gloves and sit on flowered chintz sofas, chatting or perhaps having tea. The perimeters of their social world—usually the theater or the park—are their only backgrounds. They are not beautiful women in the sense of being pretty, but neither are they fragile. Most of them are quite plain, stocky, and healthy looking. Their real beauty is in a strength of character, a certain spirit or presence that Cassatt reveals.

FIGURE 2.37 • Thomas Eakins, Ladies modeling class at the Pennsylvania Academy of Fine Arts, ca. 1883, (photograph).
Philadelphia Museum of Art.

More than a third of her work is devoted to the theme of "Mother and Child." *The Bath* is one example (fig. 2.38). It is a candid scene, a single moment stopped in time by the artist's brush. Soon the mother's hand will move the child's foot—or so it seems. The daughter's hand braced against her mother's knee, like her concentration on her own feet, will last seconds at best. The mother's arm around her daughter and the touch of her hand on the plump, wet foot reveal the artist's quick perception and her skill in making pose and gesture "speak." The language is universal: differences of time, place, status, religion, and race do not exist, or at best are inconsequential. The picture is every loving mother and child, every moment as tender and fleeting.

One characteristic of Cassatt's style is to bring you close to a scene. She accomplishes this by composing the picture as if you were sitting or standing just a few feet away looking slightly downward. Filmmakers use a similar technique with above eye-level angle shots that make the viewer an invisible participant. This is exactly what Cassatt did. To strengthen the effect, she blurred the background, much as a photographer might adjust the depth of field to obtain a clear, sharply defined subject against a slightly out-of-focus background. Notice how the rug pattern in *The Bath* is distinct in the foreground but just barely perceptible in the background. The flower-decorated chest and the floral wallpaper are not clearly defined either; instead, they are made from scrumbled, irregular brushstrokes.

Another characteristic of this artist's style is the use of color relationships to reinforce a subject's dominance in the picture. Notice how she harmonized light tints of blue, violet, and green to make a single unit of the mother and child, pitcher and basin. This unit holds your attention. Her use of red in this picture was highly selective. Red can easily grab attention, but Casset didn't allow this to happen because she used it solely for contrast. Like everything else, it is background and of related but secondary importance to "Mother and Child."

Halfway across the world from Mary Cassatt in France, another woman hiked the Canadian wilderness to record the last vestiges of a vanquished society. Emily Carr, a remarkable but neglected Canadian artist, painted what was left of Native American totem poles in villages that had been deserted long before she came across them. She painted lichen covered, disintegrating houses and totems not so much as she saw them but as she felt them to be—as symbols of a once vital civilization.

Emily Carr was born in 1871 in Victoria, the provincial capital of British Columbia. Victoria was and is very British in its customs and charm; it is, however, totally incongruous with its location on Vancouver Island. The island is five hours by boat from the mainland and is so thickly forested that as late as 1960 cougars roamed its uninhabited areas. Since Victoria in the late 1800s offered nothing in the way of art instruction, Carr moved to San Francisco for a brief time and later to England for four years of study before returning to her birthplace.

A trip to Alaska in 1907 inspired her to paint what remained of the great totem poles that were carved during the late eighteenth and nineteenth centuries. Subsequently, she made eight solitary journeys into some of the most remote, mountainous areas of mainland British Columbia and the equally

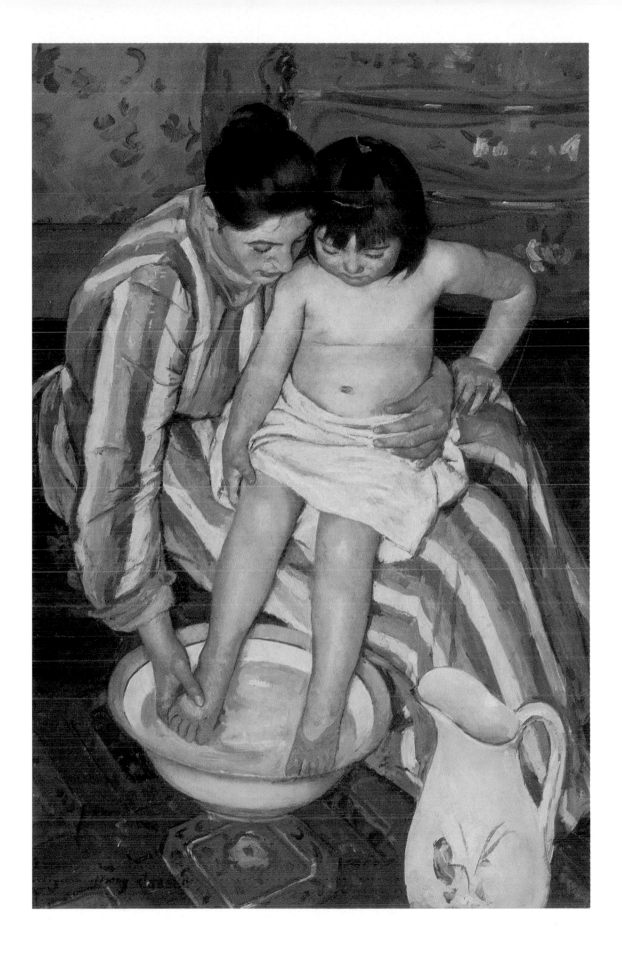

rugged Queen Charlotte Islands. Carr wrote about her experiences: "I slept in tents, in roadmakers' toolsheds, in missions, and in Indian houses. I traveled in anything that floated in water or crawled over land."[8] Her sketches and paintings are the only record of many old villages that have disappeared along with their art.

How were her paintings received? In a letter to the National Gallery, Ottawa, Carr wrote

> When I sent to an exhibition they dishonoured my work in every way, putting it behind things, under shelves,or on the ceiling. My friends begged me to go back to my old way of painting, but I had tasted the joys of a bigger way it would have been impossible had I wanted to, which I did not. Whenever I could afford it I went up north among the Indians and the woods and forgot all about everything in the joy of those lonely wonderful places. I decided to try and make as good a representative collection of those old villages and wonderful totem poles as I could, for the love of the people and the love of the places, and the love of the art, whether anybody liked them or not I did not care a bean.[9]

Carr did care. Rejection and lack of money put an end to her painting for ten years, a time when she supported herself by renting out apartments, hooking rugs, and raising sheep dogs. Largely through the encouragement of two other artists, the Canadian Lawren Harris and the American Mark Tobey, she was brought back into the mainstream of North American art. Reacquainting herself, she traveled east to see several major art shows and in a few years saw her own work exhibited in Canadian cities and to a lesser extent in the United States and Europe.

Carr began this new period of work with renewed vigor and a mature style that fully expressed her personal philosophy (fig. 2.39). The year she painted *Big Raven* she wrote: "I want to paint some skies so that they look roomy and moving and mysterious and to make them overhang the earth, to have a different quality in their distant horizon and their overhanging nearness." *Big Raven* was based on sketches made during an earlier trip to the village of Cumshewa on the Queen Charlotte Islands. There she had found a very old carved Raven marking the location of a mass grave for Haida Indians who died in the smallpox epidemic of 1860. When Carr saw the grave site in 1912, almost nothing was left except Raven and the encroaching forest. She painted the scene the way she remembered it affecting her: as a "great lonesomeness smothered in a blur of rain."[10]

FIGURE 2.39 • Emily Carr, *Big Raven* (Cumshewa), 1931. Oil on canvas, 87.3 × 114.4 cm.
Vancouver Art Gallery. 42.3.11. Emily Carr Trust.

How does an artist transfer mood and feeling to a piece of canvas? How does an artist manipulate colors and shapes to transmit loneliness or mystery? Carr's solution was to use the rich, dark colors of forests and mountains and to turn their shapes into abstractions. Everything in *Big Raven* is solid, yet nothing is static. Ground forest wraps around Raven's base like ocean swells advancing and retreating with unseen, unbridled energy. Behind Raven, a slim pole of a tree trunk supports layered sheafs of leaves. Above Raven, a dark cloud "overhangs the earth" and becomes "moving" and "mysterious." A "blur" of rain behind the mountains, falling in heavy white shafts, fails to touch Raven. And Raven? Carr's Raven is a symbol, not the authentic totem. Old wood carvings lose their paint and are left, at best, with only dull splotches of stain—faded reminders of what was once color. Old wood cracks, letting lichens and moss and shoots of new trees into its narrow crevices. Old wood weathers, carved contours soften, and gradually the original grain hides a carver's work. Carr's Raven shows no age. He is strong, arrogant, proud, ageless. He stands, a solitary sentinel guarding the dead.

PROTEST AND IDEOLOGY:
Pablo Picasso (1881–1973) and Romare Bearden (1913–1988)

On April 26, l937, German bombers destroyed the Basque city of Guernica in northern Spain. Germany was not involved in the ongoing Spanish Civil War, but it gave unofficial support to General Francisco Franco, leader of the Spanish Fascists. Although Guernica was never a military target, German dive bombers totally demolished its buildings and killed inhabitants to test the saturation bombing and strafing they would use later during World War II. Pablo Picasso, a Spaniard by birth, was enraged by this massacre and *Guernica*, considered by many art historians and critics to be his masterpiece, is the result of his fury channeled into a surge of creativity (fig. 2.40).

FIGURE 2.40 • Pablo Picasso, *Guernica*, mural 1937. Oil on canvas, approx., 11′ 6″ × 25′ 8″.
© S.P.A.D.E.M., Paris/© A.R.S. New York.

What makes *Guernica* a masterpiece? Very simply, the originality of its theme and its style. Picasso turned an atrocity into a universal statement about the horrors of violence. To this end, he distorted observable reality by changing people, places, and things into abstract symbols—a creative process that is anything *but* simple.

The painting is enormous: more than eleven feet high and twenty-five feet long. Consider the reduction necessary to fit its photograph on a single page of this book. The way you look at its photograph depends, of course, on how you hold this book, but you might want to prop up the book until the painting is vertical. Then, try to imagine yourself walking through the doorway of an immense room and seeing the actual painting on the opposite wall. If you walk up to it and stand to the left, you will see the screaming woman's face slightly

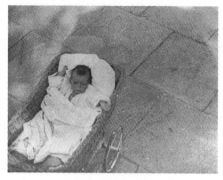

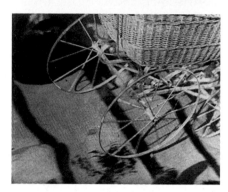

FIGURE 2.41 • ''Odessa Steps Sequence'' from Sergei Eisenstein, *Battleship Potemkin*, 1925.
Courtesy of the Museum of Modern Art, Film Stills Archive.

above eye level. Look down and you will be staring into the face of her dead child. By taking a step to the right or by turning your head slightly you will look directly into the face of the beheaded man. Then you know that man's widely separated eyes and his open hand, rigid in death, look *right*. If you look up, the bull looms over you. Since you must tilt your head to look at him, the angle of his eyes and the twist of his body make him seem in motion—a sensation that for some people produces a slight vertigo. The picture's length makes it necessary to walk alongside it, and much of what you see is not only larger than life but fragmented. The entire experience is similar to watching a violent movie scene in which images and partial images flash across the screen in quick and disorienting motion (fig. 2.41a–h). *Guernica* is black, white, and grey. Picasso chose not to paint with color but to use instead the same black and white tonal qualities found in photos and films of the 1930s. His effects, however, could never be achieved photographically. The most obvious effect is the abstraction. Bodies are hideously distorted: arms are severed; hands reach and clutch and are strangely disconnected; mouths are open and screaming. A woman, her arm and neck stretched like rubber, leans from a window holding a lamp, and just above her, a lightbulb burns with knifelike flames. More piercing flames surround the woman on the far right, incinerating her.

This picture has layers and levels of meaning. The broken sword is a universal symbol of military defeat, but does the flower symbolize hope or loss? The artist's intent is unclear and open to interpretation. In other paintings and prints Picasso used bulls and horses as victims of Spanish bullfighting, but he also used a bull as the Minotaur, a creature from ancient Greek mythology symbolizing irrational violent forces that demand sacrifice. Which meaning is implied here?

Guernica has strong elements of Cubism. Like Impressionism, Cubism was an art movement, but its aims and styles were quite different. Cubist artists changed a subject—literally abstracted it—into various geometric shapes. What resulted were multiple views of a subject presented simultaneously. Picasso was one of the founders of the Cubist movement, but by the time he painted *Guernica* his style had changed. Nevertheless, strong elements of Cubism remain in this work.

Cubist influences are also apparent in Romare Bearden's *The Prevalance of Ritual: Baptism* (fig. 2.42). Bearden's work is a collage, a word meaning "paste-up" in French and used to designate pictures created from fragments of photographs and other materials. Most obvious in *Prevalence of Ritual: Baptism* are its distorted shapes, but given the work's title, are they actually dis-

FIGURE 2.42 • Romare Howard Bearden, *Prevalence of Ritual: Baptism,* 1964 (66.410). Photomechanical reproductions synthetic polymer and pencil on paperboard, 9 1/8 × 12 in.
Hirshhorn Museum and Sculpture Garden, Smithsonian Institution, Gift of Joseph H. Hirshhorn, 1966. Photographer: Lee Stalsworth.

torted? The title is not "A Baptism in the United Methodist Church" or " A Sunday Morning Baptism" or even "A Baptism."

What *does* "Baptism" signify in this instance? Does it have connotations and implications that extend beyond religion? Considering the other half of the title, "The Prevalance of Ritual," what *is* the significance of "ritual" in society? *Is* it prevalant? Does it play a role in the lives of Americans? Since Bearden's inclusion of a Christian church together with African masks was not accidental, what is their connection?

Romare Bearden's subject is conceptual, and its ideas, like its images, are kaleidoscopic. The more you look at the work, the more your own thoughts turn and move in new directions. Ideas that at first may seem disjointed and unconnected suddenly come together to make bold new thought patterns, and you find yourself creating, expanding, and recreating ideas. Intellectually *you* become the artist giving shape and color to ideas in your mind.

Impossible? Difficult? Not at all. Style and sense work together. Notice how Bearden splits faces into fragments, some of them African masks; then ask yourself how faces actually do change expression. How does a shout or a cry or a grimace change a face? What happens to the eyes? To the mouth? What *do* faces reveal as people watch or participate in a baptismal rite? Or any rite? What do hands reveal? Look how the hands in this picture touch, hold, clasp, and reach, some of them outward toward you. Look at the color and size of the hand at the bottom left, then the hand at the top center with a thin stream of water across its palm. Water reappears at the very bottom center, where it flows right off the picture. To the right of that shape of water are three other shapes that change from river-brown to shallow-white to the clear blue-green of deep water. Immersed under those three shapes is a youth, his mouth open in a shout, his arms reaching upward and outward. Are his hands over-sized? Only if you fail to notice that this is a multiple view. A hand held close-up to a camera will always look over-large and distorted. This is a visual phenomenon and a perspective artists understand and use.

Bearden's memories and experiences came from his life in New York and his visits to the South. His grandmother sparked his interest in art by encouraging him to enter a poster contest, and he won it. Bearden's interest never wavered. After graduating from New York University he studied at the Art Students League in New York, and later, after serving in the Infantry during World War II, used the G.I. Bill to study at the Sorbonne in Paris. Eventually he became one of America's most prominent black artists, but the early years of his career were often discouraging. Bearden kept a journal during that time, and a portion of one entry reads:

> I see difficult times ahead for myself in relation to my finding those who will either understand, or make the effort to understand, my painting. The sincere artist would hope to address his work to those capable of intellectual comprehension—but where are the intellectuals of today? This is a land, a wilderness, peopled by the middle class.[11]

ENVIRONMENTAL SCENES

Landscape painting began in China sometime during the fifth century. Its long and important history is explained by a reverence for the environment that is deeply rooted in the country's three dominant religions. From **Taoism** came the contemplation of nature as the *Tao* (Way) of living in harmony. From **Confucianism** came the respect for nature that denotes a person of good character. From **Buddhism** came the profound regard for all living things. Together, these religions cultivated a veneration for nature that includes an appreciation for paintings of nature. The Chinese believed valuable lessons of life could be learned from the natural environment. Mountains and waterfalls were visible evidence of nature's tremendous energy. Tall, old pine trees were sentinels made noble by years of endurance. Stunted or gnarled pine trees indicated a strong will to survive despite life's hardships. Bamboo, because it bends in the wind and remains green through the winter, symbolized resiliency and persistence. Plum blossoms symbolized fortitude, an analogy to the tree's early flowering, even in the snow. Herons and cranes were birds of patience and refined character; eagles were birds of great courage. This deeply ingrained, environmental philosophy fostered a history of landscape painting very different from Europe's.

European landscape painting had a sporadic history. Initially popular with the Romans, landscapes and cityscapes were painted on the walls of their villas. The practice ceased with the beginning of Christianity. Landscapes reappeared in the fourteenth century in religious pictures and portraits, then gradually became the sole or dominant subject. Albrecht Dürer included an authentic landscape scene in his print *The Virgin with the Monkey* (fig. 2.25); and Leonardo da Vinci included an autumn landscape in his portrait of Ginevra de'Benci (fig. 2.30).

TWO VIEWS—EAST AND WEST:
Kuan Tao-Sheng (1262–1319) and John Constable (1776–1836)

Chinese artists assumed that people appreciated nature paintings because they were already familiar with the subject and were searching for something more. A Westerner might ask, "More of what?" One answer is found in an aphorism attributed to Confucius: "The wise men find pleasure in water; the virtuous men find pleasure in mountains." Another answer is offered by the Chinese word for landscape painting, *Shan-shui,* which means "mountain-water" picture. Merely looking at Chinese landscape paintings will not merit their full appreciation. Contemplating them is a more rewarding experience because they were originally created to be emotionally absorbed while intellectually analyzed.

Part of their analysis begins with a perception of the calligraphy. Calligraphy was considered the highest form of art, and skills of brushwriting carried over into painting. In calligraphy, line quality and balance are extremely important, and "bony"—meaning strong and spontaneous—strokes are admired. Analysis also considers the overall size and shape of the painting, because

FIGURE 2.43 • Kuan Tao-Sheng, *A Bamboo Grove in Mist*, ca. 1300.
Yale University Art Gallery, Hobart and Small Moore Memorial Collection.

this determines how it is contemplated. *Bamboo Grove in Mist* is a *Shou Chüan* (hand scroll) painting nearly six feet in length (fig. 2.43). Hand scroll paintings were viewed by first laying them on the floor or a table and then unrolling them slowly from right to left. The scrolls were designed to take the viewer on an imaginative and leisurely stroll past one small scene after another until, at the end, the whole, wonderful panorama was revealed. Whatever the viewer's thoughts during this imaginative journey, and by whatever circuitous route those thoughts may have traveled, ultimately they reached a destination.

In figure 2.43 you see *Bamboo Grove in Mist* in its entirety and greatly reduced in size, but you might want to view the scroll as it was meant to be contemplated. Beginning on the right, what you see is the most distant: the high mountain peaks that break through empty spaces of sky and cloud cover. Beneath these mountains, the trees are mere dots and the rocks black pinpoints. As your eyes "stroll" to the left, they encounter groundfog behind the first clumps of bamboo and soon the mist surrounds you. Closer to the center of the picture, a stream spills over a miniature falls. Everywhere paths lead toward sheltered, unseen places. Terrain is rough and uneven—grass-covered in some areas, rock-covered in others—making it difficult to distinguish ground from water and water from mist. Eyes are deceived. What is solid? What is empty? Where does the earth vanish into the sky? A Buddhist paradox?

The artist Kuan Tao-Sheng was an acclaimed thirteenth century calligrapher whose fame came from unique and perfected skills in copying Buddhist scriptures and in painting bamboo and plum blossoms. Kuan Tao-Sheng was also a woman artist living in a society that did not favor women. Few women, even among the noble class, were literate. Her husband Chao Ming-Fu was also an artist-calligrapher and a government official during the reign of the Mongol ruler Kublai Khan. Kuan Tao-Sheng found employment at the royal court as a calligrapher, and her biographers write that she was greatly admired professionally and personally. Only because of her social and political status and that of her husband's was she permitted to do something as unconventional as accompany her husband on official trips. At a time when women were confined to the home or at best to perimeters of the court or neighborhood, Kuan-Tao Sheng traveled beyond the gates of cities to actually experience the beauty of mist covered groves and mountains.

John Constable was a British landscape painter whose life and career bridged the eighteenth and nineteenth centuries. He was the son of a farmer, and his boyhood memories of brown plowed fields against green hills stitched with hedgerows were the single most important influence on his art. He loved nature, and his pictures inevitably included people who worked and lived in harmony with nature.

Constable's approach to art was a combination of science and romanticism. He was particularly interested in meteorology—then a new branch of science—and would go off "skying," as he called it, to watch and sketch cloud formations. He filled entire notebooks with sketches and written observations of the effects of light and weather on landscape, and he could describe, to the smallest detail, the movements and countermovements of tree branches in the wind or eddies in a stream. But if one part of him was scientist, the other was romantic. Constable greatly admired the poet William Wordsworth, who used words—as he used paint—to praise and extol earth's beauty.

Constable made his initial sketches of Salisbury Cathedral in 1820 during a visit to John Fisher, Bishop of Salisbury. During the next few years he developed several paintings from those sketches, two at the Bishop's request. Each painting is different—for example, his first version has a dark storm cloud that he eliminated in the version shown in figure 2.44. In this newer version, the cathedral stands under a sunny sky with great white clouds. Rather than make the cathedral the sole subject of the picture, Constable had it share the stage, so to speak, with its natural setting. Since the cathedral was 600 years old, it truly belonged with its setting of ancient trees and grassy clearing. Constable included the Bishop of Salisbury in the scene as a matter of record. The Bishop stands on the path pointing something out to his wife. The artist added a minor note of interest by including a woman, distant but plainly seen walking along the same path toward the Bishop and his wife. He also added what was probably at the time a common sight: Suffolk cows grazing on the commons.

Constable gave viewers a glimpse of an uneventful ordinary day in the English countryside, but he took that ordinary scene and made it a tribute to nature and architecture. How did he accomplish this? By his use of light and color. Constable's painting methods were a direct result of his scientific observations and his flair for the dramatic. In his correspondence, the artist often mentioned what he called "the chiaroscuro of nature." **Chiaroscuro** literally

FIGURE 2.44 • John Constable, *Salisbury Cathedral from the Bishop's Garden*, ca. 1825. Oil on canvas: 34 5/8 × 44″. (88 × 111.8 cm.) The Metropolitan Museum of Art. Bequest of Mary Stillman Harkness. 1950.

means "clear" and "obscure" in Italian, and refers to methods of manipulating light and shadow to make objects appear solid and dimensional. British art historian Sir Kenneth Clark equates Constable's "chiaroscuro of nature" term with two related but different effects in his pictures.[12] Clark calls one effect "a keynote of feeling," meaning the visual drama inherent in nature's own reflections and shadows. In *Salisbury Cathedral from the Bishop's Garden* that keynote of feeling is obtained by the contrasts between sun and shadow that appear throughout the picture. Notice, for example, how sunlight envelops the building and how it makes green grass appear both light and dark. Notice how the tree's dark shadows transmit the sensation of coolness that occurs when you first step out of sun and into shade. Notice, too, how the clouds' shadows give the sky an appearance of motion and dimension.

A second effect, according to Sir Kenneth, is the "sparkle of light, 'dews—breezes—bloom and freshness. . . .' " Constable achieved this by using short, broken brushstrokes of lighter colors mixed with flecks of pure white. Note, for example, the twisted branches that hang high above the heads of the Bishop and his wife: notice how their "bone" comes from the slender streaks of lighter color that make them look solid. Notice how the colors of foliage include white flecks that glisten in the sun like the undersides of leaves turning on a breezy day. A similar juxtaposition of white, this time with darker colors, produces rough and mottled textures on tree trunks.

NATURE TRANSCENDED:
Claude Monet (1840–1926) and Vincent van Gogh (1853–1890)

Claude Monet's (mo NAY) painting *Impression-Sunrise* was first shown as part of a group exhibit in Paris in 1874 (fig. 2.45). It was singled out by French critics for the harshest insults, and the word "impressionist" became their derisive label for the entire group of paintings displayed. Critics considered the paintings' techniques unfinished, their styles unrealistic, and their subjects far too ordinary and commonplace. The exhibit was held in a studio belonging to the photographer Nadar because major galleries unanimously refused to show the Impressionists' "unacceptable" art. The antagonism that greeted Impressionism was slow to disappear. Nearly twenty years after the initial exhibit,

FIGURE 2.45 • Claude Monet, *Impression—Sunrise*, 1872. Oil on canvas: 19 1/2 × 25 1/2". (49.5 × 64.8 cm.) Musée Marmottan, Paris.

when a collection of Impressionist paintings was willed to the Louvre, old criticisms of "filth" and "moral slackening" returned to echo through the offices of government officials. As a result, the Louvre refused to accept a considerable part of the collection.[13] If there is any irony to Impressionism's initial bad press, it is the theft of Monet's *Impression-Sunrise* a century later in the 1980s, a decade that witnessed thefts of masterpieces worldwide. Fortunately, with the help of INTERPOL, this painting was recovered.

Monet, of all Impressionist artists, was the major exponent of the movement's aims. These objectives, mentioned earlier in the discussion of Mary Cassatt, were to present informal, candid views of a subject and to emphasize the effects of natural light on color. Monet never deviated from these initial objectives, and he devoted his entire career to their pursuit. He advocated painting what you *see*, not what you *know;* he prefaced that belief by remarking that if what you see looks like a blur, paint the blur! This meant, of course, that images dematerialized. Edges became soft and sometimes disappeared into backgrounds that were themselves indistinct. This is apparent in *Impression-Sunrise*, a painting of the Le Havre harbor on a day when industrial smoke mixed with early morning mist made everything in view hazy and unclear— and, in Monet's eyes, violet-tinged and incredibly beautiful.

Monet once said "Light is the principal person in the picture," consequently the prismatic effects of light on color never ceased to fascinate him. He studied the works of Eugène Delacroix and Joseph M.W. Turner, two painters who had experimented in quite different ways with color, and he searched scientific journals for any ongoing experiments with light. All natural phenomena relating to color perception fascinated him, and he began to paint serial pictures of Rouen Cathedral and Westminster Bridge, of grainstacks, poplars, and water lilies. In each series he painted the same subject in different weather conditions and at different times of day. The results, so remarkably unalike, are a revelation that asks what is visual truth?

The dominant image in Vincent van Gogh's (van GO) painting *Olive Trees* is the sun (fig. 2.46). Like some great yellow revolving sphere it lights up a yellow sky. The sky itself is no longer background but a vibrating, gyrating shape in a picture where everything appears to move. Pale and distant mountains, veiled by atmosphere, seem more like a mirage than solid rock. Trees refuse to stand still. Their trunks twist and turn, and only black outlines keep them from being as fragile and impermanent as leaves. The leaves—ordinarily a pale grey-green—are now burnished like silver to reflect the light. Shadows, naturally dark, are indefinite here, colored mostly grey and black and painted over an undulating terrain of golden orange-red. The earth seethes with life.

Few artists have put a more personal stamp on landscape painting than Vincent van Gogh. His colors are luminous and his shapes and lines are textured by the thick paint he applied with brushes and palette knives. Van Gogh painted what is not always visible to the eye. Whereas Monet painted what his eyes saw, van Gogh painted what he felt. In a letter to his brother Theo, Van Gogh wrote, ". . . I wish you could spend some time here, you would feel it after a while . . . you feel colour differently." In another letter he wrote, "To express hope by some star, the eagerness of a soul by a sunset radiance. Certainly there is no delusive realism in that, but isn't it something that actually exists?"

Van Gogh painted the world he knew. He painted miners and peasants in the Dutch villages of his homeland; he painted the streets and shops of small French towns where he lived. He painted his postman, his landlady, and his doctors. He painted hospital corridors and public gardens, flowers growing in the sun and more flowers cut and arranged in vases. He painted his own small bedroom and gave lasting fame to a plain wooden chair and a narrow bed with a straw mattress. Paintings of the environment became his greatest challenge. Van Gogh was particularly interested in developing serial paintings of olive trees, cypress trees, and mountains but was able to complete only the twenty-painting series of olive trees.

The artist's career was cut short by suicide. The remarkably large outlay of work he left behind actually covered only a ten year period. Unlike Con-

FIGURE 2.46 • Vincent van Gogh, *Olive Trees*, 1889. Oil on canvas, 29 × 36 1/2.
The William Hood Dunwoody Fund. 51.7.
Minneapolis Institute of Arts.

stable and Monet and even Kuan Tao Sheng, who received recognition during their lifetimes, van Gogh sold only one painting. He was unknown to all but a small circle of family and friends in his native Holland and in France, where he died at thirty-seven believing himself a failure.

So much misinformation exists about this artist, it might be helpful to explain several widespread and erroneous rumors. To the misinformed he is that "mad" artist who painted unreal pictures. Was he "mad"? Not to anyone who reads the voluminous correspondence between the artist and his family and friends. His mind was sharp, incredibly perceptive, and possessing a rare combination of imagination and logic. His analysis of an illness doctors could neither diagnose nor cure reveals a strong will to survive. The current medical consensus is that he may have suffered from severe epileptic seizures or from intensely painful attacks of Ménière's syndrome or acute intermittent porphyia. Whatever the reason, he was often incapacitated and hospitalized for weeks and months at a time. Answers about why and how he cut off the lobe of his ear are pure guesswork. The fact is that it happened at the onset of a particularly violent seizure. A fact of far greater significance is that art became his refuge from terrifying fears and frustration. He was, after all, a lonely man living with the constant dread of recurring seizures. Four months before his suicide van Gogh wrote his brother, ". . . Oh, if I could have worked without this accursed disease—what things I might have done."

THE CITY:
Childe Hassam (1859–1935) and Richard Estes (1936–   )

Nature is one aspect of the environment, and cities are another. In cities, however, the creative forces are not of nature but of human beings. The American artist Childe Hassam was fascinated by rural coastal areas and cities alike. He drew and painted landscapes and seascapes of his native New England and historic scenes of Newport, Provincetown, East Hampton, and other coastal towns. Among his best known works are the serial paintings titled "Avenue of the Allies" dedicated to the city of New York.

Fifth Avenue, Noon, is not from the series, but it is similar in projecting the look and spirit of the United States at the turn of the century. The picture shows a few city blocks teeming with life on a sunny day in 1916 (fig. 2.47). It is a slice of life captured by an artist who was strongly influenced by the Impressionists. Hassam's perspective on the scene and his use of light are directly attributable to Impressionist techniques. His perspective positions you high above the scene, as if inside a building looking down from a second or third story window. Photographers call this an aerial or **bird's eye shot,** and it was favored by early photographers and by the Impressionists. It can produce a feeling of omniscience, as if you were standing on high, godlike, removed from the scene yet able to observe everything taking place. Playwrights and novelists are apt to use narrators in much the same way when they want to "distance" the audience, thus allowing them greater objectivity. Hassam's visual distancing makes the people in the picture completely anonymous. A few individuals are isolated from the crowd, but even they are indistinct. Some of

FIGURE 2.47 • Childe Hassam, *Fifth Avenue, Noon*. Etching. 1916. 10" × 7 1/8".
American Art Heritage Fund. Art Museum, Arizona State University, Tempe.

them stand in full sunlight, but most are blurred, darkened and tucked into shadows of the buildings. In other parts of the picture, shadows help define the architectural details of turn-of-the-century buildings.

To Childe Hassam, New York City was a microcosm of the country. The economic climate in 1916 was one of tremendous optimism. Banks were prosperous and stable, railroads and manufacturing industries were operating at peak performance. The first of several child labor laws had been enacted, and the Suffragette Movement was gaining strength. World War I had started two years earlier, but the mood of the country was secure in its belief that the United States would avoid involvement in "Europe's War." That optimism is reflected in the picture. American flags wave from the roofs of distant build-

FIGURE **2.48** • Richard Estes, *Central Savings*, 1975. 36 × 48 in. Oil on canvas.
The Nelson-Atkins Museum of Art, Kansas City, Missouri.

ings, and the streets of New York's most exclusive shopping district teem with life. Automobiles and doubledecker buses share Fifth Avenue with horsedrawn carriages, and people are everywhere.

Sixty years later Richard Estes painted New York without its people. In *Central Savings*, a normally busy little restaurant is closed, and one of the city's business districts takes on its weekend look (fig. 2.48). Estes is a Photorealist: one of a group of artists who paint with a hard-edged precision. He develops his initial ideas from photographs that he takes on Sundays when, as he says, fewer people are out and no trucks park in front of his camera. Choosing from hundreds of photos of different scenes, Estes bases his decisions on the mood of a particular building or group of buildings and sites. Using photos of a selected scene, he develops several composite sketches. From these he adds, deletes, and changes specific details, then chooses a color range, and gradually develops what will be the final oil painting. The process usually takes from three to five months.[14]

Estes' eye for detail and his skill are immediately apparent in *Central Savings*. The slick red formica counter and red plastic stools are the brightest shapes in a picture where everything fights for your attention. Chrome and more chrome, mirrors, and window glass bounce reality and illusion back and forth like a row of funhouse mirrors. What *are* you looking at? Into? Through? How many counters *are* there? How long does it take to find the title *Central Savings*? How long to find Estes' signature in another sign?

The artist's juxtaposition of objects with reflections can sometimes create bizarre effects. Where, for example, are the restaurant's ceiling light and its vent? Are they just hanging there minus the ceiling or are they floating in the air outside? And why does the reflection of a fire hydrant have more substance than the shadow figures of passers-by? The sky is a fairly solid looking patch of blue, and except for the shadow-people, is the only image of something that was not manufactured. Once, when asked about his proclivity for painting metal, glass, chrome, and concrete instead of trees, grass, and clouds Estes gave an answer Monet would have appreciated. He said, "I think the explanation is that for the past twenty years I've lived in a man-made environment and I've simply painted where I've been . . . You look around and paint what you see."[15]

FORCES MADE VISIBLE

Phenomena known to exist but only recently seen have always preoccupied humankind (fig. 2.49). Mythmakers personified them. Scientists investigated them. Artists felt them. Hundreds of years before Monet painted light's transience and van Gogh painted a universe in motion, Leonardo da Vinci filled his notebooks with drawings of the energy of natural cataclysms.

Shapes with no counterpart in nature have also interested artists, scientists, mathematicians, and philosophers. In the *Philebus*, written in the fourth century B.C., Plato presents a dialogue between Protarchus and Socrates concerning pleasure and beauty. At one point, Socrates says:

> I do not mean by beauty of form such beauty as that of animals or pictures, which the many would suppose to be my meaning; but says the argument, understand me to mean straight lines and circles, and the plane or solid figures which are formed out of them by turning-lathes and rulers and measurers of angles; for these I affirm to be not only relatively beautiful, like other things, but they are eternally and absolutely beautiful.

What is absolute? Or eternal? Plato would seem to prefer an abstract art in which there is no appearance, no connection to the natural world *as people see it*. Today many artists agree with the philosopher.

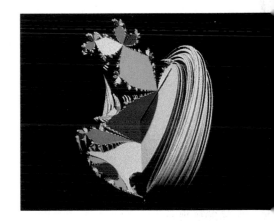

FIGURE 2.49 • Mathematics. This image illustrates a type of fractal known as a quaternion Julia set. Visualization helps mathematicians understand certain processes which are often too complex to conceptualize otherwise.
Courtesy of John C. Hart, EVL, The University of Illinois, Chicago.

ABSTRACTION AS CONCEPT:

Constantin Brancusi (1876–1957) and Isamu Noguchi (1904–1988)

The sculptor Constantin Brancusi stated his philosophy in two brief comments. "It is time we had an art of our own time," and "I give you pure joy!" The first remark originated with the artist's personal views about art history. In essence he believed that sculpture from any given historical period reflected and often endorsed the dominant power structure of its society, whether religious, political, military, economic, or artistic. By artistic power structure he meant those influential critics, museums, galleries, and magazines that control an artist's exposure by their acceptance or rejection.[16] His own exhibits, like those of the Impressionists before him, were mostly group shows held outside the art establishment, so Brancusi was fifty years old before his work received wide public recognition.

The sculptor's second remark originated with his personal dislike for anything monumental or grandiose, anything tragic or emotionally charged. He believed that art should be therapeutic, possibly humorous, and always positive. His sculpture ". . . never addresses itself to the passions, but always to the quieter functions of the inner life—contemplation, memory, the affections."[17] To communicate this briefly he simplified and resimplified his sculptures until their forms became more and more abstract.

Like Monet, Brancusi serialized his subjects. He would work on a series intermittently, exploring and developing its potential in relation to different materials, then stop to let the idea rest while he explored other ideas and different subjects. Once, when he was asked how long a particular sculpture took to complete, he answered "Fifteen years!", a reference not only to the actual work but to the amount of thought that went into it.

"Bird in Space," Brancusi's most famous series, originated with an earlier series called "Pasarea Maiastra," later shortened to "Maiastra," a name from Rumanian folklore meaning "magical bird" (fig. 2.50). The white marble *Pasarea Maiastra* shown here is the first in that series. A tightly structured form, it is a composite shape carved from a single piece of marble. Notice how Brancusi carved its beak, head, and neck in one continuous curve that expands to a thick and bulbous body. Supporting the egg-shaped body are two sturdy legs that narrow and angle at the base. Except for the eyes, the artist eliminated detail: you see no feathers, claws, or separate beak; only basic, abstracted shapes. Similarly, he did not give the bird any natural colors or textures but instead emphasized the stone's natural whiteness and smoothness. What remains in this stone is a birdlike stretch or reach upward. This effect is nearly impossible to grasp in photographs where the base is deleted to show the bird more clearly. In reality the base is so tall the closer you stand to *Pasarea Maiastra*, the more you find yourself looking up at it. Although this effect varies with a person's height, it remains quite extraordinary.

Brancusi described some of the changes in his subsequent versions of *Maiastra,*

"I wanted to show the *Maiastra* as raising its head, but without putting any implications of pride, haughtiness or defiance into this gesture . . . it was only after much hard work that I managed to incorporate this gesture into the motion of flight."[18]

Those three words "motion of flight" best describe *Bird in Space* (fig. 2.51) carved from white marble fifteen years after *Pasarea Maiastra.* Here, any resemblance to a bird is confined to the title because birds do not fly vertically, but the dynamics in this work *are* vertical. Its shape is abstract, sleek, streamlined, aerodynamic. An upward thrust of motion through space, it is motion made visible.

If you could see the actual sculpture, you might find yourself resisting an impulse to run your hand along its curved, cold, hard body. Brancusi's sculpture appeals directly to the senses. Sculptures in his "Bird in Space" series are carved of white, black, grey, and yellow marbles and also of highly polished cast bronze. Variations are subtle from sculpture to sculpture: usually a slight shift in the breadth and balance of the curve or a barely perceptible change in height.

The American sculptor Isamu Noguchi studied with Brancusi in Paris as the recipient of a Guggenheim Fellowship. The older man's influence helped set the direction for Noguchi's life's work, but differences in their methods and styles are apparent. The most noticeable difference is in the initial concept of a work: Brancusi began with a natural form and abstracted it; Noguchi began with the abstraction.

An understanding of the strengths and weaknessess of any given stone or metal is absolutely essential for sculptors. Noguchi learned a respect for the materials from Brancusi, and Noguchi never ceased searching the secrets of stone and metal and clay. Secrets can be learned both from older master-artists and by experimenting with the material. Noguchi pursued both approaches. Two years after leaving Brancusi's studio in Paris, he traveled to Japan where he spent five months in Kyoto studying with the Japanese potter Uno Jimmatsu. Fascinated by clay's inherent sculptural potential and its earthiness, Noguchi returned to Japan several more times to study with another master potter Rosanjin Kitoji.

The inherent, expressive character of shapes, their cultural and religious symbolism, and their interaction with space provided Noguchi with other avenues of learning. Before his initial trip to Kyoto, he spent eight months in Beijing studying brush painting with the Chinese master Chi Pai Shi. In 1950 a Bollingen Foundation fellowship allowed him to visit the caves at Lascaux, France, and the monuments in Egypt and India. Earlier he had met two people from other areas of the arts who became seminal influences and life-long friends. One was architect Buckminster Fuller, whose design systems were innovative—and often utopian—in their efficient use of space. The other was the great modern dancer Martha Graham, for whom Noguchi designed a number of stage sets (see fig. 6.13).

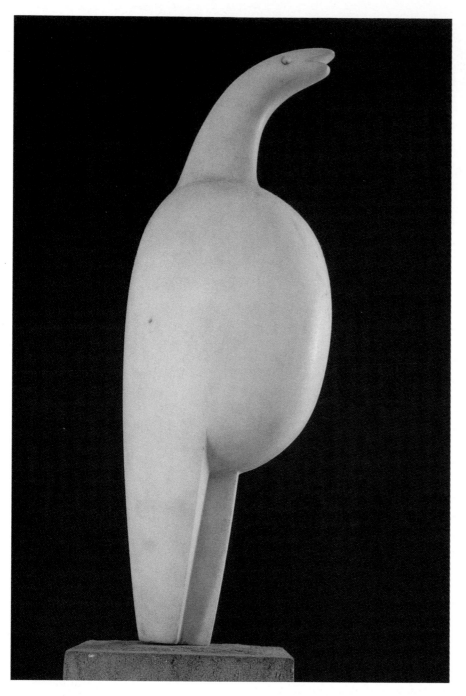

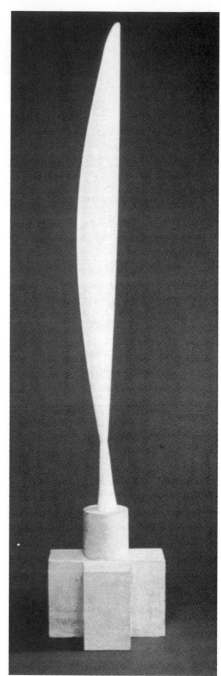

FIGURE 2.50 • Constantin Brancusi, *Magic Bird* [Pasarea Maiastra] 1910–12. White marble, 22″ high, on three-part limestone pedestal.

Collection, The Museum of Modern Art, New York. Katerine S. Dreier Bequest. Photograph © 1992 The Museum of Modern Art, New York.

FIGURE 2.51 • Constantin Brancusi, *Bird in Space*, 1925. Marble, stone, and wood: height: 3.446: 136 1/2″.

© 1992 National Gallery of Art, Washington: Gift of Eugene and Agnes Meyer.

FIGURE **2.52b** •

FIGURE **2.52c** •

FIGURE **2.52d** •

During these years, Noguchi explored two technical ideas. First was the idea of interlocking two-dimensional shapes to create three-dimensional forms. Second was the idea of harmonizing opposing forces: for example, complexity and simplicity; tension and tranquility; or strength and fragility.

Both ideas are evident in *Portal*, a public sculpture designed for the Cuyahoga Justice Center in Cleveland, Ohio (fig. 2.52a–d). The sculpture is made of welded steel pipe 48 inches in diameter and painted matt black. The material—as Brancusi would have said—is of our own time. It is also *of* Cleveland: a city whose industrial base depends on steel manufacturing. The sculpture's thirty-five foot height is colossal but is scaled to its surroundings. Today, any public sculpture on or near high-rise sites must be enormous if it is to be seen at all. *Portal's* shape at first seems deceptively simple. Humorously nicknamed "Giant Paperclip," in actuality its simplicity is complex. If you drive past the building you see one shape; but as you turn a corner and look back, you see another. If you walk up to *Portal* you see a third variation, and when you walk behind it, a fourth. These views are street level—imagine what it looks like from above.

The idea of opposing forces of simplicity and complexity is not only a technical idea but a philosophical one linking *Portal* to the building it was designed to serve. What, after all, has more facets, sides, perspectives, or opinions than *justice?* How many opinions and dissenting opinions result from the same evidence and testimony? Another aspect of this philosophical link between *Portal* and the Justice Center building is found in the word "Portal," which dennotes much more than a gate or entrance. "Portal" signifies an imposing entranceway to something of great importance. The four *toranas* of the Great Stupa at Sanchi, India, are portals (see fig. 2.13). Entrances to Gothic cathedrals are portals (see fig. 4.21). Noguchi's *Portal* does not designate sacred architecture, but it does mark the entrance to a building of great importance, a building in which human lives are significantly affected.

FIGURE 2.53 • Piet Mondrian, *Tree*, ca.
1912. Oil on canvas, 37″ × 27 7/8″.
The Carnegie Museum of Art, Patrons Art Fund,
(61.1).

ABSTRACTION AS REACTION:
Piet Mondrian (1872–1944) and Jackson Pollock (1912–1956)

"The emotion of beauty is always obstructed by the appearance of 'the object'; therefore the object must be eliminated from the picture." Acting on his words, the Dutch artist Piet Mondrian deleted all natural imagery from his paintings. He replaced "the object" with shapes, lines, and colors that have no association with the natural world.

Mondrian's earliest paintings were mostly landscapes: crisp and hard-edged and hinting at the abstraction yet to come. Within ten years, the natural images in his work became more and more abstract, resulting in paintings like *Tree* (fig. 2.53). In this picture Mondrian codified a tree's natural appearance into a composition of lines and shapes. Now, lines intersect to enclose arcs and semi-circles that fill the entire picture space. Branches are no longer branches, yet on close observation this image still resembles a tree—however abstract it

FIGURE 2.54 • Piet Mondrian,
Composition, II 1929; (Original date
partly obliterated; mistakenly repainted
1925 by Mondrian when he restored
the painting in 1942). Oil on canvas,
15 7/8 × 12 5/8″. (40.3 × 32.1 cm.)
Collection, The Museum of Modern Art, New York,
Gift of Philip Johnson. Photograph © 1992. The
Museum of Modern Art, New York.

may be. Brush strokes are also evident, and because these can be as individual as a handwritten signature, they are a reminder to the viewer that the hand of another human being *did this*. Read that way, they are a link between artist and viewer.

Thirteen years later in *Composition*, that link, together with any resemblance to the natural world, is gone (fig. 2.54). Colors have also been modified. Gradually Mondrian eliminated the shades and tints of color from his work, then he eliminated colors except for the three primaries red, blue, and yellow from which other colors are mixed. Since white and black are not considered colors, he continued to use them.

Mondrian believed—like Plato—that art could be universal only by eliminating all references to the world and to the artist. Did he achieve his goal? When you look at *Composition* do you find your own reactions influenced in any way by your nationality, race, sex, age, religion, or economic status? Does anything in the picture evoke your emotions? Stimulate your senses? Activate your memory? What *do* you actually see? Are the red rectangle and blue square in front of or behind the white rectangles and square? When you look at the black lines, where do they lead the eye? Do they direct attention off the edges of the picture? If not, what keeps your attention inside the picture space? Is the picture balanced? If so, then what keeps it from being top heavy? *Composition* is a carefully thought-out geometric problem, a totally intellectual painting directed *through* the senses, not *at* them.

Jackson Pollock's *Convergence: Number 10* (fig. 2.55) is the exact opposite in method and appearance. At first glance, the painting appears disorganized.

FIGURE 2.55 • Jackson Pollock, *Convergence*, 1952. Oil on canvas, 93 1/2 × 155 inches.
Alhright-Knox Art Gallery, Buffalo, New York. Gift of Seymour H. Knox, 1956. © 1992 ARS, NY/ S.P.A.D.E.M., Paris.

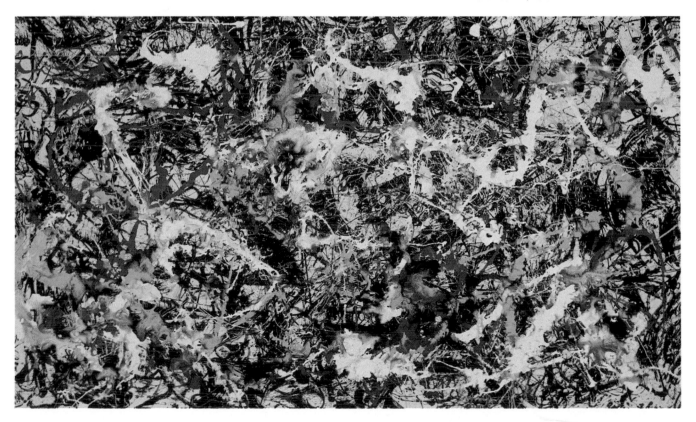

Its energy is chaotic and wild—literally bombarding the senses with erratic and explosive lines and shapes, but in content *Convergence: Number 10* is as intellectual as Mondrian's *Composition*. The paintings differ mainly in method: whereas *Composition* reveals considerable forethought and logic, *Convergence* reveals impulsive action and emotional frenzy.

Like Mondrian, Pollock excised all images of reality, thereby forcing the viewer to concentrate on shape, line, and color. However instead of neat, geometric lines and shapes, Pollock gave the viewer networks of lines, some stretching like filaments and others meandering over the picture space like a kind of bony calligraphy. Background and foreground no longer exist in this painting as lines twist, turn, cavort, and thicken into shapes and planes of different colors. Shapes are not definable; they are more like impulses or flares. Nothing in the picture holds still but there *is* order. Red, yellow, blue, and white lines and shapes make paths that are erratic but complete. If you choose to follow one, you can begin anywhere, but eventually you will return to where you started. Alluding to this, Pollock once told an interviewer, "There was a reviewer a while back who wrote that my pictures didn't have any beginning or any end. He didn't mean it as a compliment, but it was. It was a fine compliment. Only he didn't know it."[19]

Pollock was dedicated to freeing the unconscious mind. In another interview he said,

> ". . . the modern artist is living in a mechanical age and we have a mechanical means of representing objects in nature such as the camera and photograph. The modern artist, it seems to me, is working and expressing an inner world—in other words—expressing the energy, the motion, and other inner forces."[20]

Part of Pollock's interest in the unconscious stemmed from the psychoanalytical writings of Carl Jung, particularly Jung's theory of a collective unconscious. To this end, Pollock chose unusual materials, methods, and techniques, all aimed at freeing his unconscious. Besides oil paints he used a variety of glossy, commercial enamels that dried more quickly. Pollock's method was to lay his canvas on the floor, prime it, and then apply paint with sticks and hard brushes and pour, drip, and swirl it from containers. What he sought was a kind of spontaneous gesture that would, of itself, reveal the *action in painting*. Pollock never repeated himself. Every Action Painting, as they have come to be called, is unique and individual.

ABSTRACTION AS STIMULUS:
Anselm Kiefer (1945–   ) and Varda Chryssa (1933–   )

German artists were in the vanguard of the Expressionist movement from the early 1900s until the mid 1930s. Then, in the words of Siegfried Gohr, "In Nazi Germany modern art and artists were defamed and driven out of the country, destroying even that small freedom to produce art independent of the official line which had been so laboriously achieved since 1880."[21] Ironically, the inheritors of that movement today are the German artists working in a style called Neo-Expressionist. Anselm Kiefer is one of these artists.

FIGURE 2.56 • Anselm Kiefer, *Nigredo*, 1984. Oil paint on photo-sensitized canvas with acrylic emulsion straw, shellac and paper. 11 × 18 feet (330 cm × 555 cm).
Philadelphia Museum of Art 1985-5-1.

Kiefer delves into German history and myth for his subjects but remains thoroughly contemporary in his choice of materials and techniques. He began *Nigredo* using a photograph that is barely visible because he painted over it with oil and acrylic paints and shellac (fig. 2.56). Kiefer regularly applies paint by rubbing, dripping, and brushing it onto the canvas, and he wields brushes and palette knives with enough force to leave paint tracks that slash, swirl, and streak. In some areas he layers paint, either smoothing it or ridging it roughly. Where thick, crumpled layers of paint do not give enough texture, he sometimes adds straw or liquified lead. He has been known to apply a torch to areas within paintings, literally scorching them to achieve the visual "truth" of fire. You can see the kind of powerful, even brutal effects that result from these techniques in *Nigredo*.

Nigredo, the Latin word for "blackness," originates with Medieval alchemy. Alchemists were men who mixed science with magic and astrology in attempts to turn base metal into gold. Along the way, they discovered chemistry. Comparisons are often made between alchemy and creativity because both require purification, filtration, and concentration. Kiefer's comparison is direct. *Nigredo* is the first stage of alchemy: it begins when ideas are dark, muddled, and confused; when their potential is only vaguely understood and not yet realized. Kiefer compares this to the churning and upheaval of earth itself. He paints a black field where huge black boulders have been unearthed and where plowed furrows converge at some distant point on the horizon. The even, precise furrows hold remnants of some crop already harvested, but their cut-off stalks will one day be turned back into the earth. Kiefer's earth, like van

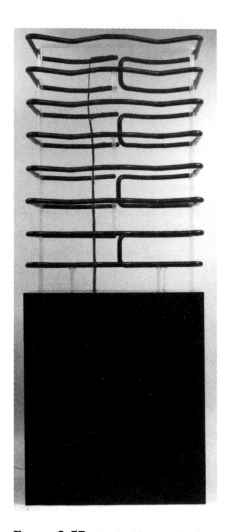

FIGURE 2.57 • Varda Chryssa, *Study for the Gates No. 15 (Flock of Morning Birds from "Iphigenia in Aulis" by Euripides)*, 1967. Black glass neon tubing with timer; 62 × 35 1/2 × 29 3/8".
Hirshhorn Museum and Sculpture Garden, Smithsonian Institution, Gift of Joseph H. Hirshhorn, 1972.

Gogh's, seethes with life, but van Gogh's brilliant and auspicious colors are replaced by Kiefer's morbid, dark tones of decay. Blackness is relieved only by a white clouded sky in the distance, far beyond the horizon. Perhaps this is a reference to *albedo*, the white stage of alchemy and creativity. With *albedo*, elements—or ideas—are broken down, recombined in new ways, and then allowed to incubate. The incubation stage can be frustrating and long, but it ends with a flash of gold—or the new idea. In Kiefer's painting, that small golden flash hides behind the title.

Nigredo is more than eighteen feet long. Viewing it in the Philadelphia Museum of Art you must step back into the adjacent gallery to see it all. Then, to see the minute details that make up its textures, you would find yourself walking toward it. Approaching the work, you discover its complexities but lose the overall picture. Kiefer's analogy between the size of this painting and the size of a creative endeavor is extraordinarily perceptive, because this pulling back, this distancing and objectivity are exactly what the pursuit of a creative idea entails. At the same time that pursuit also demands total absorbtion and immersion in details. When you experience *Nigredo* you vicariously experience both the closeness and distancing of the creative processs itself.

The sculpture of Varda Chryssa (fig. 2.57) brings together the challenge of modern materials with the goals of Minimalism. Painters and sculptors who are Minimalists pare away all but the most basic shapes and colors. Their focus—and the viewers—is on a form that relates to the space it encloses and occupies. Chryssa's materials are modern neon tubes and electricity, but the concept of using light for art is an ancient one that began with fireworks. Chryssa, who came to the United States from Greece, says that her inspiration for sculptured light comes from the neon signs that light up America! She names Times Square as the initial stimulus, comparing it to "the gold of Byzantine Mosaics or Icons." Accordingly, her most monumental work to date is titled *The Gates of Times Square*. Before completing that work Chryssa created a number of smaller pieces that she titled *Studies*. Those enabled Chryssa to experiment with different techniques and effects that she ultimately accepted or rejected for inclusion in the larger work. The *Studies*, however, are sculptured forms that stand on their own respective merits.

Flock of Morning Birds from "Iphigenia in Aulis" by Euripides: Study for the Gates No. 15 is a uniquely modern work that truly unlocks time with its reference to Euripides, the Greek dramatist who lived in the fifth century B.C. This particular play is about King Agamemnon who sacrifices his only daughter Iphigenia to assure victory during the Trojan War. If Brancusi's *Bird in Flight* *represents* motion, Chryssa's *reveals* motion through its light. Eight repeated shapes made from black glass tubing coil upward from the sculpture's black plexiglass base. When a signal is transmitted by a timer and rheostat, a soft blue light appears at the bottom of the first coil. Gradually, light rises through this coil and on to the next. The light becomes more intense as it rises, so the topmost coils are already a brilliant blue while the bottom coils are still turning from black to pale blue, the color of early morning sky. The entire sculpture fills with a luminous glow and the glow appears to fill the spaces between coils. The image of the sculpture becomes its illusion.

VISUAL LANGUAGE

Visual language, like any language, is studied to be used. When reading this chapter you encountered a number of art terms, their definitions, and their applications. In this section, the same terms are condensed, redefined, and reapplied.

STYLE, ELEMENTS, AND COMPOSITIONS

Style is an artist's consistent manner of presenting a subject. Typically an artist composes a picture or sculpture using certain combinations of **elements.** Elements are the lines, shapes, colors, and textures the artist draws, paints, or sculpts. Some styles identify art from a particular time or geographic area. Native American art from the Pacific Northwest Coast is a regional style, however it is important to remember that distinct tribal and individual styles can be identified within more general regional styles.

For example, Kadjis-du-axtc, the eighteenth century Tlingit sculptor who carved the houseposts shown in figure 2.28a–c, had a masterful style that was recognized years before his identity was discovered. His style is distinguished by a very deep method of carving that rounds shapes in a manner not seen on the more typical Tlingit pole. Kadjis-du-axtc carved eyes into lidded almond shapes; he made lips very full and with the hint of a smile; and he gave bodies a solid vital look. Not satisfied with positioning individual figures one above the other, he "wove" them into an interlocking vertical composition.

Sculptured forms are either **relief** or **in-the-round.** Houseposts, like most totem poles, are relief sculptures because they are carved from the front and sides, but not from the back. Other examples of relief sculpture are the carvings on temple columns at Karnak, Egypt (see fig. 2.5), and on toranas at Sanchi, India (see fig. 2.14). An example of sculpture in-the-round is Brancusi's *Bird in Space* (see fig. 2.51).

Analyzing the style of a work of art begins with analyzing its composition and elements. To discuss one without the other would be difficult if not impossible. For example, the most important element in Kuan Tao-Sheng's painting *A Bamboo Grove in Mist* (fig. 2.43) is its line quality. The artist's brush writing forms the shapes and textures you see. Subsequently, those lines with their resultant shapes and textures form a horizontal composition that leads the eye *across* the picture plane from right to left. In contrast, the composition of John Constable's *Salisbury Cathedral from the Bishop's Garden* (fig. 2.44) leads the eye more deeply *into* the picture plane. Here it is not Constable's line quality that the viewer notices as much as his short broken brushstrokes of color and his use of color to define textures as well as light and shadow.

Kadjis-du-axtc, Gona'x'deit Housepost, ca. 1750, Wrangell, Alaska. Cedar, height approximately 9'.
© Barry Herem.

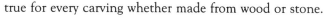

Oil painting, *Ginevra de'Benci*, Leonardo Da Vinci.

MATERIALS AND METHODS

Art materials and methods have natural strengths and weaknesses. For example, totem poles were carved most often from yellow cedar, an extremely hard and durable wood. The drawback to wood—any wood—is that its original shape restricts the size and shape of the completed sculpture. This holds true for every carving whether made from wood or stone.

Painting

Watercolor paint has a wonderful sparkle, freshness, and translucence (fig. 2.58). Those very qualities, however, are also its drawbacks. Its sparkle—isolated dots of white—comes from the heavy texture of paper that must be stretched and handled carefully. Its freshness comes from the quality of brushstrokes that must be made quickly and decisively. Its translucence—a positive characteristic of the paint—also means that mistakes cannot be painted over or erased.

Oil paint has been the preferred material since it was first developed in the fifteenth century. Its use on primed natural canvas gives it longevity, and its slow drying time allows for a variety of techniques. When thinned and applied in layers, oil paint gives rich coloristic effects. Leonardo da Vinci's *Ginevra* (see fig. 2.30) is a good example. A quite different effect is obtained when the paint is applied thickly, as van Gogh did, sometimes using a palette knife instead of a stiff brush (see fig. 2.46).

Fresco is an ancient and durable method used for interior murals. All frescoes are made on plaster coated walls, but with "true" fresco the paint is applied while plaster is still wet. The obvious disadvantage to this is the difficulty in painting directly on a wet plaster surface. Michelangelo's murals in the Sistine Chapel are true fresco (fig. 2.21).

Sculpture

Assembled sculpture is a generic term used for any work constructed or put together from almost any material. Noguchi's *Portal* was assembled by welding together lengths of steel pipe (fig. 2.52a–d).

Modeled sculpture is always made from a pliable material, usually clay, and is shaped by modeling. The soldiers and horses in the tomb of Ch'in Shih Huang-ti are modeled clay (figs. 2.9–2.12).

Cast sculpture is first modeled from a pliable material, most often clay or wax. From this a mold is made. When a durable material such as bronze or gold is poured into the mold and allowed to harden, the resultant sculpture is said to be cast. The portrait head of an Oni was cast (fig. 2.29).

Prints

Prints, as defined earlier, are multiple works of art made by transferring an inked surface to a sheet of paper, then repeating the process for as many prints as desired. The printing surface can be a wood block (see fig. 2.33), a metal plate (see fig. 2.47), a flat-surface stone, or silk fabric stretched across a frame (see fig. 2.34).

It is important to remember that, although prints are duplicate works of art, they are **original prints,** not "reproductions" or "reproduction-prints." To be considered original, a print must meet three criteria. First, the work must be conceived by its artist as a print. Second, the artist must prepare the printing surface. Third, the artist must direct the printing process and approve the editions.

Michelangelo, *The Last Judgment.* 1534–41, Sistine Chapel, The Vatican, Rome. Fresco, 48 × 44'.
Vatican Museum Photograph Archive.

Isamu Noguchi, *Portal,* 1976, black painted welded steel pipe, 35' h., Cuyahoga Justice Center, Cleveland, Ohio.
Photo: © Janet Century, Century Photography.

Kneeling Crossbowman. Terra Cotta.
Photo: Shaansi (Shensi) Provincial Studio, courtesy of Museum of Qin (Ch'in) Dynasty.

Wood block print. Shibakuni *Arashi Kitsusaboro I as Gofukuga Jubei,* 1818. Color woodblock.
Philadelphia Museum of Art, purchase of The Lola Downin Peck Fund. 70-190-8.

Head of an Oni, ca. twelfth-fifteenth century. Zinc brass; 11 5/8".
From Wunmonije Compound, Ife. Museum of Ife Antiquities, 12. © Dirk Bakker.

Notes

[1]Ange-Pierre Leca, *The Egyptian Way of Death*, trans. Louise Asmal. (New York: Doubleday & Co., Inc., 1979). pp. 52–53.

[2]John D. LaPlante, *Asian Art*. (Dubuque, Iowa: Wm. C. Brown Pub., 1985), p. 116.

[3]John R. Swanton, *Haida Texts and Myths*. (Washington, D.C.: Bureau of American Ethnology, Bulletin No. 29, 1905). See also Swanton, *Tlingit Myths and Texts*. (Washington, D.C.: Bureau of American Ethnology, Bulletin No. 39, 1909).

[4]See Steve Brown, "From Taquan to Klukwan: Tracing the Work of an Early Tlingit Master Artist," in *Faces, Voices & Dreams*, ed. Peter L. Corey. (Juneau, Alaska: Alaska State Museums, 1987). See also H., P. Corser, *Totem Lore of the Alaska Indians*. (Juneau, Alaska: Nugget Shop, 1931). Barry Herem, "A Historic Tlingit Artist," *American Indian Art*, Summer 1990, pp. 48–55. . . . G. Nagle, "Houseposts of the Nanya-ayi Tlingit," Unpublished research (Wrangell, Alaska: Wrangell Historical Museum, 1978).

[5]Ekpo Eyo and Frank Willett, *Treasures of Ancient Nigeria*. (New York: Alfred A. Knopf, 1980).

[6]John Walker, "Ginevra de' Benci by Leonardo da Vinci," *Report and Studies in the History of Art 1967*. (Washington, D.C.: U.S. Government Printing Office, 1967).

[7]For a more complete description of nineteenth century Osaka Kabuki prints see Roger S. Keys and Keiko Mizushima, *The Theatrical World of Osaka Prints*. (Philadelphia: Philadelphia Museum of Art, 1973.)

[8]Emily Carr, *Growing Pains*. Quoted in Doris Shadbolt, *Emily Carr*. (Vancouver/Toronto: Douglas & McIntyre, 1990). p. 91.

[9]Letter to Eric Brown, Director, National Gallery of Canada, 1927. See *Emily Carr*, Exhibition Catalogue. (Vancouver, B.C.: Art Gallery of Ontario, 1975). See also Maria Tippett, *Emily Carr*. (Toronto: Oxford University Press, 1979) p. 142.

[10]Carr, *Klee Wyck*, p. 21. Quoted in Shadbolt, p. 127.

[11]The Journal of Romare Bearden excerpted in *Romare Bearden: Origins and Progressions*. (Detroit: The Detroit Institute of Art, 1986), p. 32.

[12]Kenneth Clark, *Landscape into Art*. (New York: Harper & Row, 1979), pp. 147–150.

[13]John Canaday, *Mainstreams of Modern Art*. (New York: Holt, Rinehart and Winston, 1959), p. 181.

[14]For a more complete description of Estes' techniques see John Arthur's "Interview" in *Richard Estes: The Urban Landscape*. (Boston: Museum of Fine Arts, 1978).

[15]John Arthur, p. 19.

[16]For a more definitive explanation of Brancusi's personal philosophy see Sidney Geist, *Brancusi*. (N.Y.: Harry N. Abrams, Inc., 1975).

[17]Geist, p. 16.

[18]Quoted in Sidney Geist, *Brancusi*. (N.Y.: Grossman Publishers, 1968.) p. 86.

[19]"Unframed Space," *New Yorker* (Aug. 5, 1950). Quoted in Elizabeth Frank, *Pollock*, (New York: Abbeville Press, 1983), p. 109.

[20]Interview with William Wright; quoted in Francis V. O'Connor, "Documentary Chronology," in *Jackson Pollock: A Catalogue Raisonné of Paintings, Drawings, and Other Works*, vol. 4. Quoted in Elizabeth Frank, *Pollock*, p. 110.

[21]Quoted in Thomas Krens, "German Painting: Paradox and Paradigm in Late Twentieth-Century Art," *Refigured Painting: The German Image 1960–88*. New York: Solomon R. Guggenheim Museum, 1988, p. 18.

CHAPTER THREE

FIGURE 3.1 • *Yalta Conference?*
© Paul Higdon/New York Times Pictures.

Camera Arts

What is Rambo doing in a photograph of a War Powers Conference that took place in 1945 (fig. 3.1)? Britain's Sir Winston Churchill and America's Franklin D. Roosevelt *were* there. So was Russia's Joseph Stalin—although now Groucho Marx appears in his place—but Sylvester Stallone was not born until the year following the conference. This "doctored" photograph demonstrates how effectively today's computer generated images are capable of altering even the most authentic historic documents. The photograph also raises a question of truth. Philosopher Susan Sontag describes photographs as "clouds of fantasy and pellets of information." If her metaphors are applied to figure 3.1, then "clouds of fantasy" now obscure whatever "pellets of information" are contained in the original photograph. Truth, it seems, may be an illusion; but then, photography has always been something of a mystery.

ORIGINS

How *does* light create a picture? When the Frenchman Louis-Jacques-Mandé Daguerre (dah GARE) made his first successful photograph in 1837 he is said to have exclaimed, "I have seized the light—I have arrested its flight!" Photography, however, was not so much an invention as a technical and artistic evolution of global proportion. Centuries of experiments preceded Daguerre's discovery. As early as the tenth century, Chinese and Arab astronomers observed that when light entered a dark room through a tiny opening in the wall they were able to see an inverted image of the outdoors on the opposite wall. Ultimately, their findings led to the development of the **camera obscura,** used by scientists and artists as a professional tool and by magicians for optical tricks (fig. 3.2). The camera obscura, meaning "dark chamber," was able to reflect a clear and exact image, but an impermanent one. The Renaissance scientist and teacher Hironymous Fabricius noted that exposure to sunlight turned certain silver compounds from white to black, but it was three hundred years before his information became linked to the camera obscura. Daguerre made that connection when he placed a thin sheet of silver-plated copper into the camera obscura, exposed the metal to light, and developed it with mercury vapor and a bath of common table salt. Finally, light's image became permanent, and the **daguerreotype** was born (fig. 3.3).

Credit must also be given to French scientist Joseph-Nicéphore Niépce, whose published experiments with photosensitive metal plates came to Daguerre's attention and brought about their partnership. Similar kinds of inventive thought occurred elsewhere. At the time of Daguerre's discovery, English scientist Sir John Herschel was experimenting with glass negatives. In 1839, another English scientist and inventor, Henry Fox Talbot, succeeded in making images directly on paper. Five years later, Talbot perfected his process and named it **calotype.** With calotype, multiple prints could be made from a

FIGURE 3.2 • The camera obscura.
Courtesy of Beaumont Newhall.

FIGURE 3.3 • Louis-Jacques-Mandé
Daguerre, *The Artist's Studio*, 1837.
Société Française de Photographie.

FIGURE 3.4 • Muybridge's trotting horse.
Courtesy of the Library of Congress.

single negative, unlike daguerreotype which was a single, fragile metal image incapable of duplication. Although calotype was an improved method, its images were less clear and, as a result, it never achieved the popularity of daguerreotype.

Similar cross-currents of inventive thought occurred nearly forty years later when moving pictures evolved from experiments with motion-photography and from inventions and innovations in cameras, projectors, and celluloid film. Eadweard Muybridge (my bridge) is credited with making the initial breakthrough in the 1870s. Muybridge was hired by Leland Stanford—railroad president, former California governor, and horse breeder—who had bet $25,000 that a galloping horse raised all four legs off the ground. Muybridge began a series of experimental photographs at the race track, initially setting up 12 cameras, then 18, and finally 24 (fig. 3.4). Stanford won his bet, and Muybridge went on to experiment further with motion studies of other animals and humans. He published his studies in scientific journals and in a series of volumes titled *Animals in Motion* and *The Human Figure in Motion*. After inventing a projector called a zoöpraxiscope, he toured the U.S., Canada, and Europe, giving picture-lectures of his work.

Thomas A. Edison was one of the people who attended Muybridge's lectures. Soon, Edison and his assistant William Dickson were producing filmstrips made from a celluloid film only recently patented by George Eastman. Edison and Dickson devised a method of winding a filmstrip loop through a battery operated machine they named the Kinetoscope (fig. 3.5). The loops ran for just thirty seconds and could be viewed by only one person at a time, but they caught on quickly with the public. Largely through Dickson's efforts, the Edison Studio eventually replaced the Kinetoscope with the Vitascope, a projector capable of showing one and two minute films on a large screen. This invention was prompted by the phenomenal success of two French inventors and filmmakers, Auguste and Louis Lumière. The Lumière brothers produced their own movies and exhibited them using a hand cranked projector called the Cinématographe. After an initial success in Europe, the Lumières brought their "moving picture shows" to the U.S. and gave the Edison Studio strong competition.

Audiences watched this new form of entertainment in makeshift Store Theaters. When the size of audiences and profits warranted better accommodations, new buildings designed specifically for the movies made their appearance. These were the Nickelodeons—a nickel was the price of a ticket—and by the end of 1906, nearly a thousand were in full operation in the U.S.

DEFINITION

Camera Arts is a term applied to three separate but related media: still-photography, film (movies), and television. Still-photography has a close kinship with printmaking because a photograph, like a print, is a single picture complete in itself. With film and television, the single camera shot or frame is significant only in relation to what comes before and after it.

Television, like film and still-photography, transforms light into images, but it accomplishes this without film. Instead, television transforms images into electronic codes or messages and transmits them either through the air

FIGURE 3.5 • An early Kinetoscope parlor in San Francisco, 1899.
Courtesy of the Museum of Modern Art, Film Stills Archive.

or through cable. The television receiver in the home then translates or decodes the messages into images on the screen. From an audience standpoint, the most noticeable difference between film and television is the size of the screen. When a film made originally for the large size screen of a movie theater is seen on a small screen television, details are often "lost" and panoramic scenes may have less dramatic impact.

SOCIAL AND CULTURAL HISTORY: FAMILIAR FACES AND PLACES

Considering the crude equipment and materials available to early photographers, it is difficult not to be impressed by their achievements. A daguerreotype portrait, for example, required the sitter to remain absolutely motionless from ten to twenty minutes. Photographers, in an effort to keep sitters immobile, clamped people's heads in metal braces and supported their arms on a chair, a table, or perhaps an arm brace that could be hidden by a sleeve. Once a sitter was positioned, the photographer had to bring the sensitized plate from the darkroom, insert it in the camera, and expose it to light. After a long period of exposure that varied with the natural light on any given day, the sitter was finally released.

Outside the studio, conditions were even more difficult. Daumier's cartoon of the photographer Nadar taking aerial pictures from a balloon is a comical and simplistic look at what was, in reality, a prodigious feat (fig. 3.6). Years later, Nadar recalled a balloon ascent he had made with an assistant in 1858:

> Feverishly I set about organising the laboratory that I had to get into the basket, because at that date we hadn't yet reached those blessed days when our nephews could carry a whole laboratory in their pockets, and we had to do our own stuff up there on the spot . . .
>
> In the space below the balloon was hung the tent, a double layer, black and orange, which kept out all the sunlight, with a very little window of photogenic yellow glass which gave me just the amount of illumination I needed. It was hot underneath it for the worker and the work. But our collodion [a solution of guncotton dissolved in alcohol and ether and applied to glass plate negatives] and our other materials were reliable, kept in their ice-buckets . . .[1]

Because early photographers were so anxious to record familiar faces and surroundings, they inadvertently became social documentarians. Susan Sontag writes:

> Cameras began duplicating the world at that moment when the human landscape started to undergo a vertiginous rate of change . . . Like the dead relatives and friends preserved in the family album, whose presence in photographs exorcises some of the anxiety and remorse prompted by their disappearance, so the photographs of neighborhoods now torn down, rural places disfigured and made barren, supply our pocket relation to the past.[2]

FIGURE 3.6 • Honoré Daumier, *Nadar Raising Photography to the Height of Art*, 1862. Lithograph.
The International Museum of Photography at George Eastman House. Rochester, NY.

PORTRAITS

Most people think of portraits as time markers: the result of routine picture taking that often begins in a hospital nursery and continues to record birthdays, holidays, graduations, weddings, and other festive occasions. It is difficult to conceive of a time when there were no photographs because photography was a discovery that changed forever the way people viewed their societies and themselves. Early photographs were images to cherish. Children's portraits usually included pets or favorite toys (fig. 3.7a and b). Adult's portraits often included the tools of their trade or profession.

Occupational portraits were common during the late nineteenth and early twentieth centuries (fig. 3.8a–d). These little portrait photographs reveal quite individual personalities despite uniformly stiff poses and stern countenances. The carpenter, for example, either on his own or on the advice of the photographer, posed as if actually working; but he wore his "Sunday best" clothes, minus the jacket. The toolmaker wore his leather apron and rolled up his shirtsleeves, but he posed in a most formal manner. The man who holds a gold

FIGURE 3.7a • Herbert Randall, Ann Arbor, Michigan, *Girl with Doll*, ca. 1886–1895. Cabinet card, albumen print.
Collection of Wm. B. Becker, from *Photography's Beginnings* (University of New Mexico Press) © 1992

FIGURE **3.7b** • John Haarer, Ann Arbor, Michigan, *Funeral Flowers with Cabinet Card of Girl with Doll*, ca. 1886–1895. Cabinet card, albumen print.

Collection of Wm. B. Becker, from *Photography's Beginnings* (University of New Mexico Press) © 1992.

pen on top of a ledger is a bookkeeper, which may explain why the daguerreotype's paid receipt for $1.50 was found neatly folded inside the case. Occupational portraits of women were rare, and the seamstress pictured here made certain her pincushion, thimble, scissors, and thread—the tools of her trade—were prominently displayed. This particular daguerreotype case was inscribed with the woman's name, city, date, and the photographer's name: "Joseph Emrick/Degirotypist (sic)."[3]

The capacity of this new medium to record a likeness was a major factor in its immediate success. That the camera, in the hands of an artist-photographer, might capture more than a likeness was a concept not generally considered by a public more intrigued by the medium's novelty than its artistry. There were, however, a few who recognized the medium's potential for art. One was the British scientist Sir John Herschel, whose experiments with glass plates made possible the wet **collodion** process. In a letter to a photographer, Herschel describes his initial response to the photographer's work: "This last batch of your photographs is indeed wonderful . . . That head . . . is really a most astonishing piece of high relief. She is absolutely alive and thrusting out her head from the paper into the air. This is your own special style."[4]

FIGURE 3.8a • Unidentified
photographer, United States, *A
Carpenter*, ca. 1855. Ambrotype.

Collection of Wm. B. Becker, from *Photography's
Beginnings* (University of New Mexico Press)
© 1992.

FIGURE 3.8b • Addis' Lancaster
Gallery, Lancaster, Pennsylvania, *A
Toolmaker*, ca. 1850. Daguerreotype.

Collection of Wm. B. Becker, from *Photography's
Beginnings* (University of New Mexico Press)
© 1992.

FIGURE 3.8c • E. H. Benedict National
Daguerreotype Gallery, Syracuse, New
York, *A Bookkeeper*, March 23, 1855.
Daguerreotype.

Collection of Wm. B. Becker, from *Photography's
Beginnings* (University of New Mexico Press)
© 1992.

FIGURE 3.8d • Joseph Emrick, Fayette,
New York, *Mary W. McClurg,
Seamstress*, April 21, 1846.
Daguerreotype.

Collection of Wm. B. Becker, from *Photography's
Beginnings* (University of New Mexico Press)
© 1992.

The recipient of Herschel's letter was Julia Margaret Cameron (1815–1879), a fifty-one-year-old photographer, wife, and mother. Cameron's daughter and son-in-law had given her a camera as a gift, hoping it would amuse her. "Amuse" was not the word to describe what would become for Cameron a full-time occupation. Within weeks, she had turned the coal-house into a darkroom, let loose the chickens, and made the glass paneled hen-house into a studio.

Julia Margaret, her husband Charles, and their children lived in what is known as genteel poverty. The family owned a farm on the Isle of Wight and a coffee farm in Ceylon; neither enterprise was profitable. Although Charles Cameron was a respected scholar, he was not able to get an academic position, and he was never good at business. He was, however, extremely supportive of his wife's work. Julia had many requests for portraits from the writers, philosophers, statesmen and scientists, Herschel among them, who made up their circle of friends. She also exhibited widely, but because her work was not generally well received she could not help support the family as she had hoped.

What Herschel described as Cameron's "own special style," British critics saw as "inferior." One critic wrote:

> "The beholder is left to work out the idea in his own imagination, if he can; but as nine out of ten *cannot*—not being blessed with the artistic faculty— it follows that the peculiar line this lady had chosen will never allow of her works being very popular."[5]

Another critic wrote of an earlier exhibit,

> "Mrs. Cameron exhibits her series of out of focus portraits of celebrities. We must give this lady credit for daring originality but at the expense of all other photographic qualities."[6]

What were the objections to her work? Critics specifically mentioned the lack of detail and the emphasis on character and mood at the expense of a "realistic" likeness. Across the English Channel, French critics were finding the same "weaknesses" and "faults" in Impressionist paintings (p. 71). Cameron, it seems, was perfecting soft-focus photography at a time when clear-focus images were the accepted norm. In her attempts to suggest character and mood, she often concealed facial features and details by enveloping them in shadow, much as painters had been doing for centuries. The technique, called **chiaroscuro** (kee AR oh SKOOR oh), makes dramatic contrasts of light and shadow.

In *My Niece Julia Jackson* (fig. 3.9), the woman's strong profile seems almost to glow from within. This photograph, so evocative of mood, is a picture carefully, painstakingly organized into a complex circular composition of light and shadow. Notice, for example, the thin line of white along the top of the woman's head; how it emerges from the shadows on the left; widens as it moves down, delineating the profile; and then blends into the right side of her neck and the ruffled collar of her gown. Notice, too, how light changes the rows of beading around the collar into tiny sparkles. Those sparkles help direct the eye upward, completing the circle that began with the line across the top of the head. To compare any of the portraits in figure 3.8 with Cameron's is to differentiate between a competent photograph and a work of art.

FIGURE 3.9 • (Opposite) Julia Margaret Cameron, *My Niece Julia Jackson*, 1867. Albumen print.
National Portrait Gallery, London.

Cameron never lost faith in herself. Perhaps the admiration for her work shown by people whose opinions she respected compensated for the harsh words of British critics. She began writing an autobiography titled "Annals of My Glass House," a commentary on her work and an answer to criticisms leveled against it; but she never finished the book. The next year, in 1875, a move she had dreaded became a reality. Charles Cameron insisted, for financial reasons, that they return to Ceylon; and Julia Margaret, after living in England for twenty-six years, left family and friends to return with him. She died in Ceylon in 1879.

STREET SCENES

Eugène Atget (1857–1927) photographed Paris and its suburbs for thirty years. Nearly every day he was out on the streets before dawn, lugging forty pounds of equipment and waiting for the first morning light. Something about early daylight fascinated Atget almost as much as the city itself. Paris—its streets and boulevards, its buildings, fountains, and sculpture, its residents and street vendors—captivated him. Biographers say he was a man obsessed with a city.

Before Atget became a photographer he was an actor, and not a very good one. He was orphaned when very young and raised by an uncle who saw that the youth received an excellent education. After a short stint as a sailor, Atget trained and worked as an actor, but with little success. He eventually gave up acting, took up photography, and opened a small shop where he sold pictures mostly to historical institutions and private collectors. He never exhibited his photographs; and only after his death, largely through the efforts of American photographer Berenice Abbott, was his art brought to the public's attention.

Considering the scope of Atget's work, it would seem that he was attempting to preserve a Paris already in the throes of change. Frequently he photographed the same subjects again and again. He mentioned in a letter written only a few years before his death that he had all the "old streets of Old Paris . . . for example, the Saint-Severin quarter . . . the entire quarter, over twenty years, up to 1914, demolition included."[7]

Atget was a master of detail and mood, an artist capable of discovering beauty in the most nondescript *coin* (corner). In figure 3.10, an unassuming little area off the Rue Reynie assumes a quiet charm. The street with its puddles directs the eye past the child sitting on a stoop and toward an open doorway. The child might be waiting for something to happen or for someone to appear. Notice that objects in the picture—the doorway, the wagon, even the basket in the bottom right corner—are empty, as if also waiting for the usual daytime activities to begin. Quite ordinary textures of worn brick, stone, wood, and wicker are given interesting highlights; and on the arched entranceway above the wagon, a sculptured head encircled by a wreath appears chiseled as much by shadow and light as by stone. Other, smaller architectural details hint that the buildings had a past much grander than their present status. The stillness and solitude suggested here are moods typically found in Atget's work. In his pictures, skies are usually cloudless, trees, awnings, and flags motionless—as if fixed in time. People, when they appear at all, are somewhat isolated and never as prominent as their surroundings.

FIGURE 3.10 · Jean Eugène Auguste Atget, French, 1856–1927. *Paris Courtyard*, gelatin, silver print. H. 7"; W. 8¹¹/₁₆". (17.78 × 22.066 cm).
The University of Michigan Museum of Art, Acc. No. 1971/2.148.

In contrast, the people in Manuel Alvarez Bravo's (1902–) photographs are always doing something. At first glance, the significance of *what* they are doing sometimes puzzles viewers. Consider the young girl with her back to the camera in figure 3.11. Why is she standing on tiptoe peering in the window? Is she speaking to someone inside the building? Is she watching something take place? Is she looking for a particular person or is she merely curious?

Manuel Bravo's pictures pose questions. They offer clues but leave the answers to the viewer's perception and imagination. In *The Daughter of the Dancers*, the title is a clue. Quite possibly it was not the young woman's curiosity but her pose that attracted Bravo's attention. Notice how she stands on her toes with arms raised at a graceful angle. She may have reminded Bravo of a dancer; but he calls her "daughter of the dancers," and with this title reaches back into Mexico's past. His reference is to the Building of the *Danzantes*: ruins of what might have been an observatory located at Monte Albán,

near Oaxaca and dating from about 800 to 200 B.C. Little remains of the building except its large stone reliefs, believed to be of dancers. Bravo bestows on the anonymous woman in the photograph a certain nobility by associating her with one of the great achievements of their common ancestors.

In another photograph, *Parabola Optica* (fig. 3.12) Bravo turns the expected into the unexpected. This, too, is an ordinary street scene made extraordinary. It is, as Bravo's title suggests, a parable. What the eye sees, the mind rejects as false, and camera's "truth" becomes another illusion.

When Bravo is asked for interviews he is likely to suggest that his photographs be interviewed instead. He does not intend to be rude, but he recognizes what so many people, including interviewers, sometimes forget: that he communicates with *visual* images. Photographs of Mexico's people and city scenes are the core of his work. Together with an affinity for the country of his birth, he credits Atget's photographs for teaching him to "see and relate to daily life." Bravo likes to remind younger photographers that the art of photography is a matter of "discovery and expression." His advice has merit for audiences as well.

FIGURE 3.11 • (Opposite) Manuel Alvarez Bravo, *La Hija De Los Danzantes (The Daughter of the Dancers)*, 1933. © Manuel Alvarez Bravo. Courtesy of the Witkin Gallery, Inc.

FIGURE 3.12 • Manuel Alvarez Bravo, *Parabola Optica (Optic Parable)*, 1931. © Manuel Alvarez Bravo. Courtesy of the Witkin Gallery, Inc.

FAMOUS PEOPLE AND PLACES

Figure 3.13 is a photograph of Sarah Bernhardt, a famous French actress of the nineteenth century. The picture first appeared in the *Galerie Contemporaine*, a French periodical of the arts that included photographs and biographies of current celebrities. Bernhardt, known as "the divine Sarah," was enormously popular with audiences. Only a few years after posing for this portrait, her career reached its zenith during a long tour in which she played the tragic heroine in *Camille* (p. 314).

The photographer Tourtin posed Bernhardt with one hand resting gently against her cheek and looking off-camera, suggesting a slightly pensive mood. The pose was a common one for women and considered very fashionable. Bernhardt's gown is equally fashionable, and the actress complements it with pearl earrings, strands of pearls around her neck and wrist, and a flower in her hair. The camera records every detail, presenting the eye with a veritable feast of textures. Pearls, velvet, silk, lace, ruffles, buttons, shirring—the eye does not know where to rest.

FIGURE 3.13 • Tourtin, *Sarah Bernhardt*, 1877. Woodburytype.
International Museum of Photography at George Eastman House, Rochester, N.Y.

FIGURE 3.14 • Nadar (Gaspard Felix Tournachon), *Sarah Bernhardt*, 1865. Albumen print.
Bibliothque Nationale, Paris.

Another photographer interpreted the actress quite differently. He posed her wearing a cloak or shawl that has no association whatsoever with fashion—or time (fig. 3.14). The pose itself is unusual, theatrical but classic, and it draws attention to her extremely graceful hands. Notice that Bernhardt's hair is loose rather than styled and, except for small earrings, she wears no jewelry. Nothing in the picture detracts from the actress's face with its penetrating gaze that meets your eyes so directly.

Nadar—the man who took aerial pictures from a balloon—was the photographer who made this second portrait. Although Nadar is perhaps best known for his innovative aerial and underground photography, he was considered a masterful portrait photographer. Deeply committed to all the arts, he gave the Impressionist painters exhibition space in his studio at the time when museums and major galleries were refusing to show their work (p. 71).

While many enterprising nineteenth century photographers were opening shops and studios in cities and towns, others were setting off on arduous journeys to remote areas of the world. These explorer photographers produced pictures that let thousands of people see environmental and architectural wonders heretofore experienced by only a few intrepid travelers. Explorer photographers were a brave group undaunted by danger or by the ponderous and fragile equipment they had to carry and transport. They climbed the Himalayas, the Alps, and the Rockies and trudged across African deserts and American prairies, sometimes alone and sometimes as members of survey expeditions.

Certain adventure photographers made historic architecture their specialty. Félice Beato traveled to India and the Orient, while her brother Antonio made Egypt his base (fig. 3.15). These photographers—and their counterparts today—are like portrait photographers in the sense that they attempt to capture the inherent personality or character of a building or scene. Antonio Beato's photograph of the Temple of Horus at Edfu did not come about by the mere click of a shutter.

Is it possible for a building to have an aura? Can age or fame imbue a building with certain qualities sensed but unseen? American photographer Edward Steichen shared an interesting anecdote about one famous building, the Parthenon in Athens, Greece. It seems Steichen had gone to Greece to film Isadora Duncan, considered the "mother" of modern dance. After Steichen arrived in Athens, Isadora changed her mind about the film, but she did agree to dance at the Parthenon and to pose there for still-photographs (fig. 3.16). Steichen describes what happened:

FIGURE 3.15 • Antonio Beato, *Interior of Temple of Horus, Edfu,* ca. 1862. Albumen print.
National Gallery of Canada, Ottawa.

FIGURE 3.16 • (Opposite) Edward Steichen, *Isadora Duncan at the Portal of the Parthenon.* 1921. Gelatin-silver print, 19 5/8 × 15 1/4 in.
Collection of the Museum of Modern Art, New York. Gift of the photographer. Reprinted with permission of Joanna T. Steichen.

So I borrowed a Kodak camera from the head-waiter at the hotel, and we made several trips up the Acropolis to the Parthenon. But, every time, she said she couldn't do it; it was too much; she felt like an intruder when she started to move.

Finally, one day, I coaxed her into standing in the portal of the Parthenon. The camera was set up far enough away to include the whole portal wall. The idea was that she was to do her most beautiful single gesture, the slow raising of her arms until they seemed to encompass the whole sky. She stood there for perhaps fifteen minutes, saying, 'Edward, I can't. I can't do it. I can't do it here.' But finally, after several tries, I saw the arms going up. This was the moment . . .[8]

CREATING THE MEDIA HERO

An historic six-day political rally took place in Nuremberg, Germany, in 1934. Planned as a paean to Adolf Hitler and an experiment in propaganda, the event was staged—in every sense of the word—with a cast of thousands. Hitler personally requested Leni Riefenstahl (reef en schtahl) to film the rally, and he gave her an unlimited budget. Riefenstahl had a staff and crew of 120 members, 22 chauffeured cars, and a special police detail. She engineered preproduction planning to dovetail key camera shots and scenes with the most dramatic parades, ceremonies, and speeches. To facilitate the precision this feat would entail, she ordered special ramps, towers, and bridges built to accommodate the dollies and cranes needed for sixteen cameras. In addition, she ordered special platforms and camera braces mounted on cars and trucks. She used four sound trucks to record cheering crowds, drum and bugle corps, and marching and singing troops. Later, when editing the film, she put all this on a sound track, then added speeches and music that imitated the style of German composer Richard Wagner.[9]

The film is titled *Triumph des Willens* (Triumph of the Will), and it is propaganda at its best. Watching the first sequence, with its stunning camera work and ingenious editing, can be a disconcerting experience because this sequence became the prototype for television coverage of political campaigns. Substitute a jet for Hitler's prop plane, update clothing and uniforms, and the scenes fall into place with alarming familiarity. The sequence begins with a number of aerial shots taken from a plane; these alternate with ground shots of waiting dignitaries, members of the military, and an expectant crowd. The plane lands, taxies up the runway, stops, and the Führer disembarks (fig. 3.17a, b). Cheering crowds line the streets and give the Nazi salute as Hitler passes by in an open car (fig. 3.17c). Along the parade route, hundreds of smiling and shouting people lean from apartment and office windows.

The remainder of the film consists of speeches enlivened by torch light parades, precision military formations that include Hitler's Youth Corps, and the ever-present cheering crowds. Close-ups of healthy, handsome Aryan faces alternate with birds-eye views of the German military might. One birds-eye view appears in a scene about half-way through the film and shows Hitler, flanked by Joseph Goebbels and Rudolph Hess (who escaped by plane to England before the war's end), walking from a flag draped stage toward a monument erected to the Third Reich (fig. 3.17d).

FIGURE 3.17a •

FIGURE 3.17b •

FIGURE 3.17c •

FIGURE 3.17d •

FIGURE 3.17a–d • Scenes from *Triumph of the Will*, 1934, directed by Leni Riefenstahl.
Courtesy of the Museum of Modern Art, Film Stills Archive.

By definition, **documentary films** are nonfiction and therefore based on fact. It is important to remember, however, that the camera records only as much as the cinematographer chooses to select. **Editing,** the process whereby camera shots are cut and joined into scenes and the scenes into sequences, imposes another layer of selection on the final work. Adding music, sound-effects, or narration during the editing process constitutes a third layer.

In the annals of documentary film making, *Triumph of the Will* is a masterful work. It accomplishes exactly what it was made to do, namely to glorify Adolph Hitler, the Nazi Party, and the German war machine. Hitler had seen enough of Riefenstahl's earlier films based on Germanic themes to recognize her talent for this type of work, and he chose her over the objections of Joseph Goebbels, his Minister of Popular Enlightenment and Propaganda.

Riefenstahl's tragedy was in using her talent for an abhorrent political regime that came close to destroying the Western world. Still, she believed in that regime and understood the power of film as propaganda. In her own words: "That the Führer has raised film-making to a position of such pre-eminence testifies to his prophetic awareness of the unrealized suggestive power of this art form."[10]

CREATING A NON-HERO: FICTION FROM FACT

Orson Welles' (1915–1985) film *Citizen Kane* is fictional, but because its plot so closely resembles the life of newspaper tycoon William Randolph Hearst (1863–1951), it had a remarkable history of its own. Hearst, an extremely powerful and wealthy man, tried to have the movie destroyed before its release in 1941. Failing that, he used his media clout to severely curtail the film's distribution. Simultaneously his newspapers and radio stations vilified Orson Welles, calling the actor-director, among other things, a Communist and draft-dodger.

What caused this fury were some remarkable "coincidences" between the life of William Randolph Hearst and the life of the film's central character, Charles Foster Kane. Here are a few of the more obvious similarities. Hearst's fortune originated with his family's mining interests. After graduating from Harvard, he established a newspaper chain noted primarily for phenomenal growth and "yellow journalism." Hearst had a lifelong interest in politics, although he served only a single term as a California State Representative. After years of marriage to an Eastern socialite, he obtained a legal separation and a mistress who lived with him until his death. His mistress, Marion Davies, was a pretty blonde actress who never quite achieved Hollywood stardom despite Hearst's support. During the Depression years, Hearst built an enormous estate at San Simeon, California, and literally filled his mansion—nicknamed Hearst Castle—with the art and antiques he avidly collected.

In the film, Citizen Kane's mother becomes rich overnight from mining stock, and he inherits millions while still a child. After being expelled from some of the world's most prestigious schools, he takes over *The New York Daily Inquirer* (fig. 3.18a). Disregarding his own best intentions, he builds a publishing empire noted for sensationalism. He marries a socialite, is divorced, and marries a pretty blonde "singer" who fails in opera because she can't sing.

After an unsuccessful run for governor (fig. 3.18b), Kane builds a huge estate in Florida, names it Xanadu, and fills it with so many possessions some are never unboxed.

The film contains more "coincidences," but its reputation as a masterpiece is not based on its fiction-from-fact plot but rather on its achieving a nearly perfect balance between concept and technique. The film describes the

FIGURE 3.18a • Two scenes from *Citizen Kane*, 1941, directed by Orson Welles.

FIGURE 3.18b •

character and career of a tycoon by following the parallel paths of a man's private and public life. This two-pronged plot lays bare all the intricate webs of human relationships that exist in professional and private lives. In addition to five in-depth interviews with the people closest to Kane, the film includes a newsreel that summarizes events from his life in the manner of celebrity obituaries. Interestingly, *Citizen Kane* begins with the death of its central character and moves backward in time, presenting the newsreel and interviews in flashback sequences.

This film makes a statement about the Charles Foster Kanes of the world and about the people whose lives are indelibly marked because of them. One after another, the film's flashback sequences describe power's corruption of ideals, power's egoism, paternalism, and possessiveness. Love is also described in scenes that portray the emotional repercussions and lasting effects of a traumatic childhood loss. These and other themes give the film's characters and narrative both substance and universality.

Taken as a whole, the film's techniques were as daring and flamboyant as its twenty-five-year-old actor-director. Orson Welles was lured from New York to Hollywood in 1939 with a substantial offer of money and an unprecedented amount of artistic freedom. Studio moguls were impressed by Welles' work with the Federal Theatre Project, one of many government sponsored WPA programs, and with The Mercury Theatre that Welles had formed in partnership with actor-director John Houseman. Welles was also something of a celebrity after his 1938 radio broadcast of H.G. Well's *The War of the Worlds*. This program describing an invasion from Mars was intended as a Halloween joke. The joke backfired, however, when the program caused a near panic across the country.

Many of Welles' films develop themes of power around central characters who are fascinating, larger than life, and very definitely non-heroic. *The Stranger* (1946) has for its dominant character a villainous Nazi war criminal, and *Touch of Evil* (1958) has a corrupt police official. *The Magnificent Ambersons*—made a year after *Citizen Kane*—examines the moral disintegration of a prominent Midwestern family. With these films and others, Welles presents characters whose fates are determined less by circumstance than by their own very human strengths and weaknesses.

HEROES AND SCENES OF THE AMERICAN WEST

In the telling and retelling of exploits from the American West, details were added and facts embroidered until stories became legends. This is how frontier folklore was born, and it grew with the territories, accumulating more and more regional customs, beliefs, and legends along the way. During the twentieth century, western films by the hundreds added a Hollywood "folklore" that celebrated pioneers, romanticized outlaws, and denigrated Native Americans. Hollywood's role in perpetuating erroneous attitudes cannot be glossed over despite the recent filmmakers who have tried to amend past mistakes by presenting the early American West and its inhabitants with greater historical accuracy.

Genre is a term used to classify films having similar subjects and characters. In the past, the western genre typically dealt with problems solved by violence and with characters selected from a long list of stereotypes: an honor-bound hero, a sweet and usually long-suffering heroine, one or more villains, a sheriff or marshal, a gambler, a level-headed judge or doctor, one or more self-righteous citizens, a dance-hall girl or prostitute with a soft heart, a drummer (traveling salesman), Indians on the warpath, and the U.S. Cavalry arriving in the nick of time.

Only in the hands of a few directors did the genre rise above hackneyed plots and clichés. John Ford was one of those directors, and four of his most notable westerns are *Stagecoach* (1939), *She Wore a Yellow Ribbon* (1949), *The Searchers* (1956), and *The Man Who Shot Liberty Valance* (1962). Why are these films considered some of the genre's best? Uniformly they have substantial plots, strong and tenacious characters, and remarkable cinematic techniques. John Ford's characters may be stereotypical, but they are seldom superficial. The heroine of *Stagecoach* happens to be the prostitute with a soft heart—a combination of two and eight on the stereotype list—but with Ford's direction and Claire Trevor's acting, the character is interpreted as being no worse and probably a lot better than the gaggle of "law and order" ladies who march her down the street, up to the stagecoach, and out of *their* town!

One trait of the western genre is the bond that exists between characters and their environment. Backgrounds are often spectacular and actors share the camera with scenery. Landscapes of the American West are a cinematographer's challenge. Nature's ruggedness presents physical hardships to any film crew, but that same ruggedness provides opportunities for visual images on a grand scale. Monument Valley, stretching across Utah and Arizona, was director John Ford's favorite site for location filming (fig. 3.19). The areas's nearly thirty-thousand acres of mesas, cliffs, and canyons offer cinematographers an almost endless choice of compositions. Ford especially liked to contrast these free and open spaces with confining interiors. In *Stagecoach*, he repeatedly cross-cut from extreme long-shots of open terrain to medium and close-up shots inside the crowded stagecoach.

Some westerns deviate from the genre's standard format. Fred Zinneman's *High Noon* (1952) is one of the few that does not create a symbolic bond between the hero and his western background. Zinneman chose to ignore the scenery altogether and concentrate instead on his central character, a tired ex-gunslinger honor-bound to fight one more time. George Roy Hill's *Butch Cassidy and the Sundance Kid* (1969) takes an in-depth look at the psyche of two outlaws, then kills them off at the end. Robert Altman's *McCabe and Mrs. Miller* (1971), filmed in British Columbia, presents an intensely realistic picture of life in the mining and lumbering areas of the Pacific Northwest. Arthur Penn's *Little Big Man* (1970) and Kevin Costner's *Dances with Wolves* (1990) attempt to present a more accurate picture of Native American life and cross-cultural relationships in general.

FIGURE 3.19 • Monument Valley Scene from *Stagecoach*, 1939, directed by John Ford.

Courtesy of the Museum of Modern Art, Film Stills Archive.

FIGURE 3.20 • William Henry Jackson, *Photo Outfit*, 1869.
The National Archives.

True courage is found in the diaries and journals of men and women who settled the West. These are the heroes and heroines unsung and mostly unknown except to their families and descendants; yet these are the people who experienced real trials and adventures of every conceivable kind.

One such hero was William Henry Jackson, a photographer whose contribution to future generations was far more significant than chasing cattle rustlers or winning a gun duel. William Henry Jackson served with the Vermont infantry during the Civil War. After the war, he traveled West with a wagon train. He settled briefly in Omaha, where he started a photography business but spent most of his time away from the town photographing prairies and scenes of Native American life. He headed West again, this time alone and with his photo equipment on a pack mule (fig. 3.20). In 1870 he joined the Hayden Geological Survey and spent nine years traveling with the group through Arizona's Grand Canyon region, north across Utah's Unita Mountains, and into Wyoming's Yellowstone territory (fig. 3.21). Photographs taken on this and other surveys were widely distributed in attempts to persuade Congress to set aside land for national parks. Jackson became a strong advocate for national park lands, and to further the cause he printed a collection of his photographs in an album titled *Yellowstone Scenic Wonders*. In 1879, he moved to Denver, set up a studio, and proceeded to spend his time everywhere but in Denver. He did photographic work for the railroads, traveling through every state in the Union, and in the process created an extremely valuable visual history of the U.S. Jackson remained active into his nineties, and one of his last achievements was a series of pictures for the National Park Service.

FIGURE 3.21 • William Henry Jackson, *Green River.*
The National Archives.

CATASTROPHE AND CONSCIENCE

Let him who wishes to know what war is look at this series of illustrations. These wrecks of manhood thrown together in careless heaps or ranged in ghastly rows for burial were alive but yesterday . . . It was so nearly like visiting the battlefield to look over these views, that all the emotions excited by the actual sight of the stained and sordid scene, strewed with rags and wrecks, came back to us, and we buried them in the recesses of our cabinet as we would have buried the mutilated remains of the dead they too vividly represented . . .

Oliver Wendell Holmes, father of the American jurist, wrote these memorable words in 1863 after seeing photographs of the Civil War battlefield at Antietam.[11] The American Civil War, from the Battle of Bull Run to the surrender at Appomattox, was thoroughly documented in photographs.[12] Union photographers Mathew Brady, Alexander Gardner, and Timothy H. O'Sullivan and the Confederate photographer George Cook are only a few of the brave men who converted mule drawn wagons into darkrooms and worked under fire from enemy sharpshooters and artillery. Time exposures were still too long for Civil War photographers to record live action, but they did chronicle nearly everything else, including battles' terrible aftermath (fig. 3.22).

FIGURE 3.22 • Timothy H. O'Sullivan (originally printed by Alexander Gardner), *A Harvest of Death, Gettysburg, Pennsylvania*, July, 1863. Albumen print.
Rare Books and Manuscript Division, New York Public Library, Astor, Lenox, and Tilden Foundations.

SOCIAL REALISM: PERSPECTIVES

The same vision and determination evidenced by early documentary photographers is found in the men and women who succeeded them. Jacob Riis, a New York City sociologist, saw photography as a means for bringing the squalid slum conditions of the 1880s to the public's attention (fig. 3.23). Twenty years later, another sociologist, Lewis Hine, fought for legislation that would put an end to child labor. To advance the cause, he photographed children at work in coal mines and textile mills (fig. 3.24). Although his pictures of children, some of them less than ten years old, malnourished and weak from fatigue, carried a potent message, the Federal Fair Labor Standards Act was not passed until 1938.

The Great Depression of the 1930s saw the emergence of documentary photography on an enormous scale. The Farm Security Administration, Federal Art Project, and Works Progress Administration were government sponsored attempts to provide assistance and employment while documenting conditions in rural and urban America. The list of photographers and other artists who worked for these agencies include some of the century's greatest talent. When World War II brought an end to the projects, more than 270,000 photographs of American life had been collected in government archives.

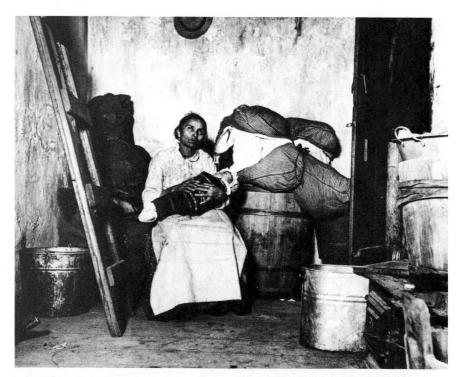

FIGURE 3.23 • Jacob Riis, *In the Home of an Italian Rag-Picker, Jersey Street*, ca. 1889.

The Jacob A. Riis Collection #157 Museum of the City of New York.

The classic film of the Great Depression is John Ford's *The Grapes of Wrath*, made in 1940 (fig. 3.25). Adapted from the novel by John Steinbeck, the film describes a farm family's disastrous odyssey from the dust bowl of Oklahoma to the labor camps of California. Plot and characters are fictional, but this is fiction drawn from the social-economic facts documented by Farm Security Administration photographers (fig. 3.26).

One FSA photographer, Dorthea Lange, was hired by the newly formed War Relocation Authority in 1942 to document another human tragedy. That year, two months after the Japanese attack on Pearl Harbor, President Franklin D. Roosevelt signed Executive Order 9006, authorizing military commanders in the U.S. to remove Japanese-Americans from their homes and move them to internment camps. Western Defense Commander Lt. General John L. DeWitt's rationale spoke for the mood of the nation: "The Japanese race is an enemy race, and while many second and third generation Japanese born on American soil, possessed of American citizenship, have become 'Americanized,' the racial strains are undiluted"[13] (fig. 3.27).

FIGURE 3.24 • Lewis Hine. *Young Millworker.*
Courtesy of Phil Davis.

When an exhibit of the WRA photographs was shown in major U.S. cities and Tokyo in 1972, art critic for *The New York Times* Hilton Kramer wrote in his review:

> . . . The documentary function is not the only interest that the art of photography can claim, but it is certainly one of its great functions, and Miss Lange was clearly one of the great practitioners of the documentary medium. In her photographs that have been brought together in Executive Order 9006 she and her colleagues have left us a moving and permanent record of a human and political catastrophe—something that no other medium could have done in quite this way, with quite this effect.[14]

Contemporary filmmakers continue the documentary tradition of conscience-raising. Godfrey Reggio's avant garde *Koyannisqatsi* (Life Out of Balance, made in 1983) and *Powaqqatsi* (Life Stolen by Sorcerers, made in 1988) describe both natural and industrialized environments. *Qatsi*, the Hopi word for life, figures in the theme and title of a third film that will complete the trilogy, *Naqaeyqatsi* (Life at War). Spike Lee's 1989 film *Do the Right Thing* is a tragicomedy exposing the absurdity of racism (fig. 3.28). In Lee's words, "I want people to know if we don't talk about the problems and deal with them head on, they're going to get much worse."[15]

Do the Right Thing concerns a chain of incidents that take place in a single neighborhood on the hottest day of the summer. Major characters are the residents and workers who make up the Brooklyn neighborhood Lee treats as a

FIGURE 3.25 • Scene from *The Grapes of Wrath*, 1940, directed by John Ford. © 1940 20th-Century Fox. Courtesy of The Museum of Modern Art/Film Still Archive.

FIGURE 3.26 • Dorothea Lange, *Migrant Homes*, 1938.
Photo Courtesy of the Library of Congress.

FIGURE 3.27 • Dorothea Lange, *American-Japanese family waiting shipment to Manazar*, 1942.
National Archives, Bureau of Agricultural Economics.

FIGURE 3.28 • Spike Lee as Mookie and Danny Aiello as Sol in a scene from *Do the Right Thing*, 1989, directed by Spike Lee.

microcosm (fig. 3.28). Mookie is a delivery man at the pizzeria and a person who goes to great lengths to avoid commitment; Sal owns the pizzeria and his two sons work for him; Buggin Out is the neighborhood activist; and Radio Raheem is the young man who won't be parted from his "beat box." The plot winds its way around seemingly inconsequential incidents that slowly rise in importance along with the summer temperature and the neighbors' tempers. Sal refuses to hang pictures of black celebrities next to pictures of Italian celebrities on the wall of his restaurant. Radio Raheem refuses to lower the volume on his radio. From this, a riot erupts and lives are irreparably damaged.

WAR: PERSPECTIVES

Since 1915, when Hollywood director David Wark Griffith released his Civil War film *The Birth of a Nation*, the genre has mushroomed in size—aided by an almost continuous progression of wars. Considering the number of films this genre includes, it might be worthwhile to compare two based on the same war.

D. W. Griffith's *The Birth of a Nation* was an adaptation of Thomas Dixon, Jr.'s 1905 play *The Clansman*, a theatrical melodrama with a racially bigoted, pro-Southern theme. Griffith, whose father had fought in the Civil War under Stonewall Jackson, readily admitted that he grew up listening to his father's bitter tales of the war and Confederate losses—the Griffith family home had been destroyed. Although Griffith's film was as controversial as Dixon's play, it became a popular and financial success. The first two years after its release, an estimated twenty-five million people paid an unprecedented two dollar ticket price to see it. The silent film premiered in Los Angeles with a live forty-piece orchestra and large vocal chorus. Similar grand openings followed in major cities across the nation, and critics wrote:

> It makes you laugh and moves you to hot tears unashamed. It makes you love and hate. It makes you forget decorum and forces a cry into your throat. It thrills you with horror and moves you to marvel at vast spectacles. It makes you actually live through the greatest period of suffering and trial that this country has ever known . . .
>
> Ned McIntosh in *The Atlanta Constitution*, December 7, 1915[16]

> The finale of the picture is Griffith's remarkable conception on the one hand of the 'human salad' of War with the blonde brute on a horse in the background striking at his helpless victims, and, on the other hand, of a Utopian brotherhood of love and peace, with some of the folks like Koreans and others like early Romans, and the figure of the Saviour blessing the glad assembly . . .
>
> Harlow Hare, *Boston American*, July 18, 1915.[17]

> Several years ago a 'professional Southerner' named Dixon wrote a sensational and melodramatic novel which has been widely read. Eight years ago Dixon brought out his novel as a sordid and lurid melodrama. In several cities the performance of this play was prohibited because of its indecency or incitement to riot. Recently this vicious play has been put into moving pictures. With great adroitness the real play is preceded by a number of marvelously good war pictures; then in the second part comes the real *Clansman* with the Negro represented either as an ignorant fool, a vicious rapist, a venal and unscrupulous politician or a faithful but doddering idiot . . .
>
> An editorial, *The Crisis* 10 (May-June 1915)[18]

The Birth of a Nation is a classic film, notable for the scope of its cinematography and editing. Griffith understood the power of visual images as few directors of his time and—like filmmaker Leni Riefenstahl who would follow twenty years later—he used the medium to express his own and Thomas Dixon, Jr.'s beliefs. The film is seriously flawed because its plot and characters are molded by the same narrow prejudicial views that dilute its major theme.

Can the American Civil War—or any war—be interpreted without imposing a particular point of view? Documentary filmmaker Ken Burns spent five years in the attempt. In 1990, his eleven hour series titled simply *The Civil War* was seen by thirty-nine million viewers, the largest audience in the history of the Public Broadcasting System. Burns' production includes letters, diaries, speeches, and newspaper reports dating from the war years in addition to 16,000 archival photos, prints, and paintings culled from more than 80 museums and libraries. Most of the visual images are portrait and documentary photographs, but maps are included to illustrate the war's territorial progress and to give viewers an opportunity to assess military strategies. The series' narrator chronicles the entire war by week, month, and year. Fact follows fact: at the Battle of Antietam 23,000 men were killed in a single day; by the war's end 620,000 men were dead (more than the American fatalities in World Wars I and II and the Vietnam War combined); black soldiers made up ten percent of the Union Army; and 100,000 Union soldiers were less than fifteen years old. Brief interviews with several Civil War historians broaden the context with explanations, conclusions, and items of human interest.

Although statistics are important, they cannot describe war's effect on human lives. Only people who actually live through a war can do this. Burns resurrects the thoughts of these people by having an off-screen narrator read excerpts from their diaries and letters. Heard most often are the penned thoughts of a Union and a Confederate soldier, and seldom do their descriptions match the glorified versions of the war seen in *The Birth of a Nation* (fig. 3.29). What these two men and others describe are loneliness, terrible

FIGURE 3.29 • A battle scene from *The Birth of a Nation*, 1915, directed by D. W. Griffith.
Courtesy of the Museum of Modern Art, Film Stills Archive.

FIGURE 3.30 • Timothy H. O'Sullivan, *Confederates captured at Gettysburg,* Civil War photograph.
Photograph courtesy of the Library of Congress.

weather, bad food, lack of food, ragged clothing and shoes, fatigue from long marches, and the worse fatigue of waiting, always waiting for the next move, the next battle, the inevitable (fig. 3.30). Providing a counterpoint to the men's descriptions, Northern and Southern women discuss the incidents and trials of life on the home front. With candor and occasional humor they reveal a keen perception of ongoing military and political events.

Burns gives extensive coverage to the period's major statesmen and leaders, but he also spotlights names heretofore unknown—Elisha Hunt Rhodes, Sam Watkins, Mary Chestnut. The lives of these people, and others, were inextricably woven into the fabric of that long war. One of the series' most poignant and personal letters was written by a man named Sullivan Ballou to his wife Sarah. While the off-screen narrator reads Ballou's letter, Burns fills the screen with portrait-photographs of young couples. The audience is not told whether Sullivan and Sarah Ballou are among them, but this missing piece of information is unimportant because the photographs, like the letter, are universal in implication. The letter is too long to print in its entirety, but these few excerpts will perhaps convey its sentiments:

My very dear Sarah;

The indications are very strong that we shall move in a few days—perhaps tomorrow. Lest I should not be able to write again, I feel impelled to write a few lines that may fall under your eye when I shall be no more . . .

Sarah, my love for you is deathless, it seems to bind me with mighty cables that nothing but Omnipotence could break; and yet my love of Country comes over me like a strong wind and bears me unresistibly on with all these chains to the battle field . . .

But O Sarah! if the dead can come back to this earth and flit unseen around those they loved I shall always be near you; in the gladdest days and in the darkest nights . . . *always, always,* and if there be a soft breeze upon your cheek, it shall be my breath, as the cool air fans your throbbing temple, it shall be my spirit passing by. Sarah do not mourn me dead; think I am gone and wait for thee, for we shall meet again . . .

Sullivan Ballou was killed at the first battle of Bull Run.[19]

LOVE AND ADMIRATION

Of all emotions the love between two adults is perhaps the most difficult to voice. Sullivan Ballou, in his letter to Sarah, succeeded where many fail, but his words were private thoughts meant to be read only by the person they concerned. How then does a filmmaker translate that same emotion into a medium designed to communicate with thousands of people? The challenge is a difficult one and requires sidestepping sentimentality and cliché. Those who meet the challenge with greatest success seem to do so only after retrieving thoughts and sensations from wells of memory and reshaping them with imagination and skill.

ARCHETYPES

Tragic love holds a particular fascination for storyteller and audience alike, and plots and characters are often archetypal. Lovers in countless tragedies confront family rivalries and different backgrounds of class, nationality, race, or religion. Shakespeare's teenage lovers Romeo and Juliet are doomed by the hatred between their families. The Broadway musical and film *West Side Story* (1961), an updated version of Romeo and Juliet, replaces feuding nobles in Verona, Italy, with fighting street gangs in New York City. Love, tumultuous and tragic, is the theme of the films *Camille* (1936), *Wuthering Heights* (1939), and *Gone with the Wind* (1939) (fig.3.31). *Camille*, adapted from the stage drama (see p. 314) is the tragic story of a heroine whose past life as a courtesan makes her socially unacceptable to her lover's family. *Wuthering Heights* and *Gone with the Wind* reverse roles by having the male lovers considered socially unacceptable.

In a more recent film, *Jungle Fever* (1991), the male lover is black and the female white. The man is also married. This complicates the plot by adding a romantic triangle theme to the complex theme of interracial love. The romantic triangle is another archetypal theme: Greek mythology gave the Mars-Venus-Vulcan triangle comic overtones, and Celtic mythology treated the Tristan-Isolde-King Mark triangle as a tragic conflict between passion and honor. Another combination of love and honor is found in *Casablanca* (1943), a film that ends unhappily rather than tragically. Cultural traditions of love and honor in India lead to a romantic triangle in Satyajit Ray's *Home and the World* (1984). Like so many of Ray's films, this one has a twin theme of social injustice. The film concerns a woman who is urged by her husband to break the rule of *purdah*, whereby high-caste women remained hidden from the sight of men and strangers. She agrees, only to fall in love with her husband's friend.

FIGURE 3.31 • Rhett Butler (Clark Gable) and Scarlett O'Hara (Vivian Leigh) in a scene from *Gone With the Wind*, 1939.
© Metro-Goldwyn Mayer.

When obsession replaces love, the theme is apt to be either the "*femme fatale*" (deadly woman) or the "woman as enchantress." *Femme fatale* is the theme of Jean Renoir's *La Chienne* (The Bitch) (1931); *Scarlet Street* (1945), an American version of the same film; and *Fatal Attraction* (1989), the most violent of its kind to date. "Woman as enchantress" has an ancient history. In Homer's *Odyssey*, Circe is the irresistibly beautiful and dangerous enchantress who entices Ulysses and detains him from his homeward journey—and his wife—for more than a year. In the film *The Blue Angel* (1930) the enchantress is also the *femme fatale*: a cabaret singer who seduces a lonely, middle-aged, unmarried professor. Once they are married, she plays with him like a cat with a mouse, humiliating, degrading, and finally destroying him.

Love stories, ancient and modern, often involve journeys, quests, and trials. Orpheus ventured into Hades, where he underwent a series of trials in an attempt to bring his beloved Eurydice back to life. Countless adventure films involve similar rescues, but journeys, quests, and trials can take quite different forms. Nick, in *The Great Gatsby* (1974), pursues a hopelessly idealistic quest to regain a woman's love by following her into the world of the very, very rich. If a heroine undergoes a trial, it is apt to follow the theme of such stories as "The Frog Prince," "Beauty and the Beast," and "Cupid and Psyche." A variation on the trial theme is the make-over theme, in which one lover must change or grow in some way to meet the requirements of the other. This is the theme of the Pygmalion myth, the story of a sculptor named Pygmalion who creates a woman so perfect he falls in love with her. The same theme is found in the Broadway musical and the film *My Fair Lady* (1964), both adapted from George Bernard Shaw's play *Pygmalion*.

TRUE STORIES

Love and admiration, although closely related, are not identical. Love may be defined as a personal and sometimes passionate affection for another person. Admiration is a feeling of wonder or approval, and the object of admiration is not always human.

Out of Africa (1985) is a film about love and the lovers' admiration for each other and for Kenya, where they choose to live (fig. 3.32a and b). The film is based on ten years in the life of Karen Blixon, who wrote under the name of Isak Dineson. Kurt Luedtke, who wrote the screen-play, compressed the eighteen years Blixon actually lived in Kenya to ten, but except for that bit of dramatic license, created a consistently authentic drama. Luedtke based the screen-play on three sources: Isak Dinesen's book *Out of Africa*; Judith Thurman's biography of Dinesen, *The Life of a Storyteller*, and Errol Trzebinski's biography of Karen's lover, Denys Finch Hatton, *Silence will Speak*.

The film begins in Denmark in 1913 when Karen Dinesen becomes engaged to Baron Bror Blixen. She follows him to Africa where they are married. After the wedding, Bror spends as little time as possible with his wife, leaving her to manage a financially risky coffee farm he started with her money. On the occasions when Karen and safari hunter Denys Finch Hatton meet, it is obvious they are attracted to each other. Nevertheless, their love affair does not begin for several years, and then it is ignited as much by admiration as by passion. Denys admires Karen's tenacity and bravery, her compassion, and her unique talent for storytelling. Karen admires his fierce independence, his empathy with nature, and his intellect. They share a great many interests, foremost their admiration for the natural beauty of Kenya, as yet unspoiled. Their relationship grows and deepens along with their fascination and respect for this part of the world. Change, however, is inevitable. The same nature that sustains life consumes it. Floods damage the coffee crop, and what can be saved is later destroyed by fire. Karen loses everything but refuses Denys' help.

Because director Sydney Pollack found the pastoral quality and romantic overtones of Dineson's writing so moving, he insisted that the film retain that same quality. Director of Photography David Watkin's success in fulfilling Pollack's request is evident from the film's beginning. Initial scenes behind the credits set a serene and tragic mood. The first image is a solitary tree silhouetted against an African sky of burnished gold. Soon Denys, rifle slung over his shoulder, appears on the horizon. Off-screen, Karen's voice describes scenes of unforgettable beauty. When she reveals that Denys' greatest gift was in helping her comprehend the world, you see his small plane soaring through clouds until it disappears into an endless blue sky. With that last image, scenes

FIGURE 3.32a • Robert Redford and Meryl Streep in a scene from *Out of Africa*, 1984.

of Africa come to an end. Next, you see a woman, no longer young, lying in bed and dreaming fitfully; then the bed is empty, the covers thrown back, and the woman sits at her desk, writing. Outside, snow is falling, and when the woman at the desk says softly that she had a farm in Africa, the story unfolds in a single long flashback.

David Watkin was Director of Photography for *Chariots of Fire*, filmed four years earlier than *Out of Africa*. In the earlier film, Watkin's cameras sought out the natural beauty of England and Scotland much as they would later explore the hills and plains of Kenya. Watkin's aerial shots of Great Britain's Olympic team members running along the beach at Dover are spectacular. Filmed from a crane-mounted camera, the scene opens with an expanse of beach and sea. The men appear no larger than dots. As the athletes run, the camera moves closer, following them and bringing you—the audience—closer

FIGURE 3.32b • Denys (Robert Redford) and Karen (Meryl Streep) in a love scene from *Out of Africa*, 1984, directed by Sidney Pollack.

until finally positioning you alongside a group of bystanders on the beach. Now, you are able to see the men more closely and as individuals.

Chariots of Fire is based on two British gold medal winners at the 1924 Paris Olympics: Harold Abraham and Eric Liddell. Harold Abraham is one of the few Jewish students at Cambridge University in 1924, and his determination to be an Olympic medal winner stems from his desire to bring honor to his family. Eric Liddell is a dedicated Scottish missionary who believes that if God had a reason for making him a missionary God must also have had a reason for making him such a fast runner. Although the film revolves around the two men, it emphasizes the admiration shared by pursuers of excellence. To reveal the forces that can shape determination the film stresses Harold's and Eric's personal relationships as much as their arduous training sessions. Camera shots of cheering crowds at the Paris Olympics, back-slapping teammates, spewing bottles of champagne, and other accolades were edited into fast-paced segments that alternate with shots filmed in slow-motion. Invariably, slow-motion prolongs action and when combined, as it is here, with medium and close-up shots, brings audiences close enough to experience the full effect of an athlete's straining muscles and labored breathing as he pushes toward the finish line. You are, in effect, there, right alongside the runners.

VARIATIONS ON A THEME

The title *sex, lies, and videotape* (1989) tells you exactly what the film is about. Ann and John are "the couple," supposedly in love, married and living a "happily-ever-after" life in a "good" neighborhood in Baton Rouge. Ann is a pretty woman in her late twenties or early thirties who wears a casual femininity like designer-label clothes. She has the sweet and vacuous look of young women who have been pruned into beautiful and egocentric objects. Ann has acquired a psychiatrist, and in the film's second scene, she is sitting in his office discussing her worry about the world garbage crisis. When he asks about her marriage, she assures him that everything is fine—except she no longer wants her husband to touch her. With those words, the next scene introduces John. John is a successful lawyer. He is glib, deceitful, and self-centered. He is also handsome with an eighties "look-for-success" image, complete with wire-rimmed reading glasses and suspenders. He sits in his law office and spins his wedding ring across the desk; the symbolism is patently obvious. Is he concerned about Ann's lack of interest in sex? Not at all, since his afternoons are spent in bed with Cynthia.

Cynthia is Ann's sister. She is a painter whose talents obviously lie elsewhere, and she supports herself by working in a gritty bar. Dark-haired like Ann, she is a dusky, husky-voiced beauty who finds sex a thoroughly enjoyable pastime. The fact that her current bed partner happens to be her brother-in-law simply adds to the excitement.

Into this triangle comes John's old college buddy, Graham. Graham has been on-the-road for nine years, but he decides to stay in Baton Rouge, at least temporarily, and he rents a nondescript apartment in a less than "good" neighborhood. Graham, of course, is the catalyst who comes with his own hang-ups. He has become a voyeur who relates to women only by videotaping them as they talk about their sexual experiences. Their camcorder confessions are stacked neatly in two boxes that travel with him cross-country. Graham considers them a file of sexual information that may help him come to terms with a rejection experienced nine years ago.

The Ann-John-Cynthia triangle evolves into a rhombus that eventually breaks apart, and in the process Ann and Graham's insecurities are erased. This is not a film of grand passion, heroics, and tragedy. These characters are simply not up to it. They are people self-absorbed and obsessed with sex or the lack of it. Filmmaker Stephen Soderbergh underscores this point by planning the entire film as a series of interior scenes. Even during the brief times when characters are outdoors, they are framed by a building or a car. Interiors, so carefully conceived, are private little environments. Ann's house, for example, is a pristine mix of designer contemporary and antique formal. In contrast, Graham's apartment is bare-bones functional and otherwise unimportant to him. Every interior set includes a window, but the characters never look outside. To all four people, that outside world is relatively unimportant or, at best, less important than their immediate concern with themselves.

Maurice (1987) is a film in which the social practices and values of a particular time mold plot, theme, and character. The time is 1913, and the locale centers around educational institutions and homes of the British well-to-do. When the film begins, Maurice Hall is a teenager attending his father's old boarding school. His father is deceased, so Maurice's family consists of his mother and two sisters, whom he sees only during brief vacations from school. The substitute family he sees on a day-to-day basis is made up of male teachers and schoolmates.

During Maurice's second year at Cambridge University, he meets Clive Durham, an extremely bright, articulate scholar whose future as a barrister and member of parliament is a matter of family tradition. Maurice is intelligent but not brilliant and, being neither handsome nor talented, is quickly attracted to Clive and soon infatuated. Clive initiates a relationship in which the men become more than friends but not lovers in the strict sense of the word. Director James Ivory treats the closeness and the awkwardness of their relationship sensitively. For example, during Maurice's first visit to Clive's family's country estate, Ivory introduces two insightful scenes. The first begins when Maurice is unpacking and Clive bursts into the bedroom and embraces him. The door opens and a maid enters. Quickly she turns her head away from the two men, but not before the camera catches her look of shock and repulsion. In the second scene, Clive's mother asks Maurice if there is someone important in Clive's life, since he seems so happy. The mother assumes, of course, that Clive has become interested in a girl. Maurice, immensely pleased by the remark, knows otherwise. The relationship between Maurice and Clive lasts three years and ends when a mutual friend is tried, publicly disgraced, and imprisoned for homosexuality. In 1913, Great Britain had a strictly enforced moral code against homosexuality.

The episode terrifies Clive, and after much soul searching, he breaks-off with Maurice and marries. Outwardly Maurice is fine. He is a successful stock broker in his father's old firm, he lives at home with his mother and sisters, and spends an occasional weekend with friends at Clive's country house. Inwardly, Maurice is torn apart. He cannot see the artificiality of Clive's marriage, only that Clive is now "normal" and he is not. He visits a doctor whom he feels he can trust and a hypnotist, but their advice, stemming as it does from their own ignorance and obvious distaste, is no help. From the hypnotist he learns only one small but important piece of information: that in France and Italy, homosexuality, while not condoned, is not considered a crime.

Later, Maurice's emotional turmoil kindled by his feelings of rejection and fear, threatens an earnest relationship offered by Alec, a young gamekeeper working on Clive's estate. In time, Maurice comes to understand that the love he shares with Alec is honest, sincere, and strong enough to withstand the obstacles they will have to face.

Maurice was adapted from the novel by E.M. Forster. Although Forster wrote the book between 1913 and 1914, it was not published until a year after his death in 1970. The novel includes an addendum of Forster's notes, and in one he explains: "A happy ending was imperative. I shouldn't have bothered to write otherwise. I was determined that in fiction anyway two men should fall in love and remain in it for the ever and ever that fiction allows, and in this sense Maurice and Alec still roam the greenwood."

SUSPENSE AND FANTASY

Alfred Hitchcock defined film as "life with the dull parts left out." Hitchcock, a master at creating suspense, knew that the very act of watching a film makes you a willing participant. If you choose to see a scary film, it is because you want to be scared; hence you are never completely passive. All competent filmmakers know that if they can just trigger your imagination, you will readily accept their illusions.

With fantasy anything is possible. In cartoons, animals of every sort talk and walk upright and act human. In *The Wizard of Oz* (1939) a girl dances with a scarecrow and a tin man and it seems perfectly natural (fig. 3.33). In *The Gold Rush* (1925), Charlie Chaplin dines on spaghetti made from his shoe lace and steak made from the sole of his shoe (fig. 3.34). In *A Trip to the Moon* (1902), space travel is a delightful, mythical fantasy (fig. 3.35). In the *Star Wars* trilogy (1977, 1980, 1983) (fig. 3.36), space travel, now a reality, reverts to a kind of high-tech mythology complete with quests, trials, fair maidens, heroes, and villains.

A FASCINATION WITH CRIME

The story idea for Fritz Lang's suspense film M (1931) came from a series of child murders in Dusseldorf, Germany. When the film begins, eight children have been murdered, reward signs are posted on kiosks throughout the city, and citizens are fearful. After the first few scenes establish this information for the audience, the murder sequence begins.

To create suspense, Lang used **parallel editing**, cross-cutting from scene to scene and thereby prolonging dramatic action. Lang begins the murder sequence with a scene of Mrs. Beckmann standing at the door of her apartment discussing the child killings with a neighbor. When a cuckoo clock, followed by a school bell, signals noontime, the scene shifts to a nearby school where children are piling out the door. Most children cluster together as they hurry

FIGURE 3.33 • The Scarecrow (Ray Bolger), Dorothy (Judy Garland), and the Tin Man (Jack Haley) in a scene from *The Wizard of Oz*, 1939.
© Metro-Goldwyn Mayer.

FIGURE 3.34 • Charlie Chaplin in a scene from *The Gold Rush*, 1925.
© 1925 Janus Films. Courtesy of The Museum of Modern Art Film Stills Archive.

away, except one little girl who walks alone, bouncing a ball on the sidewalk. Immediately, you sense that this child, singled out by the camera, is probably victim number nine. The scene changes back to the apartment where Mrs. Beckmann busily prepares lunch and sets the table. The next scene moves to the street, where the little girl bounces her ball against a kiosk bearing one of the reward signs. Suddenly, a man's shadow looms over the sign, and a voice asks the girl her name. She answers, "Elsie Beckmann." Immediately the scene shifts to the apartment where her mother keeps glancing from the clock to the window. When the postman comes to her door, she asks if he has seen Elsie. His answer is no, but he assures her the girl will probably be along soon. The

FIGURE 3.35 • A scene from *A Trip to the Moon*, 1902, by Georges Méliès. Courtesy of the Museum of Modern Art Film Stills Archive.

FIGURE 3.36 • Luke Skywalker (Mark Hamill) in a scene from *Star Wars*, 1977. ("Star Wars")™ & © Lucasfilm Ltd. (LFL) 1977 All Rights Reserved. Courtesy of Lucasfilm, Ltd.

camera, however, reveals that Elsie is with a man who stands with his back to the camera while buying her a balloon. At the apartment, Mrs. Beckmann hurries to the open window and calls in a frightened, plaintive voice, "Elsie! Elsie!" She steps into the hallway, leans over the stairwell and resumes calling. Her voice, edged with panic now, is the only sound as the roving camera reveals the empty lobby and basement. When the mother walks back inside her apartment, the camera moves from her face to the clock to the table and back again. Elsie's plate, silverware, and napkin, laid so neatly on the table are the scene's last image. The next scene opens soundlessly on an isolated patch of flat bare ground crisscrossed with shadows of thick overhanging bushes. Slowly, a little ball rolls from behind a clump of bushes and stops. The camera cuts to the sky where a balloon, snared by a web of electric wires, hangs motionless. There is no sound: no whimper, scream, or solemn music; no telltale pool of blood, no twisted, maimed body. The violence takes shape in your mind.

In the scenes that follow this, you watch a man, identified as Franz Becker, accost another little girl. Later, you see him captured, not by the police, but by a network of criminals operating in the city (fig. 3.37). Even crooks are repulsed by a child killer, but they also want him off the streets to cut back on police vigilance.

The film's last scene between the criminals and Becker makes M a classic of the genre. The criminals hold a mock trial in a vacant building, and here

FIGURE 3.37 • Peter Lorre as Franz Becker in a scene from M, 1931
Courtesy of the Museum of Modern Art, Film Stills Archive.

Fritz Lang raises the question of ethics. Becker readily confesses his crimes but pleads for his life, saying he cannot help himself. Peter Lorre as Becker creates a thoroughly repulsive character who whines and whimpers and gestures with plump little white hands. Admittedly he is a psychopath, he tells his "jurors," but this is precisely why he is *not* a criminal. Unlike the men and women who judge him, some of them admitted murderers, he cannot control his actions. He kills by compulsion and therefore cannot—as they are able to do—choose between right and wrong.

Alfred Hitchcock's *Psycho* (1960) is another film about a deranged killer, and its last two scenes neatly tie together any uncertainties left by the plot. The film introduces no moral or ethical issues of consequence but concentrates entirely on the suspense that gives the genre its name. And what suspense! Its shower murder scene has achieved classic status, largely as a result of its editing.

Prior to the shower scene, a young woman, Marion Crane, steals money from her employer. Traveling alone, she rents a motel room for the night. The motel owner, Norman Bates, invites her to share a light supper. Afterward, Marion retires to her room, undresses, and steps into the shower.

Hitchcock filmed the scene with cameras mounted above, below, and to the sides of the bathtub. Later, he chose camera shots from as many angles and distances as possible, then edited them into a **montage** of images. What do you see? Medium shots, close-up shots, and extreme-close-up shots give quick glimpses of Marion stepping into the tub, turning on the shower, holding a bar of soap, pulling back her wet hair, and turning her face to the water. Together with these images you hear the exaggerated sounds of water spraying and paper crackling as Marion unwraps the bar of soap. When these expected sounds turn into unexpected birdlike shrieks and loud dissonant music, you see the shadow of a knife-wielding woman on the other side of the plastic shower curtain. In quick succession, other images flash across the screen. The camera lets you witness a murder, but not once do you see the knife actually penetrate the body (fig. 3.38).

One of the most horrifying and fascinating images is the match-cut that ends the scene. The match-cut begins with an extreme close-up of the round drain hole into which water, now tinged with blood, runs in a steady stream. As soon as the image of the round drain completely fills the screen it is replaced by its match: an extreme close-up of Marion's eye, round, open and sightless in death.

Audiences of 1960 never anticipated this scene. Killing off the star half way through a film was unconventional, to say the least, but murdering her in the shower was unheard of. Still, the unexpected *is* a mark of Alfred Hitchcock's style, a style that includes exciting and precisely executed cinematography, editing, and special effects, mixed with a dash of humor and a thorough knowledge of the elements of drama.

Hitchcock understood the rules for creating and maintaining peak emotions, and one rule is to give audiences *dramatic relief*. Every tragic drama includes the occasional scene that gives audiences a chance to laugh or at least to relax from long periods of sustained emotion. If dramatic relief is not forthcoming, audiences will create their own: often by laughing during scenes not intended to be funny. Hitchcock relieved audience tension from the shower murder scene by following it with a scene more slow paced and unwinding.

FIGURE 3.38 • Marion Crane (Janet Leigh) in shower murder scene from *Psycho*, 1960, directed by Alfred Hitchcock.

Courtesy Paramount Studio.

This is the scene where Norman Bates removes the body and cleans the room, but even a relaxing scene needs something more interesting than Norman with his mop and pail. Hitchcock solved the problem by using the victim's packet of stolen money to introduce a new element of suspense. Unknown to Norman, the money is hidden inside a folded newspaper on the night stand, and as he mops and straightens the room, the camera keeps returning to the money. Will Norman be able to cover up the crime and get the victim's money, too? The camera "watches" as he stuffs the victim's belongings in her suitcase, puts her body and all her belongings in her car, checks the room, and stops to straighten a picture. Norman overlooks the folded newspaper! He gets ready to drive off in the victim's car when—as Hitchcock would have it—he stops, goes back inside the room, spots the newspaper, picks it up, and tosses it in the car. Norman will never know how much money disappeared in the lake along with the victim and her car.

WISHES AND ILLUSIONS

Picture a little boy standing in front of his house looking somewhat puzzled because the sun is shining through the rain. His mother tells him to stay inside, then, as if to explain her wishes, tells him that foxes hold their weddings on days like this and they do not want to be watched. As soon as his mother returns to the house, the boy heads for the woods. He is a young child, only about five or six, and he looks very small walking among the trees. The woods are truly enchanted on a day like this. Thin shafts of sunlight slip between the dense trees and turn raindrops into glistening, crystal threads. Mists rise magically from the forest floor and hover over the ground like clouds. Suddenly, foxes emerge from the mist (fig. 3.39). The little boy hides behind a thick tree and watches the foxes follow one another in solemn procession, their steps a perfect cadence. Every so often they stop. Suspiciously, furtively they glance about in the way of foxes, then continue their ritual parade. They hesitate, stop again, and stare in his direction. They see him! The boy runs home, only to find his mother outside, waiting for him at the gate. She tells him a fox came looking for him and—worse—left him a terrible punishment for intruding on the foxes' privacy.

FIGURE 3.39 • The Fox wedding scene in "Sunshine Through the Rain" sequence from *Akira Kurosawa's Dreams*, 1990.

So begins "Sunshine through the Rain," the first of eight fantasies in *Akira Kurosawa's Dreams* (1990). Japanese filmmaker Akira Kurosawa was eighty when he wrote, directed, and edited this film that is so different from any of his previous work. As he explained, "An event in a dream is a strange phenomenon which cannot possibly happen in reality . . . and yet it has sensuous feelings as if it were actual experience."[20]

With one dream for each decade of his life, Kurosawa mixes fantasy with reality, past and future with the present, and wish fulfillment with fear. The dream "Crows" lets the filmmaker indulge his admiration for the painter Vincent van Gogh (see fig. 2.46). Not content with bringing van Gogh back to life, Kurosawa imagines himself a youthful artist following van Gogh across the fields he loved to paint (fig. 3.40). Then, like Alice stepping through the looking-glass, he walks into a van Gogh painting, and then into another one. From landscape to landscape, he treks across pen and ink drawings and oil paintings, stepping over small brush strokes, dwarfed by others. His journey ends in the painting of crows and wheat fields that is van Gogh's last masterpiece.

In Woody Allen's *The Purple Rose of Cairo* (1985), a film character steps off the screen, into the audience, and changes from black and white to color. Illusion? Absolutely. The story takes place in New Jersey during the Great Depression of the 1930s. The central character is Cecelia, a fragile and indecisive young woman married to an unemployed lout. Her husband spends most of his time drinking with buddies when he should be job hunting and the rest of his time pushing Cecelia around. Cecelia supports them both by working as a waitress—unfortunately, not a very good one because her mind is always on some movie. Movies are Cecelia's escape. When her boss fires her after repeated warnings, she heads straight for the local theater where "The Purple Rose of Cairo" is playing. Cecelia sees it five times. Then, fiction in-

FIGURE 3.40 • "I" (Akira Terao) and Vincent van Gogh (Martin Scorsese) in the "Crows" sequence from *Akira Kurosawa's Dreams*, 1990.

trudes on reality and she catches the eye of a character in the movie, a hand-some explorer named Tom Baxter. Tom calls a halt to his scene, turns toward Cecelia, and remarks that she must *really* like the movie. With that, he steps off the screen and approaches her. Cecelia doesn't know whether to be shocked or enthralled, but she grabs Tom's hand and rushes from the theater with him.

Meanwhile, the movie's other characters, stuck on screen, complain that since the movie cannot continue without Tom Baxter they have nothing to do. Soon they are quarreling among themselves and with the confused theater audience. One befuddled usher runs up and down the aisles with her flashlight, and the manager calls the local police and the film studio. The police arrive followed by Hollywood moguls who bring their lawyer and the actor who played Tom Baxter. Confusion compounds. Meanwhile, Cecelia and Tom, oblivious to everything but each other, walk hand-in-hand through a deserted amusement park.

The Purple Rose of Cairo is a variation of Woody Allen's short story "The Kugelmass Episode" (1977). In the story, a humanities professor named Kugelmass finds himself in the middle of the novel *Madame Bovary*. He falls in love with the heroine and manages to get her out of the novel and into the "real" world. This, unfortunately, causes problems not only for himself but for all the students in literature classes across the country who are trying to figure out why a strange character suddenly appears on page 100!

Allen's fantasies are not the first to bring fictional characters to life. Luigi Pirandello's stage play *Six Characters in Search of an Author* (1921) is about a family who interrupts a play rehearsal demanding that somebody turn their tragic lives into a theatrical drama. Comedian Buster Keaton's silent film *Sherlock, Jr* (1924) is about a projectionist who leaves the projector running while he walks to the front of the theater, climbs into the screen and gets stuck. Because Keaton, who plays the projectionist, is unable to escape, the scenes continue to change around him, each time putting him in a different predicament.

A still-photograph is not like a film with a beginning and an end. A photograph freezes time and place. Whatever subject it represents is *now* and nothing tells you what came before or after. It is precisely this quality that Sandy Skoglund's photographs explore (fig. 3.41).

Skoglund constructs life-size scenes of fantasy and then photographs them. She creates sculptures, places them in carefully designed room settings, and paints everything in bright and often unrealistic colors. Her installations are like movie sets, but with one important difference. Movie sets are backgrounds for fully defined characters and plots; Skoglund's installations are more like suggestions that allow you to define the characters and create your own plots.

Consider her photograph *Revenge of the Goldfish* (fig. 3.41). Two people are in a bedroom. A woman lies asleep on the bed and a young boy sits awake on the edge of the bed. Who are they? Why is the bedroom, its walls and furniture the same blue-green color? Why are nearly a hundred goldfish floating around the bedroom—if it is a bedroom and not a humanized, oversized fishbowl? This photograph offers as many plots as you choose to create but, like the photographs of Manuel Bravo, it provides no specific answers. This is fantasy inviting you to participate with your own imagination.

FIGURE 3.41 • Sandy Skoglund,
"Revenge of the Goldfish, 1981."
30 x 40".

Courtesy of Castelli Graphics, N.Y. © 1981, Sandy
Skoglund.

CAMERA ARTS LANGUAGE

Camera arts language consists of selective terms and elements from the visual arts, music, and dramatic arts. Photography is a form of visual art in which cameras and developing room processes take the place of brushes and paint. Film, also a form of visual art, incorporates elements of drama, music, and dance.

STYLE, ELEMENTS, AND COMPOSITION

A painter begins with a blank canvas and then adds paint to create a picture. A photographer, however, begins with everything in sight and then subtracts to create a picture. This generalized explanation highlights a fundamental difference between the two visual arts. To a photographer, the camera viewfinder is the tool used to select the image as visualized. A photographer's technical methods involve the use of cameras, developing processes, and selections of film and paper. A photographer's creative methods involve elements of *line*, *shape*, *texture*, *color*, and *light*.

Figures 3.42a and b demonstrate how two different photographers progressed from an initial concept to the final picture. Ansel Adams' seascape *Surf and Rock, Monterey County Coast* (fig. 3.42a) is a vista evoking the mood and feel of the Pacific. Adams' photograph brings you close enough to sense the grainy texture of sand, close enough to recall the feel of its gritty warmth between your toes. The picture-image is sharp enough for you to see the water's foam where it eddies around rocks and along the shore. The scene's rough and jagged rocks glisten in the sun and lead your eye back, into the picture and beyond the last outcropping of rocks, to where the ocean, meeting the sky, disappears over the horizon. Elements of line, shape, texture, and light work in a balanced composition arranged by nature but isolated and framed by the photographer. This picture is not the result of a quick look and click of the shutter. Often, when Adams discussed his pre-photo planning and his tech-

FIGURE 3.42a • Ansel Adams, *Surf and Rock, Monterey County Coast, 1951.*
Photograph by Ansel Adams © 1992 by the Ansel Adams Publishing Rights Trust. All rights reserved

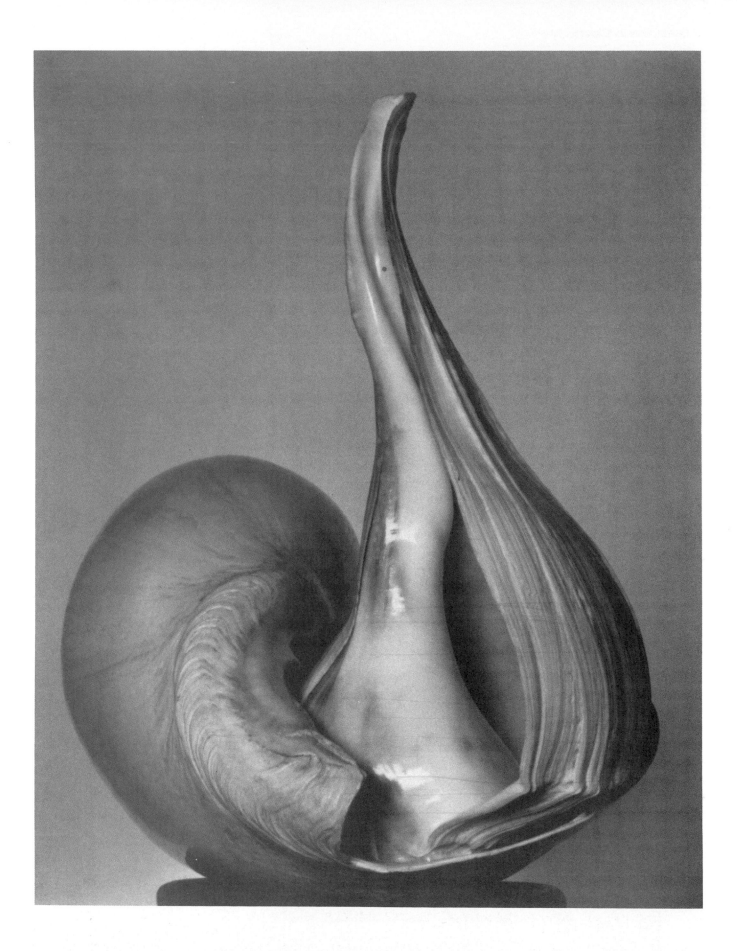

niques and methods, he mentioned "visualization," describing it, ". . . not as the way the subject appeared in reality but how it felt to me and how it must appear in the finished print."

Photographer Edward Weston used the term previsualization when referring to his total control over a subject's lighting and pictorial composition. Weston explored the shapes and textures of various shells. With few exceptions, Weston photographed the shells in his studio. Taking them out of their natural surroundings gave him total control of lighting and allowed him to eliminate anything he might consider a detraction. The results are like portraits. By "posing" a single shell against a plain background, Weston let its unique beauty and character dominate. Notice in figure 3.42b, how light and shadow dramatize the nautilus shell's spiral form. Notice how its smooth and fragile surface changes to a linear pattern that folds like drapery. Its globular shape bears another kind of pattern, this a series of upward spiraling coils that diminish as they recede into shadow. It is as if Weston is saying to the viewer "Stop and look at one of the ocean's minutia but see it and think of it as one of nature's sculptures."

Although many still-photographers continue to work with the black and white film preferred by Adams and Weston, most cinematographers are committed to color. Consider, for example, David Watkins' cinematography in Franco Zeffirelli's film *Hamlet* (figs. 3.43 and 3.44). In scene after scene, Watkins' cameras panned the castle's grey stone walls and probed its dim murky interiors. Objectively, these shots communicate the castle's bone-chilling coldness and oppressiveness; subjectively, they help communicate fear, intrigue, and murder. Even more powerful are the sunny exterior shots contrasting the castle and its hidden turmoil with the colorful beauty of its open natural setting.

FIGURE 3.42b • (Opposite) *Shell, 1927.*
Photograph by Edward Weston. © 1981 Center for Creative Photography, Arizona Board of Regents.

FIGURE 3.43 • Scene from *Hamlet,* directed by Franco Zeffirelli, 1990.

FIGURE 3.44 • Hamlet (Mel Gibson) and Queen Gertrude (Glenn Close) in a scene from *Hamlet*, 1990.

Parallel editing

EDITING

Editing, as defined previously, is the process whereby camera shots are cut and joined into **scenes** and the scenes into **sequences**. The process includes mixing sounds previously recorded and adding them, along with music, to the sound track. Although the editing process is highly technical, it is also a creative process crucial to a film's success.

Every scene in a film is edited for continuity. In the film-still from *Star Wars*, Luke Skywalker runs to his land-speeder in an attempt to warn his aunt and uncle of the Imperial Storm Troopers' search party. The next camera shot must tell the audience what happens by continuing or concluding the dramatic action begun here.

Parallel editing extends continuity by cutting to one or more different scenes and then alternating between scenes. Parallel editing is an effective way to build anticipation or suspense. Its effectiveness in *Triumph of the Will* (fig. 3.17) and M (fig. 3.37) has already been discussed.

Montage is another important editing technique. Alfred Hitchcock's montage of the shower murder scene in *Psycho* (fig. 3.38) was discussed previously, but the technique originated thirty-five years before Hitchcock used it. The man given credit for montage, which he called a "montage of collision," was Latvian filmmaker Sergei Eisenstein (1898–1948). He first used the technique for "The Odessa Steps" sequence in his silent film *The Battleship Potemkin* (1925). In one scene, Russian Cossacks open fire on unarmed citizens, massacring them. Eisenstein edited this action scene into a series of kaleidoscopic shots that juxtapose angles and distances (fig. 3.45). Because the length of time a single image remains on screen determines a scene's tempo, Eisenstein edited camera shots into shorter and shorter lengths until, at the massacre's climax, images flash on screen with the rapid fire of the Cossack's rifles. The effect is one of fractured reality, a sensation people often experience in traumatic situations.

FIGURE 3.45 • Camera shots from "The Odessa Steps" sequence in *The Battleship Potemkin*, 1925.
Courtesy of the Museum of Modern Art, Film Stills Archive.

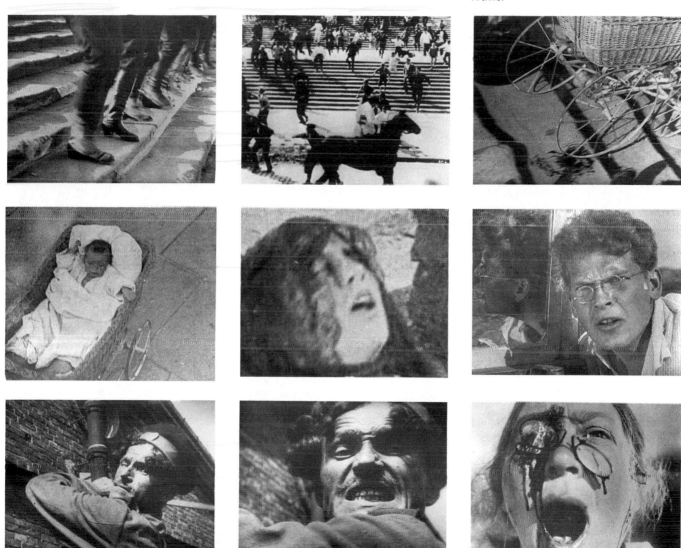

Music signals impending action in M.
Courtesy of the Museum of Modern Art, Film Stills Archive.

"Somewhere Over the Rainbow" from
The Wizard of Oz.
© Metro-Goldwyn-Mayer.

FILM MUSIC

Film music functions in several different but related ways. It can help establish time or location. For the television series *The Civil War* Ken Burns selected popular songs of the era and, to lend further authenticity, had them performed on piano, banjo, guitar, fiddle, and cello. Sydney Pollack and four sound editors combined African and European music to lend authenticity to *Out of Africa* (fig. 3.46). George W. Senoga-Zake, Professor of Music at Kenyatta University, Nairobi, researched traditional songs from the years between 1914 and 1930 and directed the performing and recording of the music in Nairobi. Traditional instruments like the ndule, a Masai flute, were used whenever possible. Because the character Denys was particularly fond of Mozart's music, the soundtrack includes short segments from four Mozart compositions: *Concerto for Clarinet and Orchestra in A*; *Sonata in A Major*; *Sinfonia Concertante in E Flat Major for Violin and Viola*; and *Three Divertimenti*.

Music is an important factor in helping set mood or in shifting from one mood to another. For "Village of the Watermills," the last dream sequence in *Akira Kurosawa's Dreams*, the filmmaker used music that was *not* authentic. Although composer Shinichiro Ikebe wrote most of the film scores, for this particular sequence Kurosawa insisted on using "In the Village" from *Caucasian Sketches, Suite for Orchestra*, by the Russian composer Mikhail Ippolitov-Ivanov.

Bernard Herrmann, who was one of Hollywood's most prolific composers, wrote the scores for *Citizen Kane* and *Psycho*, and they make an interesting comparison both musically and dramatically. The music in both films supports dramatic action from scene to scene. In *Psycho*, Herrmann's use of dissonant chords helps establish and prolong a kind of nervous anxiety on the part of the audience.

In suspense films, music can signal impending action. In M, the killer whistles the same little tune before committing his crimes. Once the audience makes this connection, a pattern is established, and thereafter merely hearing the music puts them on edge. The tune Franz Becker whistles is from "In the Hall of the Mountain King" from *Peer Gynt Suite, No.1* by Edvard Grieg.

In musical films, melodies and lyrics can provide narration, express one character's feelings about another, or function as a **soliloquy** in which the actor reveals his or her innermost feelings or intentions to the audience. When a musical composition is repeated or featured in some way, it becomes a musical's theme, for example, "Somewhere over the Rainbow" from *The Wizard of Oz*.

FIGURE 3.46 • Karen (Meryl Streep) with members of the Kikuyo tribe in Kenya, *Out of Africa*, 1984.

NOTES

[1]Part of evidence presented to a tribunal 12 December 1857. Bibliothèque Nationale Cat. des Estampes Na 163/41. Quoted in Aaron Scharf, *Pioneers of Photography*. New York: Harry N. Abrams, Inc., 1975, p. 106.

[2]Susan Sontag, *On Photography*. New York: Farrar, Straus and Giroux, 1977, pp. 15–16.

[3]John B. Cameron and Wm. B. Becker, *Photography's Beginnings: A Visual History*. Albuquerque, New Mexico: University of New Mexico Press, 1989, pp. 160–161.

[4]Quoted in Aaron Scharf, *Pioneers of Photography*. New York: Harry N. Abrams, Inc., Publishers, 1976, p. 78.

[5]Benjamin Wyles, "Impressions of the Photographic Exhibition," *The British Journal of Photography*, 9 December 1870. Quoted in Scharf, p. 74.

[6]*The Photographic Journal*, 15 February 1865. Quoted in Scharf, p. 74.

[7]Ben Lifson, *Eugéne Atget*. Millerton, New York: Aperture, Inc., 1980, p. 7.

[8]Edward Steichen, *A Life in Photography*. New York: Bonanza Books, 1984.

[9]Leni Riefenstahl, *Hinter den Kulissen des Reichsparteitagfilms*. Quoted in Erik Barnow, *Documentary*. London: Oxford University Press, 1974, pp. 102–105.

[10]Riefenstahl in Barnow, p. 103.

[11]Oliver Wendell Holmes, *Atlantic Monthly*, 1863.

Quoted in Aaron Scharf, *Pioneers of Photography*. New York: Harry N. Abrams, Inc., Publishers, 1975 p. 123.

[12]See Naomi Rosenblum, *A World History of Photography*. New York: Abbeville Press, 1984, pp. 178–208. *See also* James D. Horan, *Mathew Brady: Historian with a Camera*. New York: Crown, 1955 and James D. Horan, *Timothy O'Sullivan: America's Forgotten Photographer*. New York: Bonanza Books, 1976.

[13]Milton Meltzer, *Dorthea Lange: A Photographer's Life*. New York: Farrar, Straus, Giroux, 1978, pp. 238–249.

[14]Quoted in Meltzer, p. 244.

[15]Quoted in "*Do the Right Thing* Production Notes," *Universal News*. Universal City, California, 1989, p. 1.

[16]Quoted in Fred Silva, *Focus on The Birth of A Nation*. Englewood Cliffs, New Jersey: Prentice-Hall, Inc., 1971, p. 34.

[17]Silva, p. 40.

[18]Silva, p. 64–65.

[19]Geoffrey C. Ward, Ric Burns, Ken Burns, *The Civil War, An Illustrated History*. New York: Alfred A. Knopf, 1990, pp. 82–83.

[20]*Akira Kurosawa's Dreams*, Production Information. Los Angeles, California: Warner Bros. Inc., 1990.

CHAPTER FOUR

ARCHITECTURE

FIGURE 4.1a • Gare d'Orsay, Paris, Victor LaLoux.

FIGURE 4.1b • (Opposite) Musée d'Orsay, Paris, ACT, R. Bardon, P. Colboc, J. P. Philippon, and Gae Aulenti.

Vanni/Art Resource.

Architecture bears a human imprint. Today's buildings are impressive markers of society's dominant interests and needs, and aged buildings with their patina of accumulated history are equally impressive. Consider the great Cathedral of Notre Dame, Paris, more than eight hundred years old. Here, beneath its stone vaults and stained glass windows, Parisians mingle with tourists and walk in the footsteps of kings. Here, French monarchs were crowned, and Napoleon seized the crown from the hands of the Pope and proclaimed himself emperor. Here, General Charles de Gaulle celebrated a victory mass at the end of World War II. Today, the great cathedral stands solid and beautiful but not without scars. In the eighteenth century, French Revolutionaries ransacked the church, destroying most of its relics, and demolishing its portal statues of kings. In the twentieth century, a German World War I bomb tore through the church roof.

Paris has an affinity for its buildings. One, the Gare d'Orsay, a combination railway station and hotel built in 1900, was empty and unused in 1970. Civic leaders, faced with a derelict structure, focused on the building's potential instead of its obsolescence. The building offered an enormous expanse of space and an adequate source of natural light—two requirements for a museum—and Paris had outgrown its museums. In 1973, French President Georges Pompidou appointed a civil commission, judiciously selecting its members from government, science, and art. In 1978, the commission initiated an architectural competition and in 1986 saw the realization of its goal with the dedication of Musée d'Orsay, one example of recycled architecture (fig. 4.1 a and b).

MONUMENTS

Time dulls much of the controversy that so often greets public buildings and monuments. Who would believe that the Washington Monument, a simple and dignified marble obelisk, caused such a furor its completion was delayed for more than a hundred years? The monument had been authorized by Congress in 1783, but political squabbling kept postponing construction until 1848. When the monument was still less than half finished, the Civil War halted construction again. Finally, in 1884, the monument was completed, but it took four more years to install a steam-operated elevator. Even the elevator became controversial: it was considered too dangerous for women, who were, nevertheless, permitted to climb the Washington Monument's 897 steps.

Because monuments are symbols, representing concepts much broader in implication than their actual forms might suggest, inevitably they invite conflict. Architectural critic Wolf Von Eckardt believes this is the reason successful monuments cannot be labeled: "None of these is 'good art' or popular art, abstract or representational, 'modern' or 'traditional.' They are simply powerful ideas translated into a powerful emotional experience."[1]

VIETNAM VETERANS MEMORIAL, WASHINGTON, D.C., 1986,

ARCHITECT MAYA YING LIN (1959–   )

FIGURE 4.2 • Vietnam Veterans Memorial, Maya Ying Lin; and the Washington Monument, Washington, D.C.
UPI/Bettmann Newsphotos.

People look at it in silence. After some minutes, when the initial impact has been absorbed, they resume their conversations. The Wall, as it is called, has presence (fig. 4.2). Visitors search for a name among the thousands of names that were incised by hand, not machine, into the polished black surface. Some

people stick little flags in the ground; others place small photographs or floral wreaths or a single flower on the grass. Men and women weep, bow their heads, turn from right to left as if disbelieving the size of the granite arms that hold so many names—fifty-seven thousand, six hundred ninety-two. Everyone touches the Wall.

Controversies are forgotten. People whose beliefs were pro-war stand next to war protesters, and only a nearby statue of three Vietnam soldiers reminds visitors of the dissension that accompanied the Wall's design. Many viewers are too young to remember the war or understand the antagonism toward the monument, but they are not too young to experience the Wall's impact. Because the Vietnam War was ignoble, its objectives never clearly explained to the American people, the memorial was intended solely to honor men and women of the Armed Forces who died or were declared missing. Although it was financed entirely by private contributions, the proposed site on national land involved nearly a dozen different government agencies and Congressional approval.

The Wall's artist, Maya Lin, was an architectural student at Yale when she won the design competition for the Vietnam Memorial. Dissension followed immediately. "Why is it black instead of white?" "Why is it underground?" "What is it supposed to mean?" When the Wall was completed, people *saw* the answers to their questions. Black granite reflects, white does not. Continuously, the Wall mirrors a living, moving world: sun, clouds, trees, landscape change from day to night, from season to season. Visitors become a part of that background when their reflected images, as though reasserting life, mingle with the names of deceased. Black connects. The Wall is not underground, but *of* the ground (fig. 4.3). Its height is greatest at the angle where the two

FIGURE 4.3 • Vietnam Veterans Memorial, Washington, D.C., Maya Ying Lin.
© Catherine Ursillo/Photo Researchers, Inc.

sections meet. There, it is ten feet and from that angle tapers on either side to eight inches. Its shape leads the eye to understand what Maya Lin envisioned as two arms reaching out as if to encompass humankind.[2]

PYRAMID OF ZOSER, SAQQARA, CA. 2700 B.C., ARCHITECT IMHOTEP

Greek historian Diodorus Siculus wrote in the first century B.C., "The Egyptians say that their houses are only temporary lodgings, and their graves their houses."[3] So great was the Egyptian belief in eternal life, it became the foundation for a culture that remained relatively unchanged for three thousand years. Remaining Egyptian art and architecture are a testimony to that faith.

The Tomb of King Zoser (fig. 4.4) was part of a mortuary complex that covered thirty-five acres. Most authorities agree that the complex was intended to duplicate the king's palace and grounds as a means of insuring his physical comfort forever. The tomb stands in what was once the center of the mortuary complex, and its design is a variation of earlier tombs called **mastabas.** Mastabas were blocklike structures made of brick and stone: windowless houses for the dead. Their interiors consisted of long corridors and chambers, most

FIGURE 4.4 • Step Pyramid of King Zoser, Saqqara, Imhotep.
Marburg/Art Resource, N.Y.

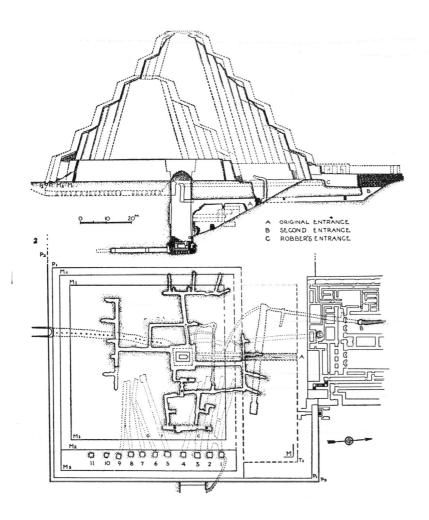

A ORIGINAL ENTRANCE
B SECOND ENTRANCE
C ROBBER'S ENTRANCE

FIGURE 4.5 • Section and plan of the Pyramid of Zoser, Saqqara, Imhotep.

From E. B. Smith, *Egyptian Architecture as Cultural Expression.* Copyright © 1968 American Life Foundation and Study Institute, Watkins Glen, NY. Reprinted by permission of American Life Foundation.

often three. One chamber held the deceased's mummy and possessions; a second was reserved for offerings of food and prayers; and a third, the serdab held the deceased's tomb statue. In an attempt to safeguard the deceased's remains, builders placed the mummy chamber at the end of a long underground shaft, which they blocked.

Zoser's architect, Imhotep, deviated from the more typical plan by building two tomb chambers, one slightly above the other. One may have been reserved for a queen's mummy or perhaps for conoptic jars containing the king's embalmed internal organs. Imhotep also changed the tomb's exterior by building a series of mastabas, graduated in size and stacked vertically to a height of two hundred feet (fig. 4.5). In making this change, Imhotep moved toward the pyramidal shape that later architects would refine by eliminating steps and letting the four sides rise uninterrupted toward their peak. Imhotep was both an architect and a priest of the Sun God Amon-Re (or Ra). As a priest he understood that just as a solar disk symbolized Amon-Re, so, too, did the pyramidal shape symbolize rays of light emanating from the sun. By creating a pyramidal shape for Zoser's tomb, Imhotep symbolically placed the deceased inside Amon-Re's protective rays of power.

Imhotep added another innovation to Zoser's mortuary complex, this a separate temple located on the north-side of the pyramid. The temple was an elaborate replacement for the traditional offering chamber inside the tomb, and it included a courtyard and separate chambers where family members and priests could bring offerings and prayers. Here, in the temple rather than the tomb, Imhotep built the *serdab* to hold a nearly life-size statue of Zoser (see fig. 2.4). The statue is intact, but little else remains. Despite the tomb's blocked shafts, false doors, maze of corridors, and Amon-Re's protection, thieves gained entry more than once. Archaeologists found the temple and tomb thoroughly plundered and Zoser's mummy literally torn apart.

TAJ MAHAL, AGRA, INDIA, 1643,

ATTRIBUTED TO USTAD AHMAD MU'AMMAR NADIR AL-ASAR

One of the world's most famous monuments, the Taj Mahal, was built by a Mogul emperor of India, Shah Jahan, in memory of his wife Mumtaz Mahal, who died in 1631 (fig. 4.6). The monument proper is a white marble mausoleum situated at the far end of landscaped grounds covering forty-two acres (fig. 4.7). When the mausoleum was still new, Shah Jahan came by boat from his palace nearby, entering the complex from the north, at the river. Visitors entered, as they do today, from the south, after first walking through an enormous gate. The gate is made of red sandstone and ornamented with the same type of carved and inlaid designs found on the mausoleum. Some designs are floral, others are verses from the Koran. One reads:

> I thou soul at peace,
> Return thou unto thy Lord, well-pleased
> and well-pleasing unto Him!
> Enter thou among My servants—
> And enter thou My Paradise![4]

The paradise visitors see is a formal landscape that follows the plan of more ancient Persian gardens. This garden is a quadrant divided by water channels symbolizing the four rivers of paradise described in the Koran. Two identical sandstone buildings flank the mausoleum; one is a mosque and the other is a rest house. Although they are important and beautiful buildings, what dominates is the Taj Mahal. Its arches thrusting upward lead the eye past smaller arches and domes to the central dome, nearly two-hundred feet high. Every shape is symmetrical and harmonious. Large as this building is, its balance and proportions prevent it from appearing ponderous or top heavy. Its silhouette, so simple when viewed from a distance, is actually a complex form of related, interlocking shapes. Huge expanses of white marble are cleft by smaller shapes, carved borders, and inlays of agate, bloodstone, jasper, and other semiprecious stones. To the eye, these appear as glistening traceries of color against the sheen of white marble (fig. 4.8). Borders of calligraphy add more rich surfaces. Calligraphy plays a prominent role in Islamic architecture and is considered the highest form of art because it makes visible the Word of God in the Koran.

FIGURE 4.6 • Taj Mahal, Agra, India.
© Lucas/The Image Works, Inc.

The mausoleum's interior consists of a central chamber, two-stories high and ringed by eight smaller interconnected chambers, four on each floor. Visitors walking through the interior rooms see the same elaborate surface decoration used for the exterior, but here the effect is very different. Natural light is diffused by the inserts of milk-glass in marble screens. The atmosphere is hushed, the mood solemn. This is a sacred place where photographs are never allowed. Inside the central chamber, an octagonal marble screen surrounds two grave markers placed over the crypt where Shah Jahan and Mumtaz Mahal are buried. High above the graves, a marble dome rises nearly eighty feet. Its illusion can be so overpowering it takes awhile for visitors to realize that it is actually a second dome placed beneath the larger exterior dome.

Who were the people so intimately involved in this monument known throughout the world as a love story in stone? Shah Jahan, like his distant ancestor Kublai Kahn, the Mogul ruler of China, was a patron of the arts. Although Shah Jahan lived lavishly, he was an able ruler and one who tolerated religions other than his own. Quite a few portraits of Shah Jahan exist but only one of his queen. Court documents record her marriage, her religion, which was Muslim, her death, and little else. Facts unadorned by fiction state that Mumtaz Mahal was married to Shah Jahan for nineteen years and died giving birth to their fourteenth child. With the help of storytellers the marriage became a romance interwoven with legends. According to one legend, Mumtaz had a premonition of her death and asked her husband to have no more children by other wives and to build her a mausoleum. Historical fact lends some credence to this particular legend because the Emperor had no more children, he mourned publicly for two years, and he ordered construction of the Taj Mahal within months of the Queen's death. Indeed, the very act of building such a magnificent monument for a wife was unprecedented and considered by certain religious conservatives as offensive. Those who found it so preferred to call the Taj Mahal the "Throne of Heaven," a name honoring the Emperor.

This story has an epilogue. Fifteen years after Mumtaz Mahal's death, their son Aurangzeb seized the throne, murdered his brothers, and imprisoned his father in a nearby fort. During his eight years of imprisonment, Shah Jahan was able to see the Taj Mahal from his window, but he was never permitted to visit it. His confinement lasted until his death, and afterward he was buried next to his wife.

FIGURE 4.8 • Taj Mahal, detail.
© Virinder Chaudhery.

SACRED PLACES

Religious buildings have many names—temple, mosque, synagogue, church—and they sometimes serve more than one religion. Notre-Dame, Paris, which is a Roman Catholic Cathedral, stands on a site considered sacred by two earlier religions. In 1711, Notre-Dame was already five hundred years old when workmen unearthed several older altars. Presently on exhibit in the Cluny Museum, two of the altars are dedicated to Roman Gods and the others to Gallic Gods.[5] The practice of rebuilding on a sacred site was a common one, and it often aided in supplanting one religion with another. During wars in which the conquest of a city involved two conflicting religions, the victors either destroyed sacred buildings or recycled them for their own use. Before its near destruction in the seventeenth century, the Parthenon, built originally as a temple to the Greek Goddess Athena, was rededicated as a Christian church and later as an Islamic mosque (fig. 4.9 a and b).

PARTHENON, ATHENS, GREECE, 447–438 B.C., ARCHITECTS ICTINUS AND CALLICRATES

The Parthenon was built at a time when the city-state of Athens had achieved its greatest military victory over the Persians. With the end of eighteen years of war, the state-city of Athens entered a Golden Age that heralded two centuries of cultural and commercial prominence. After rebuilding and refortifying the city proper, civic leaders turned their attention to the Acropolis, a dominant, fortified hilltop and a traditional center for military, civic, and religious activity. The city's patron was Athena, Goddess of Wisdom and War, and the Acropolis had always included a temple dedicated to her. Plans for a

FIGURE **4.9a** • Acropolis, Athens, view from the west.
Marburg/Art Resource, NY.

revitalized Acropolis gave her two temples: the large Parthenon, dedicated to Athena Parthenos (Virgin), and the smaller temple of Athena Nike (Victory) (fig. 4.10).

Few of the architectural achievements that marked Athen's Golden Age remain. Intervening centuries saw artillery fire, explosions, earthquakes, and thefts turn buildings to rubble. Today, the temples are empty shells, yet tourists by the thousands visit Athens every year, exploring the city and walking as close to the ruined Acropolis as permitted. What do these people see when they look toward the hill, shading their eyes against the sun? Do they picture white marble buildings standing, as they once did, tall and proud against a blue Aegean sky? Or do they see only piles of stone? Why do they come? Most tourists admit they are curious about this ancient civilization with its indelible history. Their curiosity is matched by that of the architects who come to study, measure, and admire what Ictinus (ik TIE nus) and Callicrates (Ka LIK cra tees) created.

The Parthenon is a building simple in concept, harmonious in form, and flawlessly crafted. It has a basic rectangular shape with an east-west orientation and two interior cellas (chambers). One cella functioned as a treasury and the other sheltered a forty-foot gold and ivory statue of Athena Parthenos. The temple is built entirely of white Pentalic marble, and it rests on a three-step marble **stylobate** (fig. 4.11a). Columns rise from the stylobate to support beams that once helped support a marble roof. The reconstructed scale model (fig. 4.11b) shows the height of the columns in relation to the height of an adult who stands just to the right of the picture's center. The columns are drum-shaped sections of marble fitted with lead-lined pegs, stacked, and fluted (carved into grooves). Grooves that appear so narrow in the photograph actually measure about twenty inches.

FIGURE 4.9b • Acropolis, Athens, model.

Agora Excavations. American School of Classical Studies at Athens.

FIGURE 4.10 • Temple of Athena Nike, Acropolis, Athens, Callicrates.

FIGURE 4.11a • Parthenon, Athens, Ictinus and Callicrates.
© Ewing Galloway.

FIGURE **4.11b** • Parthenon, restored model.

The Metropolitan Museum of Art. Purchase, Levi Hale Willard Bequest, 1890. (90.35.3)

The two architects devised certain optical refinements to offset the visual distortion caused by the building's size and elevated site. The stylobate is actually concave and slopes downward at the corners. Columns that appear straight actually bulge and tilt inward. Corner columns are larger in diameter than others and are positioned closer together to compensate for the difference between the sky visible between corner columns and the solid cella walls behind other columns.

Sculpture from the Parthenon that escaped destruction may be seen today in either the Athens Museum or the British Museum, London. The full significance of this sculpture, however, is best understood in relation to the temple where it was originally placed. The sculpture commemorates Greek myth, legend, and history. Sculpture on **metopes** (MET o pays) above the outside row of columns (fig. 4.12) describes various mythical and legendary battles. A continuous sculptured **frieze** above the inside row of columns illustrates the Great Panathenaia, a procession and celebration held every four years to honor the city's patron goddess. Sculpture on west and east **pediments** relate myths involving Athena. West pediment carvings describe the competition between Neptune and Venus for control of the city. East pediment carvings depict Athena's birth as a grown woman born from the forehead of Zeus, her father, and without need of a mother (fig. 4.13). Zeus is shown seated on his throne, surrounded by other gods and goddesses. Athena stands next to him holding her spear and shield, and on the far right Apollo holds the lyre described in chapter 5.

FIGURE **4.12** • Parthenon, Athens, Ictinus and Callicrates, sculptural and architectural detail.

From Richard Phipps and Richard Wink, *Invitation to the Art Gallery: An Introduction to Art.* Copyright © 1987 Wm. C. Brown Communications, Inc., Dubuque, Iowa. All Rights Reserved. Reprinted by permission.

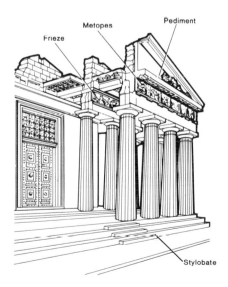

FIGURE 4.13 • Parthenon, Athens, Ictinus and Callicrates, reconstruction of east pediment, central section.
TAP Services, Ministry of Culture, Athens, Greece.

PANTHEON, ROME, ITALY, 118–125 A.D.

Considering the Pantheon's age and history, it has survived remarkably well and with its basic structure still intact (fig. 4.14). In crowded, bustling modern-day Rome, the Pantheon maintains an impressive historical-architectural presence. This temple to many gods was built during the reign of Hadrian, and the emperor may have been its architect. Blazoned across its portico frieze is the Latin inscription "M. Agrippa L.F. Cos Tertium Fecit" (Marcus Agrippa, son of Lucius, consul for the third time, built this). The entire portico was taken from an older temple that once stood nearby.[6] Emperor Hadrian's orders to dismantle the temple and use part of it for the much grander Pantheon was one way of honoring his ancestors.

You enter the temple by crossing the portico and walking between tall columns of Egyptian granite. At the end of a short aisle is a large bronze doorway. Step inside, and you stand at the edge of an enormous circular chamber. Giovanni Paolo Panini's painting of the Pantheon shows the interior as it looked in the eighteenth century, and little has changed (fig. 4.15). The circular wall is clad with different marbles and porphyry, a red-violet stone. Around the chamber are more columns and eight tall niches holding statues. High above is an enormous dome, much larger than it appears from outside. In the dome's center is an **oculus**, an open hole that provides the sole source of light. Although the oculus is actually twenty-six feet in diameter, it appears smaller because the dome rises to a height of 144 feet and has a diameter equal to its height. The dome is coffered, and these decorative indented panels lessen

FIGURE **4.14** • The Pantheon, Rome.
Alinari/Art Resource, N.Y.

the weight. The cylindrical base on which the dome rests is twenty feet thick, but the dome itself is gradually reduced in thickness from twenty feet at the base to five feet at the oculus.

On the exterior, bronze plates originally covered the dome, and white marble covered the base. Historians disagree as to when the materials were removed. Some place the date early in the seventh century, at the time Pope Boniface IV rededicated the Pantheon as S. Maria and Martyrs. Others maintain the materials were removed later in the century, when the Pantheon's gilded bronze door plates and bronze pediment sculptures were stripped and shipped to the city of Constantinople.

FIGURE 4.15 • *The Interior of the Pantheon,* painting by Giovanni Paolo Panini, ca. 1750. Oil on canvas, 50 1/2 × 39″.

Samuel H. Kress Collection, 1939, National Gallery of Art, Washington, D.C.

FIGURE 4.16a • Villa Rotonda, Vicenza, Italy, Andrea Palladio, ca. 1550.
Alinari/Art Resource, NY.

FIGURE 4.16b • Monticello, Residence of Thomas Jefferson, Charlottesville, Virginia, begun 1770.
© Alvin E. Staffan/Photo Researchers, Inc.

Even without its original adornments, the Pantheon is a spectacular building and one that reveals very definite Greek influences. Roman architects adapted elements of the Greek style much as Renaissance architects later incorporated elements of the Greco-Roman style into their designs. The sixteenth-century Italian architect, Andrea Palladio, for example, built churches, public buildings, and villas in the Greco-Roman Style (fig. 4.16a). Palladio was also one of the first architects to publish his ideas. *I Quattro libre dell' architettura* (The Four Books on Architecture), written in 1570, gained him an international reputation. Thomas Jefferson read the first English translation of Palladio's book and soon became one of his most enthusiastic admirers (fig. 4.16b).

HAGIA SOPHIA, CHURCH OF HOLY WISDOM, CONSTANTINOPLE (ISTANBUL, TURKEY), 532–537,
ARCHITECTS ANTHEMIUS AND ISODORUS

At the time Hagia Sophia (HA jeh SO fee ah) was built, Constantinople had been the capital of the Roman Empire for two hundred years. The emperor was Justinian, an able administrator, skillful military strategist, and patron of architecture. In 532, Justinian successfully put down a rebellion, but not before large areas of the city had been set afire. One of the buildings destroyed by fire was a church the Emperor Constantine had built on the site of an older non-Christian temple. Emperor Justinian immediately hired architects to design a new church, this one to honor himself. Five years later, at the consecration of Hagia Sophia, a boastful Justinian declared to everyone assembled: "Solomon, I have outdone thee."

Hagia Sophia is a remarkable building (fig. 4.17 a and b). Religious architecture scholar Professor J.G. Davies describes it as an example of the **baldachin** principle. "This means that it is the dome that is the primary space-defining element; the church as a whole is conceived as a complete baldachin . . ." or canopy. Roman domes, like that of the Pantheon, are "lids on cylinders," but Hagia Sophia is "hanging architecture." The dome appears to hang in space because the four arches underneath lend support much like four poles holding up a canopy. Inside, the baldachin principle is even more ap-

FIGURE 4.17a • Hagia Sophia, Constantinople, (Istanbul) Turkey, Anthemius of Tralles and Isodorus of Miletos.

Hirmer Fotoarchiv.

FIGURE 4.17b • Hagia Sophia, interior.
Hirmer Fotoarchiv

parent. The four arches that join to form a square floor plan are much lighter in appearance than the solid, round wall of the Pantheon. Hagia Sophia's dome is actually higher than the Pantheon's although it is smaller in diameter, rising 184 feet from a diameter of 112 feet. The dome rests on a ringlike shape formed by four arches; half-domes, vaults, and columns provide additional support. Symbolically, it hangs in space like the canopy of heaven it represents.

The exterior makes visible the building's brick and mortar construction. The interior, however, challenges the eye with an abundance of colors, textures, and decorative embellishments. Walls and columns are clad in every kind and color of marble, much of it varicolored and veined. The capitals that crown the columns are intricately drill-carved, some with Justinian's initials. Gold mosaics cover the dome, and colored glass mosaics, some applied over gold leaf, spread across arches and wall surfaces (fig. 4.18).

Interestingly, before Hagia Sophia was converted to a religious museum in the twentieth century, the public as a whole was never allowed inside. Justinian built the church solely for himself and his imperial court; and the Ottoman Turks, who conquered Constantinople in 1453, changed the church to a mosque. Outside, the Turks constructed four minarets (prayer towers), and inside, they painted and plastered over most mosaics and added Islamic callig-

FIGURE 4.18 • Hagia Sophia,
Constantinople, Mary with the child Jesus.
Justinian stands on the left and Constantine
on the right.

inside, they painted and plastered over most mosaics and added Islamic calligraphy. Each of the large round medallions visible in figure 4.17b bears a sacred name and inscription; for example the one on the left reads, "Muhammad, may peace be upon him."

TEOTIHUACAN, MEXICO (CA. 200 B.C.–750 A.D.)

Half-way across the world from Constantinople another city entered its golden age about the time Justinian began his reign. Teotihuacán (tay ah tee wah KAHN), ancient city of the Toltecs, was located about thirty-two miles from present day Mexico City. Teotihuacán covered an area of between eight to thirteen square miles and had a population that may have reached a hundred thousand. The city began as a farming community but grew to become a center for religion, government, and trade. Fertile farmlands and nearby deposits of black and green obsidian contributed to the city's growth. Obsidian, a tough volcanic glass, was used for tools and weapons before metalworking appeared in Mesoamerica sometime after the year 900. Long before then, however, Teotihuacán had ceased to exist.

What caused the city's demise may never be known, although archaeological research points to several factors, any one of which might have contributed to a mass exodus. Evidence reveals that sometime before the year 700, a large part of the city burned and the surrounding area suffered severe deforestation. Erosion caused by deforestation would have affected crops, and any climatic change would have compounded the problem by causing severe food shortages.

Teotihuacán's architecture and art help peel away some of the layers of mystery that shroud the sacred city. Teotihuacán's pyramids, buildings, and streets are laid out in an astronomical pattern with the largest monument, the Pyramid of the Sun, oriented toward a point where the sun sets over the city on the day it reaches its zenith (fig. 4.19). A broad avenue, a mile and a half long, connects the Pyramid of the Sun with the Pyramid of the Moon, and nearby stand a number of smaller pyramids. One is the Pyramid of Quetzalcótl (ket SAHL kaw AHT'l), an exceptionally well preserved example that had been covered over with a mound of stucco (fig. 4.20). The heads of Feathered Serpents projecting from the pyramid's sloping terraces are icons of the God Quetzalcótl; others are icons of the round-eyed Rain God Tlaloc.

FIGURE 4.19 • Teotihuacán, Aerial view from the northwest.
© Lee Boltin Photo Library.

FIGURE 4.20 • Pyramid of Quetzalcótl, Teotihuacán.
© Lee Boltin Photo Library.

Mesoamerican pyramids are truncated, and although resembling Egyptian pyramids, they differ considerably in structure and function. Mesoamerican pyramids were built of stone and sun-dried clay and were layered with a covering of brightly painted stucco. Some were built directly over smaller, older pyramids. Uniformly, their moundlike sloping terraces rose to a level platform where, at the head of steps—hundreds of steps—stood a single, small, windowless temple with only one door.

Eight hundred years after Teotihuacán had been abandoned, Spanish explorers and missionaries found similar stepped pyramids and temples in the Aztec city of Tenochtitlan (present-day Mexico City). Spanish logs and diaries reveal that Quetzalcótl and Tlaloc were among the gods the Aztecs worshipped. Eye-witness accounts also describe one ritual too closely linked to the Pyramid of the Sun to allow for coincidence, especially since it took place during the Aztec's annual Feast of the Sun. After choosing a war captive, the Aztecs forced him to follow their priests up the pyramid steps in a procession symbolizing the sun's ascendance in the morning sky. When the procession reached the temple, the priests stretched their victim over a curved stone and cut out his heart. Afterward, they rolled his body down the stairs to symbolize the sun's downward path from noon to sunset.[7]

Did the older Toltec civilization practice human sacrifice? There is evidence they did. In Teotihuacán, altars stood at the base of pyramids and also in courtyards of large houses. Kitchen refuse unearthed from the ruins of those houses reveal human bones, including mandibles. Historically, Teotihuacán was an important pilgrimage center, and its name means "Place of the Gods," a reference to the sacred place where Gods gathered together after the sun died. The myth tells that the Gods decided to sacrifice two of their members by fire in order to create a new sun. Nanahuatzin, God of the Poor, was the first to jump into the flames and was transformed into the Sun God. Tecuciztécatl, God of Wealth, followed and became the Moon God.

Another, stronger connection exists between Toltec and Aztec religious practices. Aztec oral history has always claimed that their rulers were taken to Teotihuacán for burial. This was contrary to the prevailing belief among scholars that Mesoamerican pyramids were solid monuments never used for burial. Recent excavations validated Aztec oral history by uncovering a secret tunnel leading to a burial cave directly beneath the Pyramid of the Sun.

CATHEDRAL NOTRE-DAME, PARIS, BEGUN 1163

When the foundation stone for the Cathedral Notre-Dame was laid in 1163, Paris was already a prosperous city of nearly a hundred thousand (fig. 4.21). The old cathedral was three hundred years old, in disrepair, and too small to accommodate the city's growing population. Churchmen, with the support of King Louis VII, decided to tear down the old church and build anew. Their decision added to a building campaign that assumed enormous proportions: in France alone, six hundred churches were built during the next hundred years.

These numbers make sense only when considering what churches meant to people of the Middle Ages. Cathedrals were much more than Bishop's domains and, taken together, all churches answered needs both secular and religious. For many people, ongoing church construction provided employment for several generations—it took a hundred-forty years to complete Notre-Dame, Paris. Churches hosted the first universities, and their holy day pageants initiated the first original drama in Europe since the Golden Age of Greece. Church grounds were used for open markets, and space inside churches was set aside for functions that could include anything from a town council meeting to a heresy trial. These and other activities generated what is known today as the "tourist trade," and as a result innkeepers, merchants, suppliers and cities as a whole prospered.

During the Middle Ages, religious services were held on a daily basis morning and evening. Charismatic preachers drew large crowds, and pilgrims traveled from town to town attending masses, listening to religious music, and comparing the different buildings. There was much to compare and admire. Pilgrims saw spires, towers, and vaults of awesome heights, portals literally covered by sculpture, dark interiors brightened by stained glass windows—and always the miraculous power of relics.

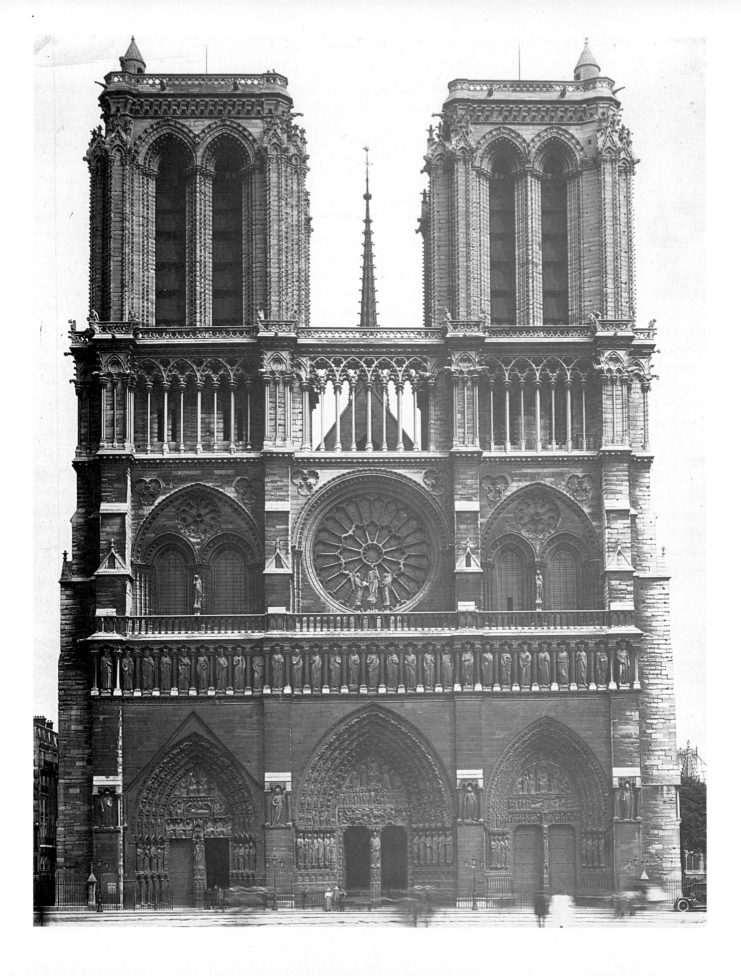

One of Notre-Dame's relics is a very special religious artifact that came to the cathedral in 1238. That year Byzantine Emperor Baldwin II offered to sell the Crown of Thorns, which was Hagia Sophia's most holy relic. Baldwin, it seems, was in dire financial need and had already pawned the relic to a Venetian businessman. When French King Louis IX heard of the offer, he immediately purchased the relic and welcomed it to the city with ceremony and fanfare. On the day the king's couriers arrived at the gates of Paris bringing the relic, Louis rode out to meet them accompanied by his personal guard, members of his court, and a bevy of priests and monks. Surrounded by crowds of onlookers, they carried the relic in procession to the cathedral, where it remained until the completion of another Paris church, Sainte-Chapelle.

The style of Notre-Dame, Paris, is "Gothic," once a derisive term for anything considered barbaric. Gradually, time erased the word's negative connotations and today it describes this important and influential style of the Middle Ages. The Gothic Style is both functional and symbolic. Gothic churches have an east-west orientation so that people entering through the west portals face east with its associated solar and Christian symbolism. Three portals are standard, three being a number associated with the trinity, and west portals are generally flanked by towers. Most churches have a cruciform floor plan (fig. 4.22). Notre-Dame, Paris, does not, but it does have the long nave so necessary for processionals. In Gothic churches, the main altar stood originally at the **crossing,** and its presence was signified outdoors by a spire directly overhead. The **choir** is a clearly defined area used originally to seat members of the choir, church, and aristocracy. Common people stood or sat on plain backless benches in the side aisles. The **narthex** held a baptismal font and served as a general multi-use area.

The height of these stone churches was a symbolic reach toward heaven, a devotional concept that resulted from a complex system of medieval architecture and engineering. An essential part of that system are the **rib vaults** (fig. 4.23). Rib vaults are skeletal arches that rise and spread from columns and piers like the ribs of an umbrella. Vaults soar, and their vast empty spaces are both impressive and emotion-charged. Adding to the wonderment, stained glass windows filter sunlight, turning it into shimmering patterns of brilliant

FIGURE 4.21 • (Opposite) Notre-Dame, Paris, West facade.
Photo © Museum of Notre-Dame de Paris.

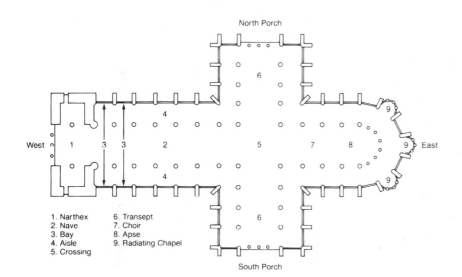

North Porch

West   1   3   3   2   5   7   8   9   East

South Porch

1. Narthex   6. Transept
2. Nave   7. Choir
3. Bay   8. Apse
4. Aisle   9. Radiating Chapel
5. Crossing

FIGURE 4.22 • Hypothetical cruciform floor plan of a Gothic cathedral.
From Robert C. Lamm and Neal M. Cross, *The Humanities in Western Culture: A Search for Human Values,* 2d ed. Copyright © 1989 Wm. C. Brown Communications, Inc., Dubuque, Iowa. All Rights Reserved. Reprinted by permission.

FIGURE 4.23 • Notre-Dame, Paris, from the height of the Western Rose Window. Scala/Art Resource, NY.

FIGURE 4.24 • (Opposite) Notre-Dame, Paris, Northern Rose Window. Giraudon/Art Resource, NY.

color (fig. 4.24). Church exteriors reveal more of the structural complexity that allows for such great heights. **Flying buttresses** give additional support to vaults and **apse** (fig. 4.25). Flying buttresses are half-arches that rise from the ground and "fly" to the walls. Supporting—buttressing—at the point of greatest stress, they carry much of the roof's weight away from the vaults and into the ground.

Nearly all Gothic churches include one or more round stained glass Rose Windows. The practice of embellishing churches with stained glass and sculpture is another characteristic of the Gothic Style. Scholars and writers have called the churches "Bibles in stone" because their art, beautiful in itself, was also a means of teaching religion and history to the largely illiterate congregations of the Middle Ages.

During this time, the Cult of the Virgin honored Mary as Mother and Protectress much as the ancient Greeks honored Athena. Notre Dame means "Our Lady," and cathedrals named Notre-Dame were built not only in Paris but in many other French cities. Two of Notre-Dame's west portals are dedicated to the mother of Jesus, and another sculpture of her stands directly in front of the Western Rose Window where its tracery and glass encircle her

FIGURE **4.25** • Notre-Dame, Paris.
Hirmer Fotoarchiv.

FIGURE **4.26** • Notre-Dame, Paris. The
Western Rose. The kings guard the
immense halo of the Virgin.
The Bettmann Archive.

like a gigantic halo (fig.4.26). Beneath Mary is a row of statues representing Old Testament kings. These replace the originals destroyed in the eighteenth century.

Kings and queens are not the only secular subjects of Gothic sculpture. Legendary heroes, zodiacal signs, birds, fish, and plant life cover portals, columns, and walls, and animals are plentiful. Some are quite lifelike but others are creatures out of a stonecutter's nightmare. All sorts of half-human, half-animal creatures appear in scenes of hell, but the most famous Gothic animals are the **gargoyles** in their rooftop perches (fig. 4.27). These are true Gothic creations: part-functional and part-symbolic. Most are down spouts, as evidenced by the open mouths, but to the superstitious people who carved the monsters, they were ugly enough to keep the devil away from the church.

During the nineteenth century, the trend toward revival architecture that began a century earlier gained momentum. Gothic Revival made its first appearance in England, then spread quickly to areas of Northern Europe, North America, and Australia where it became the popular choice for churches, universities, colleges, and government buildings (fig. 4.28).

Figure 4.27 • Notre-Dame, Paris. Gargoyle.
Culver Pictures, Inc

Figure 4.28 • Cathedral Church of St. Peter and St. Paul, "Washington Cathedral," Washington, D.C., begun 1907.
© Balthazar Korab, Ltd.

THORNCROWN CHAPEL, EUREKA SPRINGS, ARKANSAS, 1980,

ARCHITECT FAY JONES

Thorncrown is a different sort of sacred building (fig. 4.29). A nondenominational chapel built in a wooded area of the Ozark Mountains, Thorncrown began with one man's idea of what church should be: ". . . a quiet, glass chapel where people could feel like they were sitting on a tree stump in the middle of the woods."[8] The man was Jim Reed, a junior high school teacher and real estate investor, and Thorncrown was his gift to Eureka Springs and to anyone who might wish to share his idea of a sacred place.

Reed contributed eight acres of woodland, and architect Fay Jones selected a site convenient to the nearby highway but still some distance from the road. To prevent harming the fragile environment, Jones designed a building made solely from the materials two men could carry up the path to its site. This is the rationale behind Thorncrown's skeletal structure of two-by-fours and two-by-sixes—all Arkansas pine—held in place by steel truss connectors. Together with corner columns, these form a web to support the narrow, pitched roof that rises forty-eight feet. Walls are a non-supporting "skin" of glass, and a glass skylight pierces the roof.

Thorncrown is essentially a sacred shelter in the shadows of trees (fig. 4.30). Behind the small altar, clusters of dogwood, maple, and oak provide a natural backdrop for the plain steel cross. Because the church is built against

FIGURE 4.29 • (Opposite) Thorncrown, Eureka Springs, Arkansas, Fay Jones. © Wayne Sorce, photographer.

FIGURE 4.30 • Thorncrown, interior. © Wayne Sorce, photographer.

a steep slope, one glass wall overlooks the valley below, and the other faces nearby oaks, maples, dogwoods, and hickory trees. Floors are flagstone laid over a foundation of indigenous stone. Wood columns and beams are stained gray, and metal surfaces are painted a metallic blue-gray. Upholstery is a more intense blue, but the interior as a whole has a natural, informal appearance. When the church is used for evening activities or weddings, it is illuminated by lights attached to wall columns (fig. 4.31a). Jones calls them lanterns, and he designed them along with the front-door handles (fig.4.31b).

This architect's environmental sensitivity and his attention to small but important details are remindful of the American architect Frank Lloyd Wright, who died in 1959. Fay Jones is a former student of Wright's, and he shares Wright's belief that architecture must be sensitive to the needs of people and nature. Others share this philosophy. Forty thousand people visited Thorncrown the year it was dedicated, and that number has swelled to two hundred and fifty thousand annually.[9]

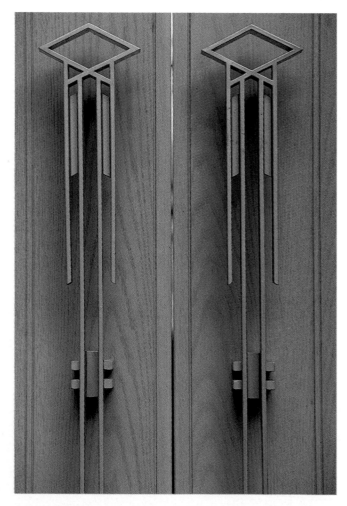

FIGURE 4.31a • Thorncrown, Fay Jones, the Lantern.
© Wayne Sorce, photographer.

FIGURE 4.31b • Thorncrown, Fay Jones, the front door handles.
© Wayne Sorce, photographer.

AN ARCHITECTURE FOR LEISURE AND THE WORKPLACE

Year after year, tourists visit the theater at Epidauros, Greece, where ancient dramas were held more than two thousand years ago (fig. 4.32). The theater is partly in ruins now, silent, unused; the only sounds are visitors', but their voices can be heard clearly all the way to the fifty-fifth tier of benches. No one has successfully explained the reason for such extraordinary acoustics, but among probable causes mentioned are the recesses behind seats and the angle of incline. The one certainty is that this theater could accommodate an audience of twenty thousand and provide them with good sight lines and remarkable sound.

In the nineteenth century, Paris theater-goers wanted considerably more. Napoleon III responded to the wishes of a prosperous and growing middle class by including several new theaters as part of his plan for a city of "grand boulevards." No theater was more grand or opulent than the Opéra built by architect Charles Garnier (fig. 4.33). Garnier's design has the same flamboyant Baroque Style as the Palace of Versailles (see fig. 4.49). You can sample that style because the Opéra is used today for ballet performances and special shows. You can walk up the grand staircase, feel the coolness of its marble banister under your hands, admire the same crystal and gilt chandeliers that impressed audiences more than a century ago (fig. 4.34). True, it is an old building and theater styles have changed, but it continues to provide beauty, function, and durability—three essential architectural requirements.

In 1871, when the Paris Opéra was nearing completion, the city of Chicago was swept by a fire that burned for three days. Of the buildings that eventually replaced Chicago's charred ruins, quite a few remain in use today. They were constructed at a time when iron and steel first became available, and

FIGURE 4.32 • Greek theater at Epidauros.
© Robert Lamm.

FIGURE 4.33 • The Opéra, Paris, Charles Garnier.
Courtesy of the Paris Opera.

FIGURE 4.34 • (Opposite) Opéra grand staircase, Paris, Charles Garnier.
Giraudon/Art Resource, NY.

these materials brought radical changes to architecture. Foremost, they did away with the need for load-bearing walls. Iron and later steel skeletons provided support, and walls provided protective cover. Any need for the "solid" look of masonry walls soon disappeared as buildings grew to new heights.

Louis Sullivan was one of the pioneers of this new architecture that would make use of vertical space. One example of his work is a steel-frame building designed in 1904 for a clothing store (fig. 4.35). The building is still a clothing store: Carson Pirie Scott & Company, located on a busy corner in Chicago's Loop District. Its display windows, so typical today, were an innovation in 1904; and Sullivan was able to introduce them only because the walls were non supporting. Although the building is plain in design, its architectural details reveal Sullivan's masterful use of ornamentation. For the roof, he designed a decorative **cornice** that has since been removed; and for display windows and the main entrance, he created flourishes of ironwork that still

remain today (fig. 4.36). Sullivan thought of display windows as pictures and decided they should have attractive frames. He then proceeded to "frame" them with an ironwork frieze running the length of the building and culminating in vertical borders alongside the entrance. He "framed" the arched doorway with a related ironwork design.

Sullivan realized that this new gigantic architecture of the workplace would have two quite different perspectives. From a distant perspective, a building's silhouette would be visible against the sky or in a cluster of other buildings. From a closer perspective, the building's individual elements would be visible to workers, customers, and pedestrians.

SEAGRAM BUILDING, NEW YORK CITY, 1958,
LUDWIG MIES VAN DER ROHE (1886–1969)

From city to city, nation to nation, high rises ring the globe. They are the International Style. Mies van der Rohe (mees VAN der ROH uh) called them "skin and bones construction." From a distance, they are giant boxes upended, massive skeletons of steel and concrete with skins of glass (fig. 4.37). Some are so tall that clouds cover their upper stories, making them true cities of the sky. From the sidewalk, their size can be overwhelming (fig. 4.38).

McGill University Professor of Architecture Witold Rybcznski writes that buildings designed by acclaimed architects "stand apart—they embody an air of detachment from the world around them." The Seagram Building fits his

FIGURE **4.37** • Seagram Building, New York City, Ludwig Mies van der Rohe and Philip Johnson.
Photograph by Ezra Stoller, 1958. Lent by Joseph E. Segram & Sons, Inc.

FIGURE **4.38** • Seagram Building, New York City, Ludwig Mies van der Rohe and Philip Johnson.
Ezra Stoller/© Esto. All rights reserved.

description. At first glance, it is the same upended steel and glass box that typifies the International Style. With more careful study, it reveals an elegance of form that sets it apart. In Rybcznski's words:

> . . what characterized all his [van der Rohe's] buildings was the careful and studied way in which they were built. There were no accidents; every corner, every meeting of materials, every point, inside and out, was specially designed to be a part of an esthetic whole. No detail was too small to be pondered.[10]

A van der Rohe building has the same geometric balance and purity of form found in a Mondrian painting (see fig. 2.54). The two men were contemporaries, and the Dutch De Stijl (the style) movement of abstraction influenced Mondrian in much the same way the Bauhaus (a German school of design) influenced van der Rohe. The architect summarized his philosophy in three words "Less is more," a belief paralleling Mondrian's philosophy that art should appear machinelike.

The Seagram building has a simplicity of form that calls attention to its rich materials. The lobby has granite floors, walls and shafts of travertine marble, and columns fitted with bronze casings. The building's thirty-nine story steel frame is clad in bronze, and the windows are bronze-tinted glass. The building site includes a landscaped plaza with a pool and fountain. Although this might be considered unprofitable space, it is, nevertheless, necessary space because it offsets the size of the building while calling attention to its form. By including the plaza, van der Rohe followed the same aesthetic principle exemplified by the gates, gardens, and pools of the Taj Mahal and other imposing buildings.

Mies van der Rohe's career falls into two phases and spans two continents. He was born in Germany, and his father was a stone mason. After graduating from trade school and serving an apprenticeship in his father's trade, Mies moved to Berlin. There, when he found that his training had been deficient in wood working, he apprenticed himself to a furniture maker. Two years later, while still in his early twenties, he designed his first house. He served as an army engineer in World War I, and afterward his career grew steadily. Appointed director of the Bauhaus in 1930, he was in the forefront of the contemporary design movement in Germany. With the rise of Nazism, that movement ended along with the Bauhaus. In 1937, American architect Philip Johnson invited van der Rohe to the United States, and three years later, van der Rohe was appointed Director of the School of Architecture at the Illinois Institute of Technology. This position gave him tremendous influence over large numbers of architectural students and brought him large and prestigious commissions during the building boom years following World War II. The Seagram Building was the eighth commission received after his appointment, and it appeared at midpoint—some say the zenith—of this second phase of his long career.

BANK OF CHINA, HONG KONG, 1989,
ARCHITECT I.M. PEI (1917–)

I.M. Pei (pay) was born in China and came to the U.S. in 1935 to study architecture at the Massachusetts Institute of Technology. Soon afterward, he became an American citizen. Among the buildings Pei has designed are the

John F. Kennedy Library, the Dallas Symphony Center, the East Wing of the National Gallery of Art, and the first of a two-phase addition to the Louvre, Paris.

His high-rise Bank of China is a milestone that moves the International Style in an entirely new direction (fig. 4.39). The Bank of China is now the tallest bank in Hong Kong—a city of banks—and the tallest building in Asia. The Bank of China rises seventy stories and has an area twice as large as the Seagram Building. More important, it is a faceted shaft of triangles that breaks with the traditional boxlike high-rise shape (fig. 4.40).

FIGURE 4.39 • (Opposite) Bank of China, Hong Kong, I.M. Pei and Partners.
Photo: © 1992 Paul Warchol.

FIGURE 4.40 • Bank of China, Hong Kong, I.M. Pei, north entrance.
Photo: © 1992 Paul Warchol.

FIGURE 4.41 · (Opposite) Bank of China, I.M. Pei, 70th floor lounge with view of Hong Kong.
Photo: © 1992 Paul Warchol.

Hong Kong's background of harbor and mountains makes it one of the world's most beautiful cities. Nevertheless, its geography presents architects with two serious problems: the city has a history of earthquakes, severe ones; and winds in the area are known to be twice as strong as Chicago's. Because the lateral loads generated by winds and other natural forces are a chronic problem with high rises, the most common solution when building to extreme heights has been to add diagonal braces to the skeletal frame. Pei did something different. He divided a square base into four triangular quadrants. As the tower rises, one quadrant ends a fourth of the way up; another half-way up; and a third three-fourths of the way, making the top floors only one-quadrant in area. Skeletal support is furnished by four columns, one at each corner, and from a central column that begins on the twenty-fifth floor. At that floor, loads from the top quadrant are transmitted diagonally to the corners. This is basic, beautiful geometry.

The exterior is clad in gray anodized aluminum with reflective glass. The tower's arched, north entrance has a wide plazalike approach off a major thoroughfare, but the other three sides are landscaped to conform with the natural slope of the site. The interior has a vaulted lobby of white and gray granite and marble. Lower floors are built around a central atrium that rises twelve stories. The top floor, with its spectacular view, is used primarily for dining and entertaining (fig. 4.41).[11]

Pei's initial concept began with bamboo. Bamboo is a tall hollow plant that grows in stages, and each section of new growth is less thick than the stalk from which it rises. Bamboo is also resilient enough to bend in the wind instead of breaking. That resiliency and the plant's ability to withstand extremes of weather made it a philosophical and political symbol in ancient China and a favorite subject for paintings (see fig. 2.33). For Pei it proved to be an inspiration.

SYDNEY OPERA HOUSE, SYDNEY AUSTRALIA, 1973,
ARCHITECT JØRN UTZON (1918–   )

Pictures of the Sydney Opera House appear in nearly all of Australia's publicity releases, and whether seen from the air, the city, or the harbor, it is extraordinarily beautiful (fig. 4.42 and fig. 4.43). It is a building where roof, walls, front, and back merge into a cluster of spherical shapes. Some call it a second Taj Mahal, but when under construction it became one of the twentieth century's most controversial buildings. In this respect, it was second only to Frank Lloyd Wright's Imperial Hotel in Tokyo, a building that preceded the Opera House by fifty years and was subsequently demolished in 1967.

The story of the Sydney Opera House begins in 1956 when the government of New South Wales decided to build an opera house on Bennelong Point, a narrow promontory. Aesthetically the site was perfect, and it held nothing but old railway yards and obsolete industrial structures. Government officials decided to hold an international competition with entries judged by a panel headed by American architect Eero Saarinen. Jørn Utzon, a Danish architect, won with a design that caught the imagination of everyone who saw it. Australian critic Robin Boyd described it as ". . . a perfect model of clarity in architectural thinking."[12]

FIGURE 4.42 • The Sydney Opera House, Sydney, Australia, Jørn Utzon.
© Balthazar Korab, Ltd.

Utzon proposed, and subsequently built, what he called a "concrete hill," a base to house mechanical equipment and service facilities. This base was the foundation for enormous soaring vaults constructed from thin shells of molded reinforced concrete. The shells were prefabricated, assembled into vaults on site, and then clad with white ceramic tile. Because these vaults are shaped like segments cut from a sphere, they blend into a single harmonious form. Roof and walls are one. The dimensions of Utzon's plan are phenomenal when you consider that this is not one building but several. The Sydney Opera House is actually a center for the arts that includes a Concert Hall, Opera Theater, and Recording Studio plus several small auditoriums, a network of rehearsal rooms, office facilities, and two restaurants.

Construction problems were caused not so much by Utzon's plan as by the lack of technology to make it work. For example, methods of computer

FIGURE 4.43 • The Sydney Opera House, Sydney, Australia, Jørn Utzon. © Balthazar Korab, Ltd.

analyses available to today's engineers and architects had not been developed in the 1960s. As a result, engineering and structural problems brought delays, more delays, and enormous cost overruns. The Opera House became, to use the cliché, a political football. In the interim a change of government occurred, the architect resigned, and the building was completed by a team of Australian architects. It was finally dedicated in 1973 by Queen Elizabeth of England.

Now, of course, much of the controversy is forgotten, and the building is Australia's architectural jewel. Its white ceramic tile surface glistens in the sun and changes with the colors of water and sky. The interior with spacious lobbies and a spectacular view of the bay is as dramatic, in its own way, as the exterior. Natural materials are used extensively. For example, the Concert Hall ceiling is made of wood, a material that is not only beautiful but acoustically suitable (fig. 4.44).

NATIONAL STADIUMS FOR 1964 OLYMPICS, TOKYO, JAPAN,

ARCHITECT KENZO TANGE (1913–)

In designing companion gymnasiums for the Tokyo Olympics, Kenzo Tange (tahn gay) faced the same set of requirements that have challenged builders of amphitheaters and stadiums for centuries. Ticket holders demand good seating and sight lines, speedy and accessible entryways, and convenient parking and transportation. In addition, the structures must provide space for necessary adjunct services and facilities. If a structure is enclosed, then light and temperature requirements are additional considerations.

Builders of ancient Roman amphitheaters met these requirements by using more than one material and structural system (fig. 4.45). The Roman Coli-

FIGURE 4.45 • Colosseum, Rome (aerial view).

FIGURE 4.46 • National Stadiums, Tokyo, Japan, Kenzo Tange.
© Osamu Murai/Time Inc. Magazines.

seum is constructed from a combination of limestone, light weight lava stone, brick, and concrete. Structurally, it is a network of concrete vaults and arches with a layout based on the semi-circular plan of Greek theaters. Successive centuries saw little variation of that plan despite the availability of more versatile materials and techniques.

Kenzo Tange's design is very different both in form, materials, and structural systems (fig. 4.46). Tange spanned space by applying the same system used for suspension bridges. His thin shelled, concrete roofs literally hang from steel cables (fig. 4.47). The roof over the larger gymnasium that seats 15,000 is suspended between two concrete towers. In the smaller gymnasium seating 4000, the cable spirals from a single concrete tower. Both buildings have wide "mouths" supported by arches that shape multiple entryways. Above the arches, rows of clearstory windows furnish natural light, and a long skylight provides still more natural light in the larger building (fig. 4.48).

FIGURE 4.47 • National Stadiums, Tokyo, Japan, Kenzo Tange. Suspension cables, detail.
Courtesy Pan-Asia Newspaper Alliance.

FIGURE 4.48 • National Stadiums, Tokyo, Japan, Kenzo Tange, basketball stadium.
Courtesy Pan-Asia Newspaper Alliance.

Louis Sullivan put the credo for organic architecture into a terse, three word sentence: "Form follows function." Tange, like Utzon, created a building complex that exemplifies Sullivan's belief. Photographs of the Tokyo Stadiums often fail to show the third building that serves as a connector; but they do succeed in revealing the gracefulness that belies this structure's size. Notice, for example, how the smaller building hugs the small slope and how both buildings are shaped like sculptures to lead the eye in a curving sweep, back and forth, from one to the other. Tange whimsically calls his achievement "two huge comma shapes out of alignment."

DOMICILE

By definition "domicile" is a place of residence. By implication it is an all-inclusive social commentary. It might even be considered a compendium of personal needs and desires. Besides meeting a basic need for shelter, domicile answers to a host of individual and often capricious wants. For some people the fantasy of a dream house remains forever a dream, unobtainable and beyond their financial means. For others, the dream house once obtained remains sadly unsatisfying. Few people seem to acquire the actuality of the dream. Most settle for what is affordable and trim their requirements to fit generic domiciles.

The domiciles described and pictured on the following pages are anything but generic. One is extravagant beyond imagination, and another is at the low-cost end of the price scale. Without exception, however, each is an example of domiciles designed to meet their respective owners' needs and desires.

PALACE OF VERSAILLES, FRANCE (BEGUN 1664),

PRIMARY ARCHITECTS LOUIS LE VAU AND JULES HARDOUIN-MANSART

Versailles is nearly a quarter of a mile long, and the people who lived there were seldom comfortable in rooms where the "water could freeze in basins" (fig. 4.49). Diaries kept by members of the Court at Versailles report that the king seldom noticed the cold or the heat and was rarely sick.[13] At the age of seventeen, King Louis XIV started to remodel the Louvre, where French kings had traditionally resided. When that plan failed to satisfy him, he decided to build the world's most magnificent palace at Versailles, seventeen miles from Paris. In the opinion of other European monarchs, who would emulate Louis in their attempts to build palaces almost as grand, he succeeded, yet Louis never stopped building. When he died at age seventy-seven, stacks of plans for renovations and additions waited his approval.

His father, Louis XIII, had built a hunting lodge—actually a twenty-room chateau—at Versailles. Here, on forest and marsh land, Louis XIV decided to build his palace away from Paris. During the years of construction, thirty-seven thousand acres of marsh were drained, and to supply fresh water for the twelve-thousand fountains that were built in the gardens, Louis' engineers diverted a river.

Extravagant? The Duke de Saint-Simon describes Louis' tastes:

> In everything he loved magnificently lavish abundance. He made it a principle from motives of policy and encouraged the court to imitate him; indeed, one way to win favour was to spend extravagantly on the table, clothes, carriages, buildings, and gambling.[14]

FIGURE 4.49 • Palace at Versailles, France, Louis Le Vau and Jules Hardouin-Mansart.
Courtesy of French Government Tourist Office.

There were, however, limits. When France's Minister of Finance Nicolas Fouquet built an enormous chateau with acres of formal gardens, the king was duly impressed. He was also suspicious enough to have Fouquet investigated, arrested, and imprisoned for embezzlement. Afterward, he hired Le Vau, Fouquet's architect.

Of the hundreds of rooms in Versailles, the most famous is the *Galerie des Glaces* (Hall of Mirrors). More than ten feet wide and two hundred and forty feet long, it was originally conceived as an architectural frame for ceiling paintings by Charles Le Brun (fig. 4.50). The paintings were meant to immortalize the French victory over the Dutch in the Wars of the 1670s, but naturally it was Louis who was featured in every panel. Le Brun depicted Louis as Apollo, Greek God of the Sun, an image that appears elsewhere in Versailles as a reminder of Louis' favorite title "Sun King." Often, Louis used the Hall of Mirrors for audiences, and it must have been a magnificent sight. The room held considerably more furniture then. Urns of blooming jasmine and orange trees stood in front of the windows, and Savonnerie carpets covered the floors.

FIGURE 4.50 • Palace at Versailles, France, Louis Le Vau and Jules Hardouin-Mansart, "La Galerie des Glaces." © Caisse Nationale des Monuments Historiques et des Sites/S.P.A.D.E.M./A.R.S., N.Y. 1992.

The king's bedroom with four ante-chambers (fig. 4.51) adjoins the Hall of Mirrors. This may seem an odd choice—so close to a public area—but it helps to remember that today's standards of privacy are very different from customs surrounding the French monarchy:

> The entire court was on hand, formally dressed, from the moment of the king's ceremonial awakening in the morning until he equally ceremoniously retired near midnight. Even when he ate alone, which was the general practice at the Petit Couvert held in the first ante-chamber at night, the court and some outside visitors and tourists lined the walls and peered through open doorways from adjoining rooms. And Louis's family hour which followed the meal was held nearby in one of the cabinets [small, private rooms] behind the bedroom, but again with the doors flung wide so that all could see.[15]

The king's entire family with their attendants and servants, lived at Versailles. Included were the queen, Louis' children, Louis' mistresses and their children by him, his brother and wife, and several cousins. Eventually the family grew to include grandchildren, their spouses and great-grandchildren.[16] Members of the court and their families also lived at Versailles. When it became necessary to construct government buildings adjacent to the palace, the need for additional housing arose, and it was not long before a town of twenty-thousand developed nearby.

FIGURE 4.51 • Palace at Versailles, France, Louis Le Vau and Jules Hardouin-Mansart. The Salon of the Œil de Bœuf (ante-chamber to the king's bedroom). Photo: © R.M.N.

The opulence of Versailles and other European palaces set standards of taste greatly admired by nineteenth and early twentieth century *nouveau riche*. Millionaire industrialists and merchants built extensively and lavishly, although on a relatively small scale if compared with Versailles. With few exceptions, they sought out builders who copied without restraint to please any rich client who might want an ersatz temple, castle, manor house, or palace. To these clients and builders, historic architecture was less a matter of preservation than imitation. New residences—with all the modern amenities—were supposed to look "historic" and, above all else, imposing (fig. 4.52 a and b).

HOUSES OF FRANK LLOYD WRIGHT (1869–1959)

Frank Lloyd Wright built houses of a different sort. Early in his career, Wright apprenticed with Chicago architect Louis Sullivan and became a firm believer in Sullivan's dictate "Form follows function." In 1907, Wright was offered a commission to build a house on a large piece of property in Riverside, Illinois (fig 4.53). As Wright remembered it: "Mrs. Coonley came to me to build her house because she said my 'work wore the countenance of principle'—a great encouragement to me at that time." Wright designed the Coonley house on two levels and without basement or attic. The lower level consists of utility

FIGURE 4.52a • W. K. Vanderbilt residence, Newport, Rhode Island, 1893–95.
© Wayne Andrews/Esto.

FIGURE 4.52b • W. K. Vanderbilt residence. Newport, Rhode Island, Gold Room, 1893–95.
© Wayne Andrews/Esto.

FIGURE 4.53 • Coonley House, Riverside, Illinois, Frank Lloyd Wright, garden view.
The Domino Center for Architecture & Design.

rooms and a large recreation room that opens onto the pool. All other rooms are on the second level: servant's quarters are in one wing, and the living room and master bedroom overlook the pool.

Although less than fifteen years separate the Vanderbilt and Coonley residences, only the latter moved with ease into the future. The wonder of the Coonley house is its openness. Entering the living room—walking into this expanse of space—is a delight. The physical and psychological effects of space never ceased to fascinate Wright. He explained his concept of space with a quote from Lao-Tzu, who founded Taoism in the seventh century B.C.: "Laotze [Lao-tzu] expressed this truth, now achieved in architecture, when he declared the 'reality of the building does not consist in the roof and walls but in the space within to be lived in.' I have built it." In Wright's words, "Space outside becomes a natural part of space within the building . . . walls are now apparent more as humanized screens. They do define and differentiate, but never confine or obliterate space."

Wright called his architecture "organic: based upon part is to part as part is to whole." Nothing was too small or insignificant for his attention. Notice in figure 4.54, how the wood panels direct attention to the ceiling with a design that culminates in friezelike bands. You will find a similar design in the balcony railing, in the window borders of stained glass, and in several exterior wall sections faced with ceramic tile. These designs constitute a **motif**: an architectural shape or pattern that is repeated. A motif is a unifying device found in music and drama as well as in the visual arts and in architecture.

FIGURE 4.54 • Coonley House, Riverside, Illinois, Frank Lloyd Wright. The Domino Center for Architecture & Design.

Wright's concept of organic architecture applies as much to the site as to the building. The Coonley House was one of the first of the Prairie Houses Wright would build in the Midwest and Plains states during the next forty years. Although no two houses are alike, they share a low horizontal roof line that harmonizes with the flat terrain. Wright truly believed in marrying a house to its site.

Taliesin, Wright's own home in Spring Green, Wisconsin, is built onto the side of a hill (figs. 4.55 and 4.56). According to Wright: "No house should ever be on any hill or on anything. It should be of the hill, belonging to it, so hill and house should live together each the happier for the other." Taliesin, a Welsh word meaning "shining brow," is an appropriate name. The house overlooks the rolling Wisconsin countryside, and its cedar-shingled roof and rough-textured stone walls, chimneys, and terraces blend into this background. Its balconies offer spectacular views and are protected by wide roof overhangs. Wright's bedroom opens onto a wide stone terrace where he liked to have breakfast on warm days. Built in 1911, the house was twice destroyed by fire and then rebuilt. Lightning caused one fire, and a deranged servant set the other fire after murdering the architect's companion and her young children. Wright was away at the time.

The architect's career, like his personal life, was subject to dynamic highs and lows. The 1930s were a definite low period, ultimately rescued by a commission to build a house that has become his most famous building (fig. 4.57). "Falling Water" is the house Wright designed for the Kaufman family in the

FIGURE 4.55 • Taliesin, Spring Green, Wisconsin, Frank Lloyd Wright.
© Wayne Andrews/Esto.

FIGURE 4.56 • Taliesin, Spring Green, Wisconsin, Frank Lloyd Wright.
© Wayne Andrews/Esto.

foothills of the Pennsylvania mountains. The site has a clear swift stream and spectacular waterfall and is dense with native rhododendrons. Most architects would have built next to the waterfall, but Wright designed the house to cantilever *over* the waterfall. An architectural and engineering marvel, it is a highly creative and adventuresome design.

Wright worked up to the time of his death at the age of ninety, designing religious buildings, hotels, public buildings, theaters, and a museum; but he never ceased designing houses. He was particularly interested in what he called Usonian Houses: affordable residences built with an integrity of materials and craft and with the same aesthetic consideration given to more expensive houses. Long before the advent of the "development house" in the 1950s, Wright warned about conformity:

> Unfortunately conformity reaches far and wide into American life: to distort our democracy? This drift toward quantity instead of quality is largely distortion. Conformity is always too convenient? Quality means *individuality*, is therefore difficult. But unless we go deeper now, quantity at expense to quality will be our national tragedy—the rise of mediocrity into high places.

FIGURE 4.57 • "Falling Water,"
Kaufman house, Bear Run, Pennsylvania,
Frank Lloyd Wright.
Western Pennsylvania Conservancy/Art Resource.

Usonian houses were Wright's solution to mediocrity, and their price tag in 1939 was $5,000. The Rosenbaum House, on a flat site in Florence, Alabama, resembles the Prairie Houses (figs. 4.58 and 4.59). The roof is in sections, raised in part to allow for clearstory windows. The roof section on the left is the carport, a Wright cost-saving feature. Walls facing the street have clearstory windows for light and privacy.

The Usonian floor plan (fig. 4.60) illustrates how this house follows an L-Shape to allow for maximum privacy while taking advantage of its landscaped view. The house is about 1500 square feet and has three bedrooms, two baths, and a study. Wright labeled the kitchen "work space" and placed it in the center—the heart—of the house. Because "work spaces" did not have outside windows, Wright gave them skylights. He also included fireplaces, acting on his own sentiment that the hearth is a symbol for family.

FIGURE **4.58** • A Usonian House, Rosenbaum House, Florence, Alabama, Frank Lloyd Wright.
© Balthazar Korab, Ltd.

FIGURE **4.59** • A Usonian House, Rosenbaum House, Florence, Alabama, Frank Lloyd Wright.
© Balthazar Korab, Ltd.

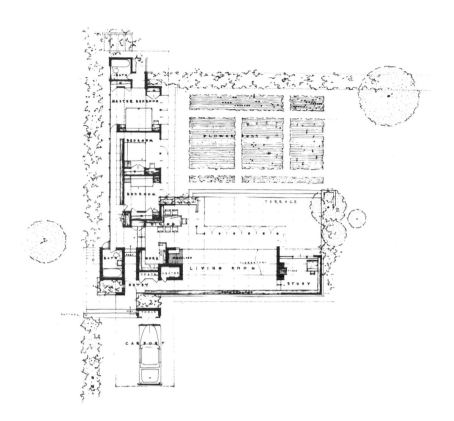

FIGURE 4.60 • A Usonian House, Rosenbaum House, Florence, Alabama, Frank Lloyd Wright, floor plan.
Copyright© The Frank Lloyd Wright Foundation.

HOUSES OF RICHARD MEIER (1934–   )

Architecture designed by Richard Meier includes museums, civic centers, and other large projects, but houses also comprise a significant portion of his work. The influence of Mies van der Rohe's "skin and bones" architecture is obvious in Meier's work. Like van der Rohe, Meier was influenced by the Dutch De Stijl movement and the paintings of Piet Mondrian. Although Meier is an architect by profession, he is also a painter. This may explain his acute sensitivity to the coloristic possibilities of white. According to Meier:

> White is in fact the color which intensifies the perception of all of the other hues that exist in natural light and in nature. It is against a white surface that one best appreciates the play of light and shadow, solids and voids . . . Goethe said, 'Color is the pain of light.'
>
> Whiteness is one of the characteristic qualities of my work; I use it to clarify architectural concepts and heighten the power of visual form."[17]

Meier was also influenced by Frank Lloyd Wright, particularly by Wright's use of multi-levels in Falling Water. It is important to note that influences are important—creativity does not take place in a vacuum—but Meier's work, like every work of art, is original both in concept and execution. An obvious feature of Meier's architecture is the dominance of a building over its site. Unlike Wright's houses, Meier's do not hug the ground. Describing the Smith House (figs. 4.61 and 4.62), Meier said:

> The white form of the Smith House is not only rooted in a New England tradition of the house as a compact, self-sufficient entity, but also expressive of a strong and extroverted attitude toward its site: beyond its internal function as a shelter, it is an object that acts as a prism to the natural scene around it.

FIGURE 4.61 • Smith House, Darien, Connecticut, Richard Meier.

The Smith House is located on one and one-half acres in Connecticut and is built on a rise overlooking Long Island Sound. It is wood with a brick chimney and steel support columns, all painted white. The interior is laid out according to Meier's plan for appropriate and functional zones and circulation systems. Circulation systems are patterns of movement from one zone or room to another. Whereas stairs provide vertical circulation, a floor plan provides horizontal circulation. This is how the architect divides zones into public and

FIGURE 4.62 • Smith House, Darien, Connecticut, Richard Meier.

private space. In the Smith House, the private zones of bedrooms and baths are on all three levels but facing the landscaped entryway. Public zones where the family meet and entertain face the water.

Meier's zones and circulation system are a means of providing maximum efficiency and privacy inside a building, but they can also delineate a building's exterior form. Meier's house in Old Westbury, New York (figs. 4.63 and 4.64) is much larger than the Smith House. The Westbury house is built on a small knoll that slopes down to a pond surrounded by landscaped grounds and distant woods. Designed for a family with six children, its private zone has eleven bedrooms and baths and its public zone has several living and dining areas on two different levels. For this reason, Meier made the circulation system "a major organizing element in the design." This system includes a ramp that zig-zags behind an expanse of curved glass, an exterior stairway, an enclosed stairway (not pictured) and what Meier calls a helical stair.

FIGURE 4.63 • House in Old Westbury, Westbury, New York, Richard Meier. Ezra Stoller/© Esto. All rights reserved.

Although most interior walls are white, certain wall sections are painted bright colors. During the day, these colors reflecting on the white walls change with the direction and intensity of light. Meier oriented bedrooms to receive morning light and brightened interior rooms with a central skylight. Meier calls this " . . . the infiltration of light from many different directions." He uses multi-directional and multi-colored light as a motif.[18]

FIGURE 4.64 • House in Old Westbury, Westbury, New York, Richard Meier.

ARCHITECTURAL LANGUAGE

The concepts embodied in architecture are based firmly on the reality of building beautiful, functional, and durable structures. What determines beauty, function, and durability are elements of shape, color, texture, space and their organization into structural systems.

BEAUTY AND FUNCTION

Is the Taj Mahal beautiful? Look at its separate shapes—its domes, arches, rectangles—and ask if they form a balanced, harmonious whole. Look at the building's silhouette against the sky and ask if it embellishes rather than detracts from the environment. Ask if this building entices the senses, uplifts the emotions.

If you were able to visit the Taj Mahal, you would see colors and textures more clearly. You would see the marble's white-on-white veining and the intricacy of floral patterns and calligraphy. You would realize that its arches define deep and shaded porticos. Stepping away from the building and looking upward, you would be able to experience, in some very personal way, the enormous dome with its golden crown.

Is the Taj Mahal functional? Having read its history and seen its photographs, will you remember this building created in memory of a wife?

STRUCTURAL SYSTEMS

Every structure, beautiful and impressive as it may be, is subject to forces of gravity and weather. *Compression* is the constant force of weight that can crush a building. *Tension* is the stress that pulls and stretches against it. For a building to be strong and durable, these ongoing forces are problems that structural systems must overcome. Simultaneously, these same structural systems determine a building's beauty and function.

Post and Lintel

The Parthenon is the most famous example of this system in which a lintel (cross beam) is positioned on posts so that together they bear the weight of the roof. Post and lintel is adaptable to either wood or stone, but its major drawback is the close placement of posts. For Athenian builders, this did not present a problem because temples were essentially shrines.

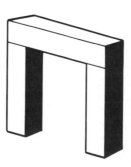

Taj Mahal.
© Lucas/The Image Works, Inc.

The Parthenon.
Ewing Galloway.

Arch

For early builders, the arch solved the problem of spanning large areas of space without the need for additional support posts. Ancient arches were built of wedge-shaped stones and were constructed from bottom to top with scaffolding used for temporary support. The last wedge-shaped stone positioned at the arch's center is called a "key-stone."

The arch has excellent load-bearing capabilities because weight and stress are distributed to the sides. Ancient builders used mostly stone and brick, but the arch is adaptable to reinforced concrete and other modern materials. Portals of the Cathedral Notre-Dame, Paris, are examples of stone arches, and the National Olympic Stadium in Tokyo includes a system of arches at its base.

Notre-Dame, Paris.
Photograph: Bulloz.

Barrel Vault

The barrel vault is a series of continuous arches. The Hall of Mirrors at Versailles is an excellent example of barrel vault construction, but it also reveals one of the system's drawbacks, namely the lack of light. Another drawback is the stress of tension along the sides. Large barrel vaults usually require buttressing.

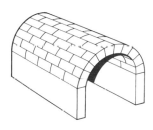

Hall of Mirrors, Versailles.
© C.N.H.M.S./S.P.A.D.E.M./A.R.S., N.Y. 1992.

Groin Vault

This system is also called a Cross Vault because it crosses or intersects two barrel vaults. Although the system is stronger than the barrel vault, it does require buttressing because sides are subject to forces of tension. Advantages include a more flexible floor plan and more light. The Gare d'Orsay, now Musée d'Orsay, is a groin vault with some archways glassed and others leading directly into lobby areas and the hotel that originally abutted the building. Now, of course, the archways lead to different galleries inside the museum.

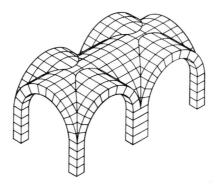

Musée d'Orsay, Paris.
Vanni/Art Resource.

Ribbed Vault

This is a variation of the groin vault in which ribs carry weight downward. The interior of Notre-Dame, Paris demonstrates how this more efficient system—with the help of flying buttresses—permits the use of large areas of glass.

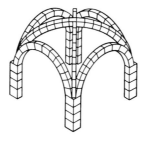

Notre-Dame, Paris.
Scala/Art Resource, NY.

Dome

Domes are various shapes and sizes and are supported in several different ways. The dome of the Pantheon rests on a circular, load-bearing stone base; the outer dome of the Taj Mahal rests on a circular drum above the base structure. The dome of Hagia Sophia rests on brick **pendentives.** Pendentives, usually of stone or brick, are triangular, concave sections that fill in the space left between a dome and the arches on which it rests. **Squinches**, also of stone or brick, are similar triangular, concave sections used when a dome rests directly on a square or polygonal base.

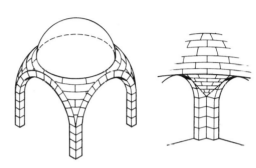

Hagia Sophia, Istanbul.
Hirmer Fotoarchiv.

Steel Frame Construction

This is exactly what the name implies: a frame or cage of steel. Although the steel frame of the Carson Pirie Scott Building is hidden behind masonry walls, the steel frame of the Seagram Building is clearly visible.

Carson Pirie Scott and Co., Chicago.
Courtesy of the Chicago Historical Society (IcHI-15065).

Cantilever

When a structure of wood, stone, metal, or reinforced concrete extends beyond its vertical support, it employs a principle of balance called cantilever. Frank Lloyd Wright considered cantilever a natural principle that can be seen in the way a tree's limbs cantilever from its trunk. Wright's Falling Water is cantilevered over the waterfall.

"Falling Water," Pennsylvania.
Photo by Bill Hedrich, Hedrich Blessing HB-4414 D3,
Courtesy Chicago Historical Society.

Truss

The truss is a wood or metal frame made from a series of triangles. Truss frames are frequently employed in bridge engineering for cantilever. In architecture they have been commonly used as roof supports and, more recently, for entire buildings. Thorncrown is a good example.

Thorncrown, Arkansas.
© Wayne Sorce.

Freeform

Reinforcing concrete with steel mesh or rods gives this molded material enormous strength and versatility and makes possible freeform buildings of every conceivable size and shape. The Opera House, Sydney, Australia, is one example.

Sydney Opera House, Australia.
© Balthazar Korab, Ltd.

Suspension

Ancient Romans used arches and vaults to span large spaces, but today's architects are likely to use the suspension system pioneered in the nineteenth century by John Augustus Roebling. Roebling was the engineer who built the Brooklyn Bridge by suspending its deck from steel cables attached to two support piers. After the development of newer lighter weight materials, this system was adapted for architecture. The National Olympic Stadiums in Tokyo are combined freeform structures with suspended roofs.

National Stadiums, Tokyo.
© Osamu Murai/Time Inc. Magazines

NOTES

[1]Quoted in Jan. C. Scruggs and Joel L. Swerdlow, *To Heal A Nation*, (N.Y.: Harper & Row, Pub., 1985), p. 52.

[2]Scruggs and Swerdlow, p. 77.

[3]Quoted in Hugh Honour and John Fleming, *The Visual Arts: A History*. 2nd ed. (Englewood Cliffs, N.J., Prentice-Hall, Inc., 1982), p. 44

[4]Quoted from W. E. Beglay, "Amanat Khan and the Calligraphy of the Taj Mahal." *Kunst des Orients*, vol. 12. in Janice Leoshko, "Mausoleum for an Empress," *Romance of the Taj Mahal*. (Los Angeles: Los Angeles County Museum of Art and Thames and Hudson, 1989), p. 58.

[5]See Allan Temko, *Notre-Dame of Paris*. (N.Y.: The Viking Press, 1955), pp. 13–19.

[6]This opinion, although not shared by all architectural historians, is put forth in Sir Banister Fletcher, *A History of Architecture on the Comparative Method*, 9th ed. (London: Butterworths, 1987).

[7]Heyden, pp. 22–24.

[8]This statement was quoted by Jim Reed's wife Dell in: Andrea Oppenheimer Dean, "The cathedral builder born 500 years too late," *Smithsonian*, August 1991, pp. 102–108. See also: Roger G. Kennedy, American Churches, (N.Y.: Crossroad, 1982) pp. 130–132.

[9]Dean, p. 103.

[10]Witold Rybcznski, "It Seems That God Isn't in the Details, After All," *The New York Times*, Sunday, Dec. 16, 1990, p. H44.

[11]Peter Blake, "Scaling New Heights," *Architectural Record*, Jan. 1991., pp.76–83.

[12]Forrest Wilson, "The Sydney Opera House: A Survivor," *Architecture*, Sept., 1989, p. 109.

[13]Described in Guy Walton, *Louis XIV's Versailles*, (Chicago: The University of Chicago Press, 1986).

[14]Walton, p. 43.

[15]Walton, p. 39.

[16]Walton, p. 38.

[17]*Richard Meier Architect*, (N.Y. Rizzoli, 1984), p. 9.

[18]See *Richard Meier Architect*, pp. 55–63.

CHAPTER FIVE

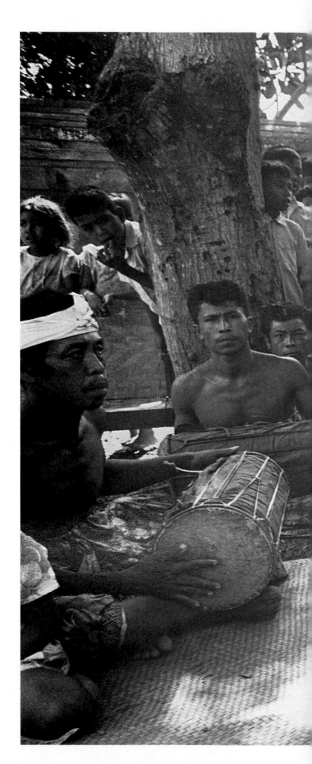

MUSIC

The Navaho believe that music maintains the essential harmony between nature and human beings. According to Navaho mythology, all music originated with the Holy People who created Earth Surface People, the Navaho ancestors. Navaho chantways, consisting of hundreds of individual songs, keep alive the stories and teachings of the Holy People who were earth's first inhabitants. Although the Holy People left the earth long ago, they still travel from place to place on sunbeams, rainbows, and lightening. When a Navaho shaman creates a sand painting during a curing ceremony, he is making images of the same deities his songs address. This is how he hopes to invoke greater supernatural powers, and this is why the sand painting must be destroyed by sunset—scattered to the winds so that it cannot be seen by evil or mischievous spirits.

An ancient Hindu belief holds that all music originates from a single cosmic vibration throughout the universe, a vibration also existing in human beings. To sing or play a musical instrument is to serve the gods, for according to the *Natyasastra*, an ancient treatise on performing arts, the god Shiva so enjoyed music he exclaimed, "I like better the music of instruments and voices than I like a thousand [ritual] baths and prayers."[1] A 900-year-old sculpture of Shiva depicts him in his dual role of God of Destruction and God of Music and Dance (fig. 5.1). The metal Shiva dances inside a ring of flames that symbolizes the cycle of energy generated by the perpetual process of life and death—destruction and renewal. In one hand Shiva holds a small drum, in another a tongue of flame. He holds his third hand in a gesture of peace and points his fourth hand down, toward the demon of ignorance he crushes underfoot.

Two thousand years before the Indian artist created this sculpture of Shiva, Egyptians proclaimed their god Hesu as the creator of music. Recognizing the importance of music, the Egyptians associated it with other deities, too. Hathor, Goddess of Love and Joy, was also known as Goddess of Music; and Thoth, God of Wisdom and Magic, was believed to have written forty-two books on astronomy, acoustics, and music and to have invented the lyre.

Like Egyptians, ancient Greeks attributed the creation of music and musical instruments to their gods. Apollo, God of Light, Healing, Poetry, and Prophesy, was also the God of Music. The Greeks linked other gods and goddesses to specific musical instruments: Athena with the trumpet and aulos; Minerva with the flute; Pan with the syrinx; and Hermes with the lyre. According to Greek mythology, Hermes made the first lyre from a turtle's shell strung with gut strings. He presented his invention to his brother Apollo who, on receiving the lyre, played it so melodically all the gods and goddesses stopped whatever they were doing to listen.

FIGURE 5.1 • *Shiva Nataraja, Lord of the Dance.* Sculpture, South Indian, Chola Period, eleventh century. Copper: 43 7/8 x 40″.

Cleveland Museum of Art, Purchase from the J. H. Wade Fund, 30. 331.

One mortal is also associated with the lyre. Orpheus, son of the Muse Calliope and a Greek prince, sang and played the lyre with such skill and feeling his music could tame wild animals, soften the hardest stone, and turn oak trees toward the melodious sounds. When Orpheus sailed with Jason and the Argonauts, his music helped the ship's rowers overcome fatigue and saved Jason and his men from the Sirens. Sirens were invisible enchantresses of the sea who sang with irresistible sweetness. The magic of their voices could make sailors change course and turn their ships onto rocks, sinking them. As soon as the Argonauts heard the Sirens' song, Jason played his lyre, overpowering the bewitching voices and keeping the ship on course.

Among ancient peoples, the Chinese were unique in *not* attributing music's creation to gods. Central to Chinese Taoist philosophy is the belief that harmony must exist between human beings and nature. Taoists believe that weather, seasons, and the physical marks of time are natural forces beyond human control, but music is not. Accordingly, in the year 2697 B.C., during the latter part of the Hsia Dynasty, Emperor Huang Ti ordered a member of his court named Ling Lun to develop the ideal pitch pipes. Fulfilling this royal order—with his life depending on its success—meant that Ling Lun first had to find the right kind of bamboo. His search took him to the distant valley of Yüan Yü Mountain, where he selected the proper bamboo and cut it into the exact lengths that would emit sounds in harmony with the natural and celestial world. The twelve *lü's*, as they were called, corresponded to the principle of opposites *yin* and *yang*: six *lü's* were considered masculine and six feminine.

PERSPECTIVES ON MUSIC: EAST AND WEST

It is impossible to separate music from the fibers of culture and society. Music is what people make of it: attitudes and practices are inextricably bound together. When people of ancient civilizations attributed the origins of music to gods and spirits, it was their way of dignifying the art, their attempt to isolate it from the ordinary and mundane but not from the mainstream of life. The Chinese, while not involving their gods directly with music, nevertheless made music essential to that fragile harmony that exists between human beings and their world. What greater compliment could they have paid it?

There is a wonderful proverb, belonging to the Dan of the Ivory Coast, that says, "The village where there is no musician is not a place where a man can stay."[2] Implied in this sentence is the overpowering need for music's recognition and appreciation.

The philosopher and teacher, Confucius (551–478 B.C.), whose guidelines for etiquette and art affected every aspect of Chinese culture and government, recognized two types of music: true and vulgar. True music, according to Confucius, is performed and appreciated by the "noble-minded man," and it is "mild and delicate, keeps a uniform mood, enlivens and moves. Such a man does not harbor pain or mourn in his heart . . ." In contrast, a "vulgar-minded man" enjoys music that "is loud and fast, and again fading and dim, a picture of violent death-agony. His heart is not harmonically balanced; mildness and graceful movements are foreign to him."[3]

Had the Greek philosopher Plato (427–347 B.C.) known Confucius, he probably would have agreed with the Chinese sage because Plato had very definite ideas about the role of music in the education of Greek men. In the third book of the *Republic*, Plato describes a conversation between Socrates and Glaucon concerning music and athletics. Socrates begins:

> Neither are the two arts of music and gymnastic really designed, as is often supposed, the one for the training of the soul, the other for the training of the body.
>
> What then is the real object of them?
>
> I believe, I said, that the teachers of both have in view chiefly the improvement of the soul.
>
> How can that be? he asked.
>
> Did you never observe, I said, the effect on the mind itself of exclusive devotion to gymnastic, or the opposite effect of an exclusive devotion to music?
>
> In what way shown? he said
>
> The one producing a temper of hardness and ferocity, the other of softness and effeminacy, I replied . . .
>
> And, when a man allows music to play upon him and to pour into his soul through the funnel of his ears those sweet and soft and melancholy airs of which we were just now speaking, and his whole life is passed in warbling and the delights of song; in the first stage of the process the passion or spirit which is in him is tempered like iron, and made useful, instead of brittle and useless. But, if he carries on the softening and soothing process, in the next stage he begins to melt and waste, until he has wasted away his spirit and cut out the sinews of his soul; and he becomes a feeble warrior . . .
>
> And so in gymnastics, if a man takes violent exercise and is a great feeder, and the reverse of a great student of music and philosophy, at first the high condition of his body fills him with pride and spirit, and he becomes twice the man that he was.
>
> Certainly.
>
> And what happens? if he do nothing else, and holds no converse with the Muses, does not even that intelligence which there may be in him, having no taste of any sort of learning or enquiry or thought or culture, grow feeble and dull and blind, his mind never waking up or receiving nourishment, and his senses not being purged of their mists?
>
> True, he said.
>
> And he ends by becoming a hater of philosophy, uncivilized, never using the weapon of persuasion,—he is like a wild beast, all violence and fierceness, and knows no other way of dealing; and he lives in all ignorance and evil conditions, and has no sense of propriety and grace.

Plato's belief that a proper education meant a balanced education was carried a step further by his pupil, the philosopher Aristotle (384–322 B.C.), who wrote in *Politics* 8:6:

> And now we have to determine the question that has been already raised, whether children should be themselves taught to sing and play or not. Clearly there is a considerable difference made in the character by the actual practice of the art. It is difficult, if not impossible, for those who do not perform to be good judges of the performance of others.

It was not the intent of Confucius, Plato, or Aristotle to train young men to become muscians. To the contrary, it was not training they were advocating but a liberal education. Plato makes this clear by delineating two separate stages in a man's education, and Aristotle clarifies his position when he writes: "Let the young pursue their studies until they are able to feel delight in noble melodies and rhythms, and not merely in that common part of music in which every slave or child and even some animals find pleasure." Aristotle is clearly making a distinction between the "common" melodies and rhythms—the simple tunes and beats—that elicit an easy and almost immediate physical response and the "noble" melodies and rhythms that are more complex musical ideas requiring thought as well as absorption.

Appreciation and enjoyment are not the same. Enjoyment is easy; almost everyone enjoys music. Appreciation, however, requires both concentration and comprehension. Twentieth century American composer Aaron Copland wrote an excellent book titled *What to Listen for in Music*. He begins by saying that listening involves three separate planes: the sensuous plane in which people listen for the sheer pleasure of musical sound; the expressive plane in which people respond to the emotional content of music; and the sheerly musical plane, in which people are able to hear—audibly picture—the music's architecture. Only by reaching the third level can people appreciate the ideas and skills—the artistry—that creates music.

That artistry is a human achievement! It is not the god Apollo playing his lyre as if by magic or Orpheus playing better music than the Sirens; neither is it the technology of the electronics industry—although this can help. Appreciation comes with the ability to perceive the human spirit—the composers and performers *behind* the sounds of their instruments.

PERFORMERS AND THEIR MUSICAL INSTRUMENTS

Information about ancient music largely comes from two sources: the written observations made by historians and travelers and the images of musicians and instruments pictured in the visual arts. Neither source discloses what instrument may have developed first or where. Whether the first musical sounds other than voice were the vibrations made by slitting a blade of grass and blowing on it or the beats made by hitting two sticks together is a moot point. The bagpipe, for example, is so old its origin has never been established. The harp came from Syria but found its way to Egypt and eventually to northern Europe, where it became Ireland's national symbol. The lute, a favorite European instrument after the Crusades, originated in Persia (Iran), but its name comes from the Arabic word *Al'ud*, meaning wood.

So often, people fail to realize how much communication actually took place in ancient times. Concerning the trading and exchanging of musical instruments, historian Curt Sachs says:

> Egyptians borrowed from Mesopotamia and Syria; the Jews from the Phoenicians; the Greeks from Crete and Asia Minor and again Phoenicia. The harp, the lyre, the double oboe, the hand-beaten frame drum were played in Egypt, Palestine, Phoenicia, Syria, Babylonia, Asia Minor, Greece and Italy. The Egyptians called lyres and drums by their Semitic names, and the harp by a term related to the Sumerian word for bow; the Greeks used the Sumerian noun to designate the long-necked lute and adopted a Phoenician word for the harp . . . indeed, they had not a single Hellenic term for their instruments . . .[4]

This traffic in musical instruments required a comparable dissemination of musical knowledge that could only have occurred when musicians, themselves, moved about. During wars, armies routinely took musicians as permanent hostages. The Greek army of Alexander the Great captured more than three hundred women musicians from the court of the Persian King Darius; and several centuries later, conquering Romans took Greek musicians as prized slaves. In times of peace, skilled and adventuresome musicians journeyed from one nation to another, sometimes voluntarily and other times at the request of their rulers. During China's T'an (618–906) dynasty, the Imperial Court invited musicians from India and the region that is now Afghanistan to take up residence at court.

Most musicians received their training and support at royal courts. Records show that during China's Chou dynasty (1027–256 B.C.), more than fifteen hundred musicians were in royal service. In Egypt, one measure of the honor accorded musicians was the closeness of their tombs to the tombs of royalty. In India, every palace had a ballroom for performances of music, dance, and song, and musical skills were cultivated among both men and women. India's caste system, however, determined the choice of instruments: for example, only high-caste Brahmins were permitted to play the *vina*, a string instrument rather like a zither with a gourd at each end.

Vina player.
© D. Chawda/Photo Researchers, Inc.

During the European Renaissance that began in the fifteenth century, royal and aristocratic patrons supported musicians and artists alike. The Medici family, who ruled the city-state of Florence and sponsored artists, including the young Michelangelo, were also patrons of musicians. Henry VIII and his successor, Elizabeth I of England, were not only patrons but accomplished musicians themselves. This was also true of the French King Louis XIV, who was an avid dancer and so enthusiastic about music and drama he was determined to make his court the showplace of Europe. He succeeded—with the help of an eighteenth century superstar, Jean-Baptiste Lully.

Lully performed, composed, and directed musical-theatrical events held at the French court. He arrived in France from his native Italy when he was fourteen. The details are vague, but it seems he was already a talented singer and violinist when discovered by the Chevalier de Guise, who brought him from Florence to Paris, where he first became a page and then a member of the court's string orchestra. In addition to his skills at singing and playing violin, Lully played guitar and harpsichord and danced. Lully wrote, choreographed, and produced ballets—often in collaboration with the playwright Molière. He also wrote and directed operas and directed the court's military bands and two small orchestras. One orchestra was the *Douze Grands Hautbois* (Dozen Grand Oboes), consisting of ten oboes and two bassoons. The other was the *Vingt-quatre Violons du Roi* (Twenty-Four Violinists of the King), a small string orchestra, consisting of violins, violas, and cellos. The string orchestra had been started originally by Louis XIII, but with Louis XIV's generous financial support and Lully's improvements its fame spread across Europe.

The English King, Charles II, in an attempt to rival the French king, organized a string orchestra of his own, and he permitted, even encouraged, his "Band of 24 Violins" to perform outside the court at afternoon concerts. In 1672, an advertisement in the London Gazette listed the time and place of concerts as "4 of the clock in the afternoon . . . at Mr. John Banister's house (now called the music school) over against the George Tavern, in White Friars." Banister, the producer of this enterprise and a member of the orchestra, charged a shilling per person, a price that included free ale and tobacco.[5] Public concerts became more firmly established in 1699 when the Playford music publishers sponsored afternoon concerts three times a week in a London coffee house. These "coffee house concerts," as they were called, reestablished the custom of public performances that had disappeared with Greek and Roman civilizations.

In both Greece and Rome, music was considered a worthy profession, and public festivals and competitions of drama and music were held regularly. Music was always performed in conjunction with theatrical events; it was, for example, an essential part of Greek drama, and theaters were open to all Greek citizens with the price of a ticket. The Roman government paid for many theatrical events that were offered free to citizens and noncitizens alike; only slaves were excluded.

During the centuries of social upheaval following Rome's decline, the Church that initially banned music as a pagan influence eventually adopted it and proceeded to regulate both its writing and performing. By the year 300, vocal music had become part of the Catholic liturgy, although instrumental music was forbidden. By the Middle Ages, vocal music called **plainsong** or Gregorian Chant had become the dominant form of religious music. Seldom is plainsong performed today, and recordings are, at best, a poor substitute since these vocal chants performed by choirs of men and boys were but one part of a much larger religious experience. Plainsong's single melodic line, minus the harmony today's listeners expect to hear, may sound thin on a recording; but try to imagine listening to this music inside one of the great Gothic cathedrals (see fig. 4.23). Imagine, if you can, the sounds of many voices soaring upward, toward the high stone vaults that amplify sound. Imagine listening to this music in the presence of sculpture and stained glass as beautiful and devout in their imagery as the music.

During the Middle Ages, **minstrels** kept secular music alive. "Minstrel" is a generic term for musicians who were mostly itinerant, although a few were lucky enough to become part of a castle's retinue. Minstrels came from all social classes and their skills ranged from excellent to merely amusing. French minstrels were noblemen called troubadours who composed and performed songs of love and chivalry. Early German minstrels were poet-singers called minnesingers (love singers). Eventually, guilds of meistersingers (mastersingers) composed of middle-class citizens took over the profession. *Jongleurs* (jugglers) and plain minstrels came from the lower classes of society, and although they performed music, they seldom composed it. One minstrel promoted himself with this description:

I can play the lute, the violin, the pipe, the bagpipe, the syrinx, the harp, the gigue, the gittern, the symphony, the psaltery, the organistrum, the regals, the tabor, and the rote. I can sing a song well and make tales to please young ladies and can play the gallant for them if necessary. I can throw knives into the air and catch them without cutting my fingers. I can do dodges with string, most extraordinary and amusing. I can balance chairs and make tables dance. I can throw a somersault and walk on my head.[6]

The European minstrel's counterpart—minus acrobatics—is found today in the African **griot.** Depending on national and tribal customs, a griot may be either a man or a woman. Some are in the paid service of a ruler and others are wanderers and street musicians. In western Sudan, griots are members of a hereditary caste whose duty is to preserve and recite past events and traditions; they are, in effect, musical historians. Griots are also noted for composing and performing praise songs, although their standard repertoire consists of set pieces for weddings, christenings, funerals, and other occasions. Certain griots are highly respected but others, usually those who perform as street musicians, are ranked very low socially. Attitudes toward griots reveal an element of fear, for in the minds of many people these musicians know too many secrets. Perhaps this is why, in the past, they were not buried in the same way as other citizens. In Senegal, for example, the bodies of griots were not buried at all but placed inside hollow baobab trees. Like the shamans of Siberia and North America, they carried the distinction of being different or special even in death.

VOICE

The most natural and flexible musical instrument is the human voice. In Ghana, Senegal, and other African nations too numerous to list, professional singers, including griots, must have voices agile enough to perform **vibratos** (slight waverings or vibrations) as well as growls, shouts, hums, and whispers. Singing through clenched teeth, singing through the nose, vibrating the tongue in the mouth—these are only a few of the vocal feats required. Vocal methods and techniques are an outgrowth of whatever subject or theme a song is meant to communicate, and a performer's method changes from song to song. Music as a whole is considered entertainment, but it is an entertainment measured as much by social relevance as by the performers' skills.

On the North American continent, traditions and customs among individual tribes established diverse vocal styles. For example, Ojibwa singing requires an open-throated tone, a high range, and a voice agile enough to perform vibratos, **glissandos** (moving up or down rapidly), growls, and shouts. In contrast, some Navaho chants require a tight and somewhat thin nasal tone and a voice capable of singing **falsetto,** which is the topmost range for the male voice.

Choral and operatic singers are grouped by the range and **timbre** (TAM ber) of their voices, soprano being highest and bass the lowest in range. A **soprano** voice has a range from approximately middle C to high C. From highest to lowest range, soprano voices are designated as *soprano, mezzo-soprano,* and *alto-soprano.* Individual soprano voices are also classified by timbre. A dramatic soprano's voice is commanding and expressively rich; a lyric soprano's is somewhat lighter and sweeter; a coloratura's is extremely agile with a high range. American soprano Jessye Norman, for example, has a voice with a range from E above high C to E below middle C.

Male voices are grouped as **tenor,** the highest; **baritone,** the middle range; and **bass,** the lowest. Tenor and bass voices are also classified by their timbre. A lyric tenor is light and impressive but a *heldentenor* (heroic tenor) is more powerful and lusty in tone. A *basso buffo* (comic bass) is extremely agile and suited for comic roles in opera; a *basso cantante* (singing bass) has a lighter quality; and a *basso profondo* (deep bass) is a powerful and expressive voice in the lowest range.

American soprano, Jessye Norman.
Foto © Both Borgman, 1992

WOODWIND INSTRUMENTS

Woodwind instruments produce sound when air vibrates either through a mouth hole or a reed. The shorter the air column, the more vibrations per second and the higher the pitch. Most woodwinds are made of wood, but exceptions are the flute, its near relative the piccolo, and the saxophone.

Flute

The flute is the coloratura soprano of the woodwinds with a high range and brilliant, silvery tone. The piccolo is shorter, an octave higher, and has a shrill, piercing sound. It is the fife in a fife and drum corps. The recorder is an end-blown flute made of wood with a whistle mouthpiece; it is easier to play than either flute or piccolo.

Flutes are usually made of silver or gold, but they have been made from bone, bamboo, clay, and commonly from wood. Today in Scandinavia and Rumania, the descendant of an ancient willow flute is made by peeling off a

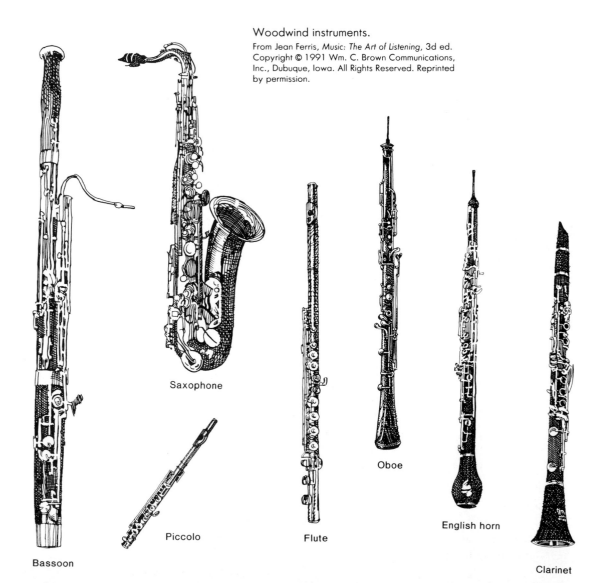

Woodwind instruments.

From Jean Ferris, *Music: The Art of Listening*, 3d ed. Copyright © 1991 Wm. C. Brown Communications, Inc., Dubuque, Iowa. All Rights Reserved. Reprinted by permission.

Saxophone

Oboe

Piccolo

Flute

English horn

Bassoon

Clarinet

Figure 5.2 • Doc Tate Nevaquaya, Comanche flute player.
New York Times Pictures.

long strip of bark while the tree is still green. When a mouthpiece is added, the instrument can be played, but only for the brief time it takes for the bark to dry out.[7] In Africa, the Masai once made a flute called a *ndule* from tree fiber. The film *Out of Africa* includes one song played by a musician of the Samburo tribe on a ndule he made by putting two holes in an aluminum tube. In Central and South America, string instruments seem not to have existed, but flutes of all kinds were popular. Some whistle flutes were made of clay in the shape of snakes, birds, and fish. Other flutes were plain in shape and similar to the wooden flutes found among Native American tribes in the North.

Doc Tate Nevaquaya, a Comanche musician, currently performs traditional flute music he learned from years of research among the elders of his own and neighboring tribes (fig. 5.2). He modeled his wooden flute on a few extant examples and from oral history descriptions. His instrument has a rich, mellow tone, perfectly suited for playing love songs and the evening songs that were Comanche lullabies.

Oboe

The oboe is the woodwind's lyric soprano and has a slightly more nasal, bittersweet tone than the flute. A variation of the oboe is the English horn with its more reedy and distant, plaintive tone. The English horn is eight inches longer than the oboe and has a bulb shape at its end.

The oboe's ancestor was the *shawm*, played in ancient Sumeria and Egypt and eventually finding its way to Europe via the Crusades. During Lully's tenure at the French court, a musician and instrument maker named Jean Hotteterre redesigned the shawm into an oboe and introduced it while accompanying one of Lully's ballets at the French Court.

Clarinet

The clarinet is the woodwind's dramatic soprano. It has a wide range from low to high and a smooth, less-reedy tone than the oboe. An agile instrument, it is capable of rapid scales and trills and is found in both symphony orchestras and jazz ensembles. The clarinet was developed in Germany during the eighteenth century from a Greek instrument, the *chalumeaux*. Similar to the shawm, the chalumeaux was made from a cane pipe.

Bassoon

Jean Hotteterre, who developed the oboe from the shawm, redesigned another ancient instrument, the *curtal*, into the bassoon. Lully was so impressed with the bassoon's timbre and its extensive range he featured it in several orchestral compositions. Lower and heavier in tone than the oboe, the bassoon is the bass of the woodwinds, but when played in a dry staccato manner has a comic effect that earned its title "clown of the orchestra."

Saxophone

The saxophone, another favorite jazz instrument, is the youngest member of the woodwind family. It was invented in 1840 by Adolphe Sax, a Belgian instrument maker, when he added a clarinet mouthpiece to a brass band instrument called the ophicleide. In tone, the saxophone has a deep, reedy sound that blends easily with other instruments, but it is also played as a solo instrument. French composer Claude Debussy (day byoo SEE) was so impressed with this new instrument he wrote a composition titled *Rhapsody for Saxophone and Orchestra*.

BRASS INSTRUMENTS

Brass instruments produce sounds through tubing and bell shapes that amplify vibrations made by performers' lips. Originally, brass instruments were horns used primarily for hunting, war, and religious rituals where their loudness provided necessary signals and dramatic fanfares. Their status from working horn to musical horn changed in the late eighteenth century after instrument makers perfected metal working techniques and invented valves.

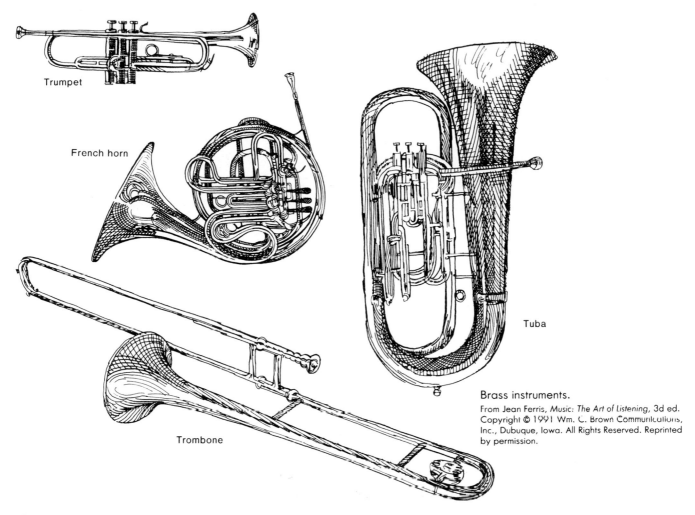

Trumpet

French horn

Trombone

Tuba

Brass instruments.
From Jean Ferris, *Music: The Art of Listening,* 3d ed.
Copyright © 1991 Wm. C. Brown Communications,
Inc., Dubuque, Iowa. All Rights Reserved. Reprinted
by permission.

Trumpet

Two trumpets, one silver and one bronze, were found in the tomb of the Egyptian King Tutankhamen (see fig. 1.1). The exact reason for placing them in the tomb is unknown, but trumpets were regularly sounded in Egyptian armies, and Egyptian priests blew trumpets when worshipping Osiris, the God to whom they attributed the trumpet's invention.

Although the Israelites, like the Chinese, did not attribute the creation of music or invention of musical instruments to a god, music played an important role in their religious rituals. The Israelites modeled the *hazozerah,* a long straight trumpet made of silver or brass, on the Egyptian trumpet and allowed only Aaronites (priests descended from Aaron) to play the silver hazozerah when calling people together for worship. Brass hazozerahs served a number of less sacred purposes that are described both in Scripture and rabbinical literature.[8]

The modern trumpet is found in nearly all orchestras, bands, and ensembles where its high pitch and brilliant tone make it easy to identify whether the music is classical, jazz, or pop. When musicians use a mute, a pear-shaped device placed in the bell, the trumpet tone changes, becoming softer and more lyrical. However, musicians can also force that muted tone into a melodious snarl and a growl.

FIGURE 5.3 • Shofar.
The Jewish Museum/Art Resource, NY.

French Horn

The French horn is derived from the rams' horn or *shofar* (figure 5.3) still used for Jewish liturgy. Shofar, which means "wild goat," originated with the Assyrians, a warlike people who overran an area that today would encompass Israel, Turkey, Syria, and Iraq. The Israelites associated the instrument with sorcery and used repeated blasts of the shofar to keep away the Accuser (Satan). It was sounded routinely every day and also for important announcements and for battles. During the Battle of Jericho, described in Joshua 6:4–20, rams' horns were blown for six days, and on the seventh: ". . . at the sound of the trumpet, when the people gave a loud shout, the wall collapsed; so every man charged straight in, and they took the city." The Talmud mentions a specific type of ram's horn as the *shipura deshikta* (a funeral bugle) sounded to frighten away any demons who might harm the body.[9]

The French horn evolved from the brass hunting horn and was a rather plain orchestral instrument until fitted with valves. Now, of course, it is an orchestral standard. In tone the French horn ranges from majestic lows to mysterious highs, and if horn players plug its bell with their hand, the tone becomes much huskier.

Trombone

The trombone is manipulated by a slide that performs much like valves. When a player draws the slide out, the tone becomes lower. This makes it a difficult instrument to play because the musician is continuously regulating pitch with the slide. Unlike other horns, the trombone has undergone few changes since the fifteenth century, when the slide was added to a long trumpet called the *sackbut*.

Tuba

The tuba has the lowest range of brass instruments, and its tone is full and mellow. When compared with other instruments, it is a youngster, dating only from the 1830s. Its close relative, the *sousaphone*, has its bell turned toward the front. John Phillip Sousa developed the sousaphone as a more convenient way to carry such a large instrument in a marching band.

STRING INSTRUMENTS

With string instruments, musicians produce sound in two ways: by plucking with their fingers or a *plectrum,* or by bowing. Plectrums are made of quill, ivory, wood, metal, and plastic. Bows are made from a single flat band of horsehairs rubbed with rosin and stretched across a thin, slightly curved wooden stick. Plucked instruments include the lute, guitar, zither, harp, and their various relatives and ancestors. Bowed instruments are all members of the violin family and include viola, cello, and double bass.

Lute

The banjo is a descendant of the long necked lute pictured in Egyptian tomb paintings. The body of the Egyptian lute was made from skin stretched over a wooden oval frame; the neck was wood, and typically the instrument had two strings. A pear-shaped lute called a *p'i p'a,* having four strings made of silk, was played in China, and it may have been the ancestor of the Arab *al'ud* that, in turn, became the European lute. The lute came to Europe sometime after the thirteenth century and remained popular until the seventeenth century, when it was replaced by the harpsichord for instrumental solos and by the guitar for vocal accompaniment.

Guitar

The guitar came to Europe from Spain and gained popularity very quickly because it was easier to play than the lute. Its familiar shape with flat back and curved body has undergone few changes. In the eighteenth century it was made slightly larger and its four courses of gut strings were increased to six, but the most radical change took place in the twentieth century when the instrument was electrified. Then both its volume and timbre changed radically. In the 1950s, the development of a new bass guitar with electromagnetic pick-ups that amplified steel strings was another major breakthrough.

Zither

The zither is a flat, shallow wooden box played in a horizontal position. It has five metal strings that play melody and several dozen gut strings used for accompaniment. The zither's ancestor is the Chinese *ch'in* with only seven silk strings. The ch'in, a most unusual instrument, was revered by Chinese scholars, but women and male actors were forbidden to play it. The ch'in's narrow tonal range was considered meditative and its performance ritualistic. A much closer relative of the zither is the *dulcimer* that is made and played in the Appalachian area of the U.S. The dulcimer is wooden, about three feet in length, and has four metal strings. One is the melody string and the others are drones, each sounding a single, reverberating tone.

Harp

Egyptian tomb paintings show the harp paired with the lute, since both instruments were used primarily for vocal accompaniment (fig. 5.4). The modern harp, dating from the early nineteenth century, is a more complex instrument with forty-six strings and seven foot pedals, giving it an extremely wide range.

Woman playing the lute.
© Historical Pictures Service.

FIGURE 5.4 • (Opposite) Wall painting of Egyptian musicians and Dancers from the Tomb of Nakht. Instruments from left to right: the aulos, long-necked flute, and harp.
The Metropolitan Museum of Art. (15.5.9)

A modern harp.
© H. Armstrong Roberts.

A variation of the harp is an instrument called the *kora* that is played in Senegal, Guinea, Gambia, and southern Mali (fig. 5.5). A combination of harp and lute, the kora is made from skin stretched over a large gourd. A wooden neck and twenty-one strings are attached to the gourd. The kora's tone has a ringlike clarity and is best described as a true blend of harp and lute tonalities. Although the kora is an ancient instrument, it has undergone few changes and is a favorite instrument among Senegalese griots. In addition to its use for vocal accompaniment, it is played solo and in ensemble performances.

Violin Family

Near-relatives and ancestors of the violin are found worldwide. In North America, Apache musicians played a small bowed instrument (fig. 5.6). Similar instruments have been found among the Kalahari Bushmen in South Africa,

FIGURE 5.5 • Two kora players, Senegal.
© M. Huet, Hoa-Qui Editions.

FIGURE 5.6 • Apache musician with
bowed string instrument, ca. 1880.

National Anthropological Archives, Smithsonion,
Washington, D.C. Photo by A. F. Randall, ca. 1880.

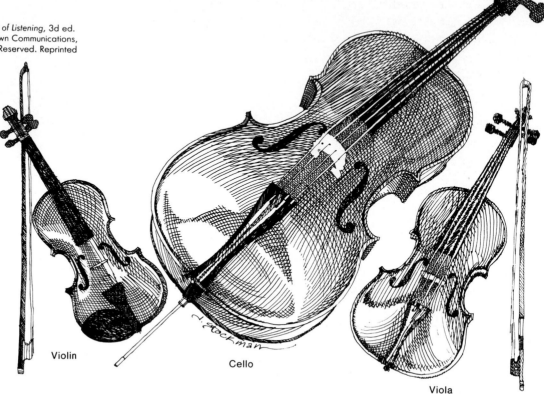

Violin family.

Violin

Cello

Viola

the Kamba in Kenya, and currently among griots in Niger and northern Nigeria. Music historians believe the oldest bowed instrument originated in Central Asia, and if they are correct, then the use of this stringed instrument spread in every direction.

Today's violin has changed very little since the late seventeenth century when two master instrument makers, Antonio Stradivari and Bartolomeo Giuseppe Guarneri del Gesù, perfected string instruments that have never been equaled for beauty of tone. Stradivari—who lived to be ninety-two—made more than a thousand violins and an unknown number of violas, cellos, and basses. Considered priceless, Stradivari and Guarneri instruments are owned and played by some of the world's most renown performing artists.

The violin is the soprano of the string family and has a clear penetrating tone. Violinists perform wonderful feats of sound with the instrument and certain effects that include *saltando* (bouncing the bow), *pizzicato* (plucking strings), *tremolo* (repeating the same note with up and down strokes of the bow), and **glissando**.

The viola is slightly larger and pitched lower than the violin. It is the alto of the strings and has a rich, full tone.

The cello or violoncello is twice the size of the violin, its neck is proportionally shorter, and its strings are longer and thicker. Cellists hold the instrument angled between their knees and rest its base on the floor. The cello is the baritone of the strings with a mellow tone both deep and sweet.

The double bass or contra bass is the lowest pitched string instrument. Since it is six feet high and played in a vertical position, musicians either stand or sit on a stool while playing it. Because it accents the rhythm, it is plucked more frequently than other members of the violin family. Jazz bass players often emphasize the rhythm in a slightly different way by slapping the strings to achieve a percussion-like effect that keeps the beat.

PERCUSSION INSTRUMENTS

Percussion instruments make sound by striking, beating, or shaking. The timpani and xylophone, found in symphony orchestras, are two of about a dozen percussion instruments that can be tuned. Many percussion instruments have origins steeped in ritual and mystery. When dancers from the Akwesasne Mohawk tribe perform the ritualistic Great Feather Dance, two singers accompanying them shake rattles made from the shells of snapping turtles. The rattles are used only for this dance, which is never performed in public. The South American maraca demonstrates a resourceful use of nature because it is nothing more than a gourd with dried seeds. The slit drum is similarly ingenious. Found in South America, South Pacific islands, and Africa, the drum is made from a hollow log placed over an open pit. The hoop drum is another globe-wandering natural instrument made from a round wooden frame with skin stretched across the top.

Other drums come in nearly every size and shape imaginable. Talking drums can be found in the Solomon Islands, New Hebrides, and most African nations. They were once used for long distance communication, but technology has not replaced all of them. Drummer and musicologist John Miller Chernoff tells about a recent humorous experience with talking drums in Ghana:

Percussion instruments.
Courtesy of Ludwig Industries, Inc.

During my first day practicing with Gideon, I was following him well until he suddenly performed a rather complicated series of rhythms and then went back to the basic rhythm he was showing me. A few minutes later a man who had passed at that moment returned with two bottles of beer.[10]

The drums, triangles, cymbals, and the oboes in a modern band and orchestra came to Western Europe by way of Turkey. Between the fifteenth and eighteenth centuries when the Turks were conquering Asia Minor and portions of Africa, Asia, and Europe, tales of the "wild music" that accompanied them in battle were carried back to Western Europe along with their instruments that produced the music.

The modern xylophone with wooden bars struck with beaters is nearly identical to one depicted in a fourteenth century relief sculpture from Java.[11] Nearly every African nation has some form of xylophone, and among *Bapende* in the Congo it is called *Madimba*, a name lending credence to the theory that the South American *marimba* came originally from Africa.[12]

KEYBOARD INSTRUMENTS

The two most familiar keyboard instruments are the organ and piano. The pipe organ is a complex and truly amazing instrument based, actually, on a very simple principle. Think of the syrinx, more commonly called pan-pipes, and how it is sounded by air blown through its pipes of different lengths. In principle, this is a pipe organ in miniature; all that needs to be added are bellows and a keyboard. Of course, adding them and making it all work took several centuries. The first pipe organs were installed in churches during the seventh century, but they were so difficult to play and sounded so raucous, they were kept for congregational singing and never permitted for liturgy. Winchester Cathedral in England had a pipe organ in the tenth century that is reported to have sounded much better, but it had 400 pipes that required two men to play it and seventy men to operate its bellows. By the seventeenth century, the pipe organ had become a truly wonderful instrument, and by the mid-twentieth century it became electric. The sound source of an electric organ is not generated by air but by an oscillator's impulses translated into sound through an amplified loudspeaker.

The modern piano was developed in the eighteenth century by an Italian harpsichord maker named Bartolommeo Cristofori. He called his new instrument a *gravicembalo col piano e forte* (harpsichord with soft and loud). Because the harpsichord's keyboard action plucks strings, the instrument has a tinkling sound and is incapable of dynamics (relative loudness or softness). Cristofori's *piano forte* strikes the strings with small wooden hammers padded with felt. In the nineteenth century, the piano's shape was changed with other structural improvements and foot pedals were added to give the instrument more dynamic versatility. In the twentieth century, it was electrified into the small, familiar keyboard instrument of rock and jazz groups and the keyboard synthesizer.

Harpsichord.
Courtesy Zuckerman Harpsichords, Inc., Stonington, CT.

A synthesizer is capable of producing, modifying, and combining sounds. It can also alter pitch, timbre, and rhythm. Initially, synthesizers imitated the sounds of acoustical instruments, thus replacing musicians, but eventually their capabilities began to change the entire concept of sound: what it is and how it is produced. Today, digital and computer programming present musicians with even greater challenges.

Synthesizers.
Courtesy ARP Instruments, Inc.

SOCIETY AND CULTURE: COMPOSERS, PERFORMERS, AND MUSIC

The Turkish army's drums, cymbals, shawms, and other instruments that made the "wild music" so strange and exotic sounding to European ears eventually found their way into European orchestras. In the years that followed Turkey's unsuccessful attempt to take the city of Vienna in 1683, vagaries of politics and wars eventually brought the Austrians and Turks together in an uneasy alliance against Russia. By 1780, when the former enemies had become almost friends, one of those quirks of fashion impossible to explain "conquered" Vienna faster than any army. It was all a matter of style: everything from hats to furniture followed the "Turkish" fad. The film *Amadeus* describes this silliness in a number of historically accurate scenes in which Mozart persuades Austrio-Hungarian Emperor Joseph II to let him create a comic opera with a Turkish background. Orchestration for that opera, *Die Entführung aus dem Serail* (The Abduction from the Harem) included cymbals, triangle, bass drum, and clarinets. Although the instruments were Turkish, putting turbans on women singers wearing the customary court fashion of white wigs and hoop skirts was hardly authentic.

What connection does this have to the appreciation of music in today's society and culture? It explains something of the enormous and complex network that connects music to society. Put simply—what composers write for one society, you hear in another. Politics, wars, fashions, attitudes, and customs are all factors affecting the creation and performance of music: so are the quality of instruments and the unique skills of individual performers. Mozart was not the first or last composer to write with a particular performer in mind. He wrote coloratura arias for Catarina Cavalieri, one of Vienna's most famous operatic divas, and the film is quite accurate in its portrayal of Catarina. Unfortunately, the film includes too little of the music written for her. *Amadeus* did succeed, however, in describing the inherent servitude of the patronage system. Mozart's patron, the Archbishop of Salzburg, did fire him, although Mozart was luckier than J. S. Bach, whose patron Duke Wilhelm of Weimer, Germany, became so angry when Bach resigned to take a position elsewhere he imprisoned Bach for thirty days, then gave him a dishonorable dismissal.

JOHANN SEBASTIAN BACH (1685–1750)
AND THE PATRONAGE SYSTEM

Bach's career was affected both negatively and positively by the patronage system. It is true that he suffered most of its more demeaning aspects. Duke Wilhelm, for example, like the Archbishop of Salzburg, required his musicians to wear the livery of servants and treated them as such. Before entering the Duke's service, Bach had been a church organist, a position of even less prestige and income. The one positive aspect of the patronage system in general was the sheer number of compositions it produced. Composers were paid to compose, and this they did. Because Duke Wilhelm was a strong advocate of religious music, during the nine years Bach was at Weimer his compositions were mostly for organ and choir. The organs Bach played, however, could hardly be compared with the noisy, cumbersome instrument that had been built in Winchester Cathedral. Organ builders were creating magnificent instruments, and Bach worked as a consultant for many of the organ makers. During this time composers in Holland and parts of Denmark and Germany—mostly Lutheran areas—wrote both religious and secular music for organ, and Danish organist-composer Dietrich Buxtehude inaugurated Sunday afternoon church concerts.

When Bach left Duke Wilhelm he entered the employment of another patron, Prince Leopold, at Cöthen, Germany. During his three years at the lively and somewhat more lenient atmosphere of the Prince's court, Bach wrote compositions for special events, holidays, ceremonies, and entertainments— as a court composer was expected to do. These compositions consisted of chamber music for instrumental ensembles, solo pieces for harpsichord and clavichord, and the six Brandenburg Concertos.

Bach left Prince Leopold to apply for the joint-post of Music Director for the city of Leipzig and Director of St. Thomas School, where musicians for the city's churches were trained. This was an important position that had been offered earlier to two other musicians who were unavailable. Supposedly, one disgruntled town council member remarked that they would have to be satisfied with Bach, a musician "of second rank." Bach remained in Leipzig until his death, and during this twenty-eight year period, performed and composed religious and secular music; he was, in fact, more famous as an organist than a composer. His music was considered by many as too "new" and much too dramatic for church services. His output of music was truly prodigious, especially when considering that his duties included directing music at four churches, teaching music and Latin to St. Thomas students, and composing and directing music for the town council's ceremonies and celebrations.[13]

Johann Sebastian Bach.
© Superstock

Clara Schumann (1819–1896),

PIANIST AND COMPOSER

The public concerts that began in England in the seventeenth century were not adopted as quickly elsewhere. The patronage system was entrenched, and it was not until 1725 that the first public concert was held in Paris. Others soon followed in major cities across the continent. During this time, music publishing became a firmly established business and music journals first appeared. These developments, together with improved musical instruments, gave birth to a new phenomenon: the virtuoso performer.

Clara Wieck Schumann was such a performer. A child prodigy, she wrote her first composition at twelve and made her performing debut as a pianist at fourteen. From her first concert until her last at age seventy-five, she was idol-

Clara Schumann, age 38, Munich.
© Omikron/Photo Researchers, Inc.

ized by critics and public alike. The celebrated pianist and composer Franz Liszt wrote a glowing review for the newspapers after hearing the nineteen-year-old Clara perform. That same week, Liszt wrote in a letter:

> Just one word about Clara Wieck—distintissimo [most distinguished]—but not a man, of course. She is a very simple person, cultivated . . . totally absorbed in her art, but with nobility and without childishness. Her compositions are really very remarkable, especially for a woman.[14]

Six years later, in 1844, a Russian critic gave a glowing review of her Moscow concert: "We have had an abundance of famous pianists here . . . and what touched the heart? We soon forgot that they had ever visited Moscow and not one of us remembers their playing. Can we say the same of Clara Schumann? Absolutely not!"

The Schumanns' daughter Eugenie noted that at one of her mother's last concerts the audience stood when the pianist made her entrance:

> At last Mamma was allowed to seat herself at the piano. She looked so beautiful . . . and Brahms himself said that he had never heard the concerto so well played. When it was over a tremendous storm of applause broke out again, there was a flourish of trumpets, and Mamma was overwhelmed with flowers . . .[15]

Clara Schumann was neither an exhibitionist type performer nor a media celebrity. She earned her fame on the solid basis of her performing artistry. A Viennese critic wrote this analysis of her work:

> To give a clear expression to each work in its characteristic musical style and, within this style, to its purely musical proportions and distinctions, is ever her main task. She seems to play rather to satisfy a single connoisseur than to excite a multitude of average listeners . . . If one were to express a preference for one aspect of her so excellently developed technique, it would be for the dazzling facility with which she plays delicate fast movements . . . [16]

What music did Schumann play? She was particularly fond of Bach fugues and Beethoven sonatas but also performed impromptus, nocturnes, etudes, and other short solo pieces. In addition to compositions for solo piano, she played chamber music with small ensembles, most often duets or trios; and when performing with a large orchestra, she performed piano concertos.

Besides performing the music of Bach, Beethoven, and Mozart, Clara Schumann played compositions written by her contemporaries Franz Lizst, Felix Mendelssohn, Johannes Brahms, and Robert Schumann, her husband. Invariably, her concerts included one or more of her husband's compositions, and it was largely through her efforts that his work was introduced to the public. Clara's admiration for Robert's music was based on the respect one professional gives to another, but it also stemmed from an adulation bordering on hero worship that carried over into their marriage.

To her public, Clara Wieck Schumann lived an exciting life. Travel, despite its discomforts, must have seemed glamorous to nineteenth century women restricted as they were by custom and convention. The public image of Clara Wieck Schumann was one of a woman both beautiful and talented, a woman who wore expensive gowns and mingled with aristocrats, politicians, musicians, artists, and writers. Here was a woman who, to use the cliché, had it all: beauty, career, marriage, family.

Schumann's biographers describe another image, one of a woman far more extraordinary than her public would ever realize. Like Mozart before her, she was taught piano by her father, who supervised every aspect of her training and career as well as her personal life. Clara met Robert Schumann when she was nine. Then when she was eleven and he was twenty, he came to the family home in Leipzig to study piano with her father. Their romance started just after her sixteenth birthday and was vehemently opposed by Clara's father. Some of Frederick Wieck's dislike for Robert resulted from his fear of losing Clara. Wieck had complete control of his daughter's concert arrangements and finances, but he loved her as a father and feared that her marriage to Robert could be disastrous, both professionally and emotionally. What he knew of Robert Schumann he did not like. He saw Robert as irresponsible, dependent on his mother for money, and generally weak in character. From their close association he also knew about Robert's fluctuating moods, his nervousness, and his generally weak health. Wieck managed to forestall Clara and Robert's marriage for several years, but his domineering attitude and harsh behavior alienated Clara, forcing her to choose between the two men. Finally, she married Robert the day before her twenty-first birthday. Afterward, her father refused to see or communicate with her for many years.

Clara Schumann's biographers agree that her love for Robert never wavered and that after his death she devoted herself to keeping his music and memory alive. Volumes of correspondence support this opinion, but the marriage was difficult. Clara had eight children, including one who died in infancy, but she continued her career. Performing was too important a part of her life; she was an artist of exceptional talent and she knew this. Equally important, however, the family needed money because neither Robert's composing nor the music journal he edited proved financially successful.

Clara and Robert each kept diaries, and it is interesting to compare their thoughts about Clara's dual-role. One year after her marriage, Clara wrote:

> My piano playing is falling behind. This always happens when Robert is composing. There is not even one little hour in the whole day for myself! If only I don't fall too far behind. Score reading has also ceased once again, but I hope that it won't be for long this time . . . I can't do anything with my composing—I would sometimes like to strike my dumb head!

Three years after their marriage, Robert made this entry in his diary:

> Clara has written a number of small pieces that show a musical and tender invention that she has never attained before. But to have children and a husband who is always living in the realms of imagination do not go together with composing. She cannot work at it regularly and I am often disturbed to think how many profound ideas are lost because she cannot work them out. But Clara herself knows her main occupation is as a mother and I believe she is happy in the circumstances and would not want them changed.[17]

They were married fourteen years when it became necessary to institutionalize Robert; two years later, he died. Clara Schumann, with seven children to support, needed the money earned from concerts. During her long career, when audiences and critics remarked about her quiet beauty and artistry, she was trying to meet household bills and the medical bills for one child with tuberculosis and another child institutionalized with symptoms not unlike his father's. After her children were grown, it became necessary for Clara to help pay her eldest son's medical bills and support his children during the years their father was ill. When Clara Schumann was asked, as she often was, why she did not perform in the U.S. her standard reply was that profits from such a long tour might be too small to cover expenses. Tactfully, what she did not admit publicly was that she could not afford to take any financial risk.

Clara Schumann's tours took her to nearly every European country, and only in later years, did her itinerary allow for long periods of rest between concerts. Frequently, these rest periods were occasioned by illness, usually arthritis. Despite the infirmities brought by age, this stalwart artist was in her seventies before ending her tours to accept a teaching position in Frankfurt.

GLENN GOULD (1932–1982),

PIANIST

Glenn Gould was born and raised in Toronto, Ontario. When he was three, his parents discovered he had perfect pitch, and his mother, who had studied piano and organ, became his teacher. Except for Gould's intense interest in music and his equally intense dislike of school, his childhood and adolescence were uneventful. At ten he began piano studies at The Royal Conservatory in Toronto and at fourteen made his debut with the Toronto Symphony Orchestra. Nine years of studying and performing followed. At twenty, he made his debut in New York City. Music critic John Briggs wrote in *The New York Times*: "The most rewarding aspect of Mr. Gould's playing . . . is that technique as such is in the background. The impression which is uppermost is not one of virtuosity but of expressiveness. One is able to hear the music." For the *Musical Courier*, this same critic wrote: "I can only call him great, and warn those who have not heard him that he will plunge them into new and unfamiliar depths of feeling and perception."[18]

Glenn Gould performing during a
recording session on his Steinway CD
318 at Goldberg Variations Recording
Session, 1955.
Photo: CBS Masterworks/Sony Classical Archive.

For the next nine years, Glenn Gould's schedule was filled with concert tours, television appearances, and recordings. Then in 1964, Gould ended all live concerts. Although he took part in network television specials and documentary films in Canada and the U.S., he never again performed before a live audience.

Why would a man with his career in ascendance suddenly withdraw from the public—the record buying public? No single answer surfaced, but there were a number of personal foibles and professional choices that made perfect sense to Glenn Gould. He had always been an intensely private person, and he became increasingly uncomfortable and nervous before a concert. This, of course, is not unusual: Clara Schumann admitted she was always nervous beforehand and terrified of forgetting some part of the music. Schumann, however, maintained a stage *presence* that Gould refused to bother with. He was never interested in appearances as such. He sat much lower at the piano than most pianists; moreover he insisted that the piano be raised on blocks while he sat—slouched actually—on a rickety old folding chair he carried everywhere. He was known to fidget and squirm, and he always hummed along with the music. Needless to say, there were not a few critics and members of the audience who had difficulty accepting Gould's behavior. But this was not a pose. There have always been performers noted for grandstanding and audiences who loved them for it. Franz Liszt played so exuberantly he broke piano strings, hammers, and keys. Clara Schumann described a performance in which Liszt broke the first piano he played and then went on to break two replacements. Another nineteenth century performer, Niccolò Paganini, turned his extraordinary skill with the violin into a set of crowd-pleasing tricks, and he did little to squelch rumors that only the devil could make such music. Glenn Gould hummed because it helped his concentration, and he sat low at the piano because, for him, it "worked" better than any other position.

Only someone who has played a musical instrument with seriousness understands the rapport and affection between a musician and his or her instrument. Gould had two favorite pianos: a Chickering made in 1895 and a Steinway CD 318.[19] Interestingly enough, it was a piano that inadvertently brought about Gould's career change. The studio piano Gould played while recording a CBC broadcast had a too-heavy bass sound. Afterward, while listening to the play-back, Gould found that by suppressing the bass and boosting the treble he could get exactly what he wanted—electronically. In Gould's own words:

> I discovered that, in the privacy, the solitude and (if all Freudians will stand
> clear) the womb-like security of the studio, it was possible to make music in
> a more direct, more personal manner than any concert hall would ever permit.
> I fell in love with broadcasting that day, and I have not since then been able
> to think of the potential of music (or, for that matter, of my own potential
> as a musician) without some reference to the *limitless possibilities* of the broad-
> casting and/or recording medium.[20]

Gould signed a contract with Columbia Records in 1955, the day after his New York debut, and from that time until his death in 1982, he recorded regularly. He firmly believed that recording techniques allow for a quality of interpretation unmatched by live performing. Gould put together his recorded performances in much the same way a filmmaker constructs a film. Parts or sections of a musical composition, like the scenes in a film, underwent any number of "takes." Moreover, they were not always recorded in the same sequence or order heard on the final cut. Gould admits that when recording J. S. Bach's *Goldberg Variations,* he saved the melodic theme until last, although it is heard first. This kind of "cut and edit" technique is, of course, possible only in a recording studio. Consequently it represents a concept many artists find totally unacceptable.

Gould's methods carry over into audience response. He believed that the perfect audience setting is in the privacy of your home where you are not disturbed by strangers and where sound quality is determined not by the location of your seat in an auditorium or concert hall but by the caliber of equipment you own. Not everyone agrees.

MUSICAL LANGUAGE

A musical composition is constructed as solidly as a building, and its essential materials are rhythm, melody, and harmony. Rhythm lays the foundation, providing the listener with a skeleton shape of the work. Think of a marching band with its drums beating a constant and relentless beat. This beat is the rhythm holding the band together and keeping its members in step. With rhythm supplying the pulse, melody fuses with rhythm to shape the work. **Melody** is the changing of pitches that are interwoven with rhythm to provide a meaningful pattern. The "Happy Birthday" song, for example, is a simple melody of changing pitches that rise and fall as it is sung. **Harmony** provides the background and context of a work. At the simplest level, harmony is the simultaneous sounding of two or more pitches.

Composers have discovered techniques for interchanging the roles of melody, harmony and rhythm. Rhythm can serve both as structure and melody; melody can unfold into harmony; and harmony can break apart into melody. As you will see, it is both the simple definitions of rhythm, melody, and harmony, and their unique relationships that form the complex art called music.

RHYTHM

Most people think of rhythm as the beat they tap a foot to. For some music, rhythm is just that. John Phillip Sousa's marches and Johann Strauss's waltzes are toe tappers that provide the structure upon which harmonies and melodies flow. A number of more complex rhythms, however, make music more exotic and interesting. Rhythms found in Africa, China, and Latin America are far beyond simple toe tapping.

One very popular technique, called **hemiola**, alternates the grouping of six notes between two groups of 3 or three groups of 2. Another technique, **polyrhythms** (many rhythms), also creates different size groups from a set number of notes. Here, however, the groupings are not alternated but are played simultaneously. For example, twelve notes can be evenly grouped into four groups of 3, three groups of 4, six groups of 2, and two groups of 6. When one voice plays one grouping and another voice plays a different grouping simultaneously, the effect is polyrhythmic.

Rhythmic Example: Leonard Bernstein, "America" from *West Side Story*

As you listen to the song "America" from the musical *West Side Story*, try tapping your foot to its beat. Notice how your beat is not steady but fluctuates between two groups of 3 and three groups of 2. This is hemiola.

Leonard Bernstein (1918–1990).
© Wide World Photos, Inc.

MELODY

Melody is one of the most easily accessible elements of music. Melody is constructed from a series of pitches (tones) that are named and ordered Do Re Mi Fa Sol La Ti (Do). The latter Do begins another octave and would sound identical to the original Do, except that it is exactly twice the pitch of the first. To the human ear, the only difference is whether the music sounds more high pitched or low pitched. For example, a man and a woman singing a single melody would usually sing one or two octaves apart. You would still hear a single melody, but the man's voice would sound lower than the woman's voice. When people sing one or more octaves apart, it is called singing in unison.

The relationship between the eight pitches Do Re Mi Fa Sol La Ti Do is important to melody. For example, the song "Three Blind Mice" begins with the pitches Mi (Three) Re (blind) Do (mice). How the human ear hears the pitch differences, called intervals, is the mechanism that allows listeners to perceive a melody.

Examples of Melody: Canon and Fugue

Because people grasp melodies quickly, composers sometimes use melodies to help listeners follow the music. For example, the children's song "Frére Jacques" is a simple melody that is repeated with various voices. Music built on a single, unchanging and repeated melody is called a **canon**. A canon presents the theme (melody), and then repeats the theme, laying it upon itself to give the illusion of many voices and harmonies.

The canon is the simplest example of a theme repeated upon itself, and the **fugue** is the most mature example. Like a canon, the fugue begins with a theme that is then repeated. Unlike the canon, however, the fugue theme can be altered in a number of ways. Turning the theme upside down is called inversion. For example, "Three Blind Mice" would be inverted from Mi (Three) Re (blind) Do (mice) to Do (Three) Re (blind) Me (mice). Notice that the notes now go up in pitch where the original notes fell. Slowing down the theme is called *augmentation*. Playing the theme faster is called *diminution*.

A good example is J. S. Bach's "Fugue No. 2" from *Prelude and Fugue No. 2, BWV 847*. The theme is stated at the beginning and as it continues, another voice begins the theme again. In total, the theme is stated six times in its original form and several times in inversion and augmentation.

To discover these musical techniques you first need to know they exist, and then it helps to listen to the composition several times. The first time, try to identify the theme in its original form. Then listen to the piece again and this time search for the inverted theme; listen again and try to discover its augmentation.

HARMONY

In the previous section, most of the harmony you heard was derived from the relationships of melodies being played simultaneously. This type of harmony is called *polyphony*. Generally, polyphonic composition reached its maturity in the seventeenth century. The eighteenth century saw the emergence of harmonies where chords shape harmonic structure and melody rests on or interacts with the harmony.

What exactly are chords? They are groupings of pitches that convey a certain sound. For example, when Do, Mi and Sol are sounded together, the resulting harmony is bright and pleasing to the ear. If Sol is changed to La, then the sound is darker and melancholy. Using these chords, composers can set musical moods and support the melody as a single voice shining above and interacting with the harmonies.

An Example of Harmony: Wolfgang Amadeus Mozart, *Serenade for Winds, K. 361; Third Movement*

As you listen to the third movement of this serenade, you will easily hear its harmonies. There is no single melodic line in the beginning, only a pulse. In the film *Amadeus*, the composer Salieri compares it to a rusty squeeze box that sets a very serene mood. Then, a single melodic line rises from the harmony as the oboe and then the clarinet play a delicate tune. As the music progresses and the melody passes between clarinet and oboe, the harmonic structure set by bassoons and French horns continues to plod along, providing a constant harmonic and rhythmic texture upon which the melody ebbs and flows. At the very end, the rusty squeeze box harmonies fade away and the entire ensemble unites to close the piece on a pure sounding and relaxed harmony.

Amadeus.

MUSICAL COMPOSITIONS

Some people shy away from learning about music because they fear it will take away the enjoyment they already experience. Usually, they worry about becoming too technical, too analytical in their approach to what should be enjoyable. Understanding music is not a matter of technical analysis, but of human assessment. No longer are sounds *just* sounds: now they are sounds created and performed with human intellect and skill. Understanding music will not distance you, but it will lead you to a greater appreciation of human achievements.

One note of caution: at times, you may find yourself listening to an excerpt several times before you discover the musical characteristics described. Never think of yourself as a slow learner; think of yourself as unlocking music's secrets. It takes skilled musicians many hearings before they grasp a piece and most admit that each time they hear something new.

THEME AND VARIATIONS: JOHANN SEBASTIAN BACH, GOLDBERG VARIATIONS, BWV 988

Bach wrote the *Goldberg Variations* originally for harpsichord, but the composition is most often recorded as a piano performance. Glenn Gould recorded it twice, each time with a slightly different interpretation.

In a **theme and variation** composition, a simple tune is played at the beginning of the piece and followed by numerous variations. The variations can range from thematic (melodic) variations to free variations where the theme is no longer recognizable.

Bach's *Goldberg Variations* is a theme and variation work where the theme is presented and then thirty variations ornament and modify both the original theme and the harmonic structure. The theme is a slow, dance-like song with the notes grouped into three's. This type of dance, called a *sarabande*, originally came from Mexico and was common throughout Europe in the seventeenth and eighteenth centuries. After the theme, a number of variations techniques are used. Variations 3, 6, 9, 12, 15, 18, 21, 24, and 27 are particularly interesting because they are canons, each using a different interval. Finally, to come full circle and close the work, Bach returned to the original theme after the last variation.

WOLFGANG AMADEUS MOZART (1756–1791), SONATA IN C MINOR FOR PIANO, K. 457, FIRST MOVEMENT

Mozart, who died at thirty-six, wrote hundreds of solo, ensemble, and orchestral works during his short life. **Sonata** is a musical form usually consisting of three or four sections called movements. Most often, the first movement is marked *allegro*: the second movement is slower and more reflective and is marked *adagio*; the last movement returns to a fast pace and is marked *allegro*.

Mozart followed the traditional sonata form, marking the three movements *allegro molto*, *adagio*, and *allegro assai*. The first movement begins forcefully to announce the piece and then follows the sonata-form. This means the first movement consists of three parts: *exposition*, *development*, and *recapitulation*. The exposition is the statement of the themes. The development section develops the thematic material, and the recapitulation restates the themes and closes the work.

JAZZ ENSEMBLE: LOUIS ARMSTRONG (1900–1971) AND P. VENABLE,

"BIG BUTTER AND EGG MAN"

Although twentieth century classical performers have developed a very sophisticated orchestral structure, their counterparts in the eighteenth and nineteenth centuries might have had more in common with modern jazz ensembles. Because there were few orchestras or concert halls in the 1700s, composers wrote for whatever group of musicians happened to be available. One day it could be a group of string players, another day a group of wind players. Every ensemble was unique, and composers wrote music to match the musicians at hand. Also, like jazz musicians, eighteenth century performers took great liberties with the music, embellishing and improvising throughout a work.

Since the very heart of jazz is improvisation, no two performances are alike and the same melody played by two different ensembles will sound different. Nevertheless, certain consistencies exist. Most ensembles have a rhythm section and melody section, and these are easily heard. In the jazz swing bands of the 1930s and 1940s, these were large instrumental sections. Now, however, a rhythm section may be a single bass violin, and the melody section may also consist of only one or two instruments.

Jazz musicians play their instruments in ways that create sounds unique to jazz: they bend, twist, and slur notes to intensify and shade tones. In jazz, the rhythmic beats can change with the duration of notes, and this makes the music "swing." These and other characteristics of American jazz have origins in the music from African nations.

Musicians play both jazz compositions and popular tunes that they restructure by theme and variation. This is easily heard during the improvised part of the music. Quite often, a jazz composition begins with the melody stated and repeated. Then improvisation follows when musicians, one by one, vary the melody. This is, in a sense, spontaneous composing on the part of each performer. Before the performance ends, the melody is usually stated again in its original form.

This is the structure you will hear in "Big Butter and Egg Man," written by P. Venable and the great jazz trumpet player Louis "Satchmo" Armstrong. The young trumpet player Wynton Marsalis, who also plays classical trumpet, recently recorded this piece with Ellis Marsalis on piano, and Reginald Veal on Bass.

Louis Armstrong.
© UPI/Bettmann News Photos.

The music begins with a walking bass (a bass line that moves like a scale) that continues until the music ends. The trumpet enters, states the melodic theme and repeats it, bending notes on the final repeat. The piano enters, playing chords while the trumpet now freely improvises on the theme. When the trumpet completes its improvisation, the piano begins improvising. Then the bass is heard in a brief solo improvisation followed by piano chords. The trumpet enters, restating the melodic theme and embellishing it while the piano does the same.

GAMELAN ENSEMBLE

"Once a year the old **gamelan** Sekati (tense heart) is brought from its place in Srimenganti Hall inside the Jogi kraton (palace) to be played for a week inside the compound of the Great Mosque."[21] These few words say a great deal about the reverence felt by musicians and audiences toward ancient and esteemed instruments. Gamelan ensembles are found primarily in Bali and Java (fig. 5.7). The old gamelan Sekati is in Java, where, according to history, it was made in 1555 by skilled metal craftsmen under the advice of Nine Holy Men.

FIGURE 5.7 • Javanese Gamelan.
© Eugene Gordon/Photo Researchers, Inc.

Even small villages in this part of the world have gamelans. A gamelan ensemble is actually a set of instruments: gongs of different sizes and pitches: sarons that are bronze keyboard instruments struck with a mallet; wooden xylophones; drums; sulings, similar to flutes; and the rebab, a two-string fiddle. These ensembles vary in size, ranging from fifteen instruments to sixty. Unlike Western ensembles made up of musicians with their own instruments, gamelan instruments are a "set" that remain together. The musicians may change but never the instruments. This is why every gamelan has its own, distinct sound.

Gamelan music is constructed from a slow, baseline melody that varies from instrument to instrument. The result is often described as shimmering layers of sound, beautiful but unusual to Western ears unacquainted with the gamelan harmonic and tuning system. Most often, gamelan music accompanies dances and puppet shows. The Javanese dance drama *Arjuna's Wedding* (see fig. 6.1) is performed to gamelan music.

ORCHESTRAL MUSIC: LUDWIG VAN BEETHOVEN (1770–1827)
SYMPHONY NO. 5 IN C MINOR, OP. 67

Symphony orchestras were an outgrowth of ensembles, but a number of factors were responsible for their continued growth and popularity. Musical instruments were being improved and redesigned, and as the number of instruments increased, so did the number of musicians. Support for large orchestras increased with the popularity of public concerts. As public concerts increased so did the demand for concert halls. Concert halls, besides accommodating larger audiences, encouraged larger orchestras, but composers also demanded larger orchestras. The German composer Richard Wagner, for example, wrote operas that required orchestras of more than 130 musicians. An orchestra today numbers between approximately 90 and 110 or 112.

In 1808 when Beethoven's Fifth Symphony was first performed in Vienna, neither the orchestra nor the concert hall would have met today's standards. The hall was unheated—in December—the audience was small, and the orchestra had not rehearsed properly. Beethoven's biographers write that at one point, the composer jumped up from his seat and shouted "Stop! Badly played!" or words to that effect.

The composed symphony has a three hundred year history, and during this time it has taken different musical forms. During much of the eighteenth and nineteenth centuries, however, symphony compositions followed a fairly standard four-movement form. Typically, the first movement was marked allegro. The second movement was slow and lyrical. The third movement was usually written in the dancelike minuet or trio style. The fourth and final movement was most often lively and quick and concluded the work.

Ludwig van Beethoven.
Free Library of Philadelphia.

Beethoven's *Symphony No. 5 in C Minor* is typical of this form. It is scored for the usual string sections plus two flutes, two oboes, two clarinets, two bassoons, two horns, two trumpets, and the timpani. The last movement calls for a double bassoon, three trombones, and the piccolo.

The first movement is in sonata-allegro form: the three-section form consisting of exposition, development, and recapitulation, discussed previously. In the exposition, three separate melodic themes are introduced or exposed. The first is the famous four-note melodic idea called "fate knocking at the door." It is repeated three times but recurs throughout this movement and the composition as a whole. A second theme is introduced by horns and bassoons. If you listen carefully while this second theme is playing you can also hear the rhythm of the opening theme. A third rather short theme is introduced by violins, and the exposition section ends. In the development section, the first melodic theme is varied extensively. In the recapitulation, it is introduced by the oboe and themes two and three are heard again.

This may be a good time to listen again to the first movement, since by now you are aware of how much is taking place. There are three melodies to remember here and all kinds of musical complexities. Depending on the level of your listening skills, it is sometimes better to concentrate on one movement before attempting another.

The second movement is in a contrasting mood, slower and more lyrical. Its form is theme and variation. The first theme is announced by violas and cellos and the second by clarinets and bassoons. The second theme is a flowing, almost soaring melody. The movement is almost equally divided between the first and second themes.

In the third movement, a moody, somewhat mysterious melodic theme is introduced by cellos and bass violins. Very soon, however, the horns announce the same four-note fate theme heard in the first movement. These two themes are passed around the orchestra and the tempo increases, then decreases near the end of the section. Here, you hear the tapping rhythm of the fate theme again, and the timpani keeps a steady beat.

The fourth movement begins immediately, and its first theme is announced by full orchestra. A short second theme is announced by woodwinds, answered by violins, and then woodwinds announce a third theme, the familiar fate melody. This last movement, so strong and imperious in mood, is in sonata-allegro form like the first movement.

VOCAL-INSTRUMENTAL MUSIC

Two of the largest and most dramatic works of vocal-instrumental music are **oratorios** and **operas**. Both are written for soloists, ensembles, and choruses and consist of **arias** and **recitatives.** An aria is an elaborate vocal solo with orchestral accompaniment, and a recitative is sung dialogue. How are oratorios and operas different? Most oratorios have religious themes and are based on Biblical literature. Unlike operas, they do not have dramatic plots or characters—there is no stage acting as such—but they do have narrators. Oratorios also place greater emphasis on the chorus. One of the best known oratorios is George Frederick Handel's *The Messiah,* usually performed during Christmas season in churches and concert halls.

Historically, opera became the oratorio's secular counterpart. From its origins in the Renaissance, opera underwent gradual but persistent modifications both in its drama and music. Among the composers who contributed to these changes, three are outstanding. One was Claudio Monteverdi, who improved the recitative and aria. Another was Jean-Baptiste Lully—Louis XIV's superstar—who heightened the dramatic aspects of opera while increasing the role of the chorus. The third innovator was the nineteenth century German composer Richard Wagner (VAG ner) (1813–1883).

Wagner was a contemporary of Giuseppe Verdi, whose opera *La Traviata* is discussed in chapters 3 and 6. Unlike Verdi, who followed the conventional operatic form that included arias and recitatives, Wagner replaced them with what is best described as endless melody. To accomplish this musical feat, Wagner increased the orchestra both in size and importance. Like Verdi, Wagner wanted the orchestra to do more than accompany singers; but where Verdi used the orchestra to support and express the emotions of the drama, Wagner went a step further by making the orchestra essential *to* the drama. He accomplished this with the *leitmotif* (light mo teef), a short melodic theme or leading motive that represents a specific person, place, or idea. As such, it is a little melody that is repeated and developed throughout the entire opera.

Wagner did not call his works operas; he called them "musical dramas" because he knew that he was truly creating a new kind of music. The initial response to his work was divided, with negative opinions having the edge. Now, however, more than a century later, his music is universally recognized for its highly innovative artistry, and the challenge to move music into unexplored territories is taken up by today's composers.

Wagner's theater at Bayreuth.
Courtesy of Opera News.

George Crumb (1929–   ), *Ancient Voices of Children*, A Song Cycle

Much of the work of American composer George Crumb is influenced by the poetry of Federico Garcia Lorca. Lorca was a Spanish poet killed by the Fascists during the Spanish Civil War, the same war that impelled Pablo Picasso to paint his monumental work *Guernica* (fig. 2.40). Although *Ancient Voices of Children* uses verses from Lorca's poems, its dramatic theme is not based on war, but instead on the simple but profound observations of children.

George Crumb is not the first composer to adapt another art form—in this instance poetry—to music. The single most dominant influence in all of Wagner's music was the literature of German legend and myth. In adapting Lorca's verses Crumb keeps the original Spanish. Printed programs and record inserts include English translations, but performances and recordings are always in Spanish.

The work calls for a unique ensemble of mezzo-soprano and boy soprano plus a global mix of instruments that includes oboe, mandolin, harp, electric piano, child's toy piano, harmonica, musical saw, maracas, marimba, Tibetan prayer stones, Japanese temple bells, and various gongs and drums including an African tuned drum. The mezzo-soprano is required to use traditional operatic skills plus vocal techniques more common to the music of Senegal, Ghana, North American Ojibwa, and jazz scat singers. The score requires unconventional whispers, hums, growls, and cries. The boy soprano sings offstage, and this distancing gives his clear delicate voice the quality of an echo.

As you listen to Song 1, "The Little Boy Was Looking For His Voice," do not expect a conventional lyrics-matched-to-music structure. Like Wagner before him, Crumb uses instruments for more than accompaniment. Harp, oboe, and piano alternate with both the soprano voices. Instrumental tones seem to fuse with the Spanish inflections, and the effect is a kind of universal harmony reminiscent of the mythical beliefs of American Navaho and Indian Hindu.

An instrumental interlude intended for solo dance follows Song 1. Here, the harp is heard again, but now with mandolin, oboe, and prayer stones. At times harp and mandolin play the same melody although not in unison. This is called heterophony and is commonly found in Javanese gamelan music.

Three songs, a second dance interlude, and a final fifth song conclude the work. Each piece is unique yet merges into the work as a whole. Song 4 is particularly intriguing and somewhat puzzling. It includes a short work by J. S. Bach played on a toy piano. The resultant sound is delicate and has the same distancing quality as the boy soprano's voice. Possibly this is why it is included; but why perform it on a toy piano? Is it meant to be whimsical, or is it a link to the lost child in us all? The composer lets his listeners decide.

NOTES

[1]Bharata, *Natyasastra*, ch. 36:27. Quoted in Curt Sachs, *The Rise of Music in the Ancient World East and West*, (New York: W. W. Norton & Co., Inc., 1943), p. 157.

[2]J. H. Kwabena Nketia, "Music in African Cultures: A Review of the Meaning and Significance of Traditional African Music." (Legon, Accra, Ghana: Institute of African Studies, University of Ghana, 1966). In John Miller Chernoff, *African Rhythm and African Sensibility*, (Chicago: The University of Chicago Press, 1979), p. 36.

[3]Quoted in Sachs, *The Rise of Music in the Ancient World East and West*, p. 106.

[4]Curt Sachs, *The History of Musical Instruments*, (N.Y.: W. W. Norton & Co., Inc., 1940), p. 63.

[5]Herbert Chappel, *Sounds Magnificent, The Story of the Symphony*,(London: British Broadcasting Corp., 1984), pp. 17, 18.

[6]*Les deux Menèstriers*, Bodleian Library, Oxford. In Howard D. McKinney and W. R. Anderson, *Music in History*, 2d ed. (NY.: American Book Co., 1957), p. 140.

[7]Yehudi Menuhin and Curtis W. Davis, *The Music of Man*, (Toronto: Methuen, 1979), p. 11.

[8]Alfred Sendrey, *Music in the Social and Religious Life of Antiquity*, (Cranbury, N.J.: Associated University Presses, Inc., 1974), pp. 189–191.

[9]Sendry, p. 193–200.

[10]John Miller Chernoff, *African Rhythm and African Sensibility*, (Chicago: The University of Chicago Press, 1979), p. 75.

[11]Sachs, *The History of Musical Instruments*, p. 238.

[12]Francis Bebey, *African Music*, trans. Josephine Bennett. (Westport, CN: Lawrence Hill & Co., 1975), pp. 84–92.

[13]K. Marie Stolba, *The Development of Western Music*, (Dubuque, IA: Wm. C. Brown Pub., 1990), pp. 399–416.

[14]Franz Liszt, *Correspondence de Liszt et de Madame d'Agoult*, ed. Daniel Ollivier, 2 vols. (Paris: Grasset, 1933), 1:217 (April 13, 1838). Quoted in Nancy B. Reich, *Clara Schumann*, (Ithaca, N.Y.: Cornell University Press, 1985), pp. 209–10.

[15]Quoted in Joan Chissell, *Clara Schumann: A Dedicated Spirit*, (N.Y.: Taplinger Publishing Co., 1983), p. 171.

[16]Chissell, pp. 141–42.

[17]Reich, p. 228.

[18]John Briggs, *The New York Times*, Jan. 12, 1955, and John Briggs, *Musical Courier* 153, no. 3 (Feb. 1, 1955). Quoted in Geoffrey Payzant, *Glen Gould: Music and Mind*, (Toronto: Van Nostrand Reinhold Ltd., 1978), p. 14.

[19]For a lengthy description of these two pianos and Gould's own description, see Payzant, pp. 104–6.

[20]Broadcast, CBC (April 30, 1967). Quoted in Payzant, p. 36.

[21]R. M. Wasisto Surjodiningrat, M.Sc, *Gamelan Dance and Wayang in Jogjakarta*, (Jogjakarta, Java: Gadjah Mada University Press, 1971), p. 1.

CHAPTER SIX

DRAMA AND DANCE

In a single day, television brings you more drama than past generations saw in a lifetime. Choices ranging from Saturday morning cartoons to *Masterpiece Theater* are available in numbers that boggle the mind. Even the innocuous commercial has taken on a new image, changing from its former sixty-second sales pitch to the current thirty-second micro-drama where characters and story do the selling on a far more subjective level. Television news has changed as well, and its alteration to a more dramatic format is not without controversy. Detractors say the news is now sensationalized by commentators who are better actors than journalists and by selective editing that blurs the line between fact and fiction.

What is drama's power that makes it so pervasive a means of communication? The answer lies with one of the first writers in the Western world to analyze drama's impact and influence, the Greek philosopher Aristotle (384–322 B.C.). In the *Poetics*, Aristotle wrote that a dramatic form must have "incidents arousing pity and fear, wherewith to accomplish a katharsis of such emotions." Aristotle's use of the word "**catharsis**" is generally taken to mean the cleansing of emotions that occurs when audiences empathize with characters enough to care what happens to them. It follows that being caught up in the human tragedies of others gives audiences an opportunity to lessen or release their own pent-up feelings. Catharsis explains why watching someone else's troubles may give you a different perspective on your own or why laughing may help you feel better.

In Aristotle's lifetime people were lucky to see one drama festival a year, and only Greek citizens were allowed to buy tickets—women were not considered citizens. Today's audiences have access to operas, musicals, dance dramas, and spoken dramas spanning every century and national origin and available live, filmed, video taped, and televised. How to sort out a menu this size? How do *you* sort it out? When you buy a ticket to a movie or play or when you push a television button, do you select a type of drama already familiar to you or do you choose something totally unknown? Do you consider yourself a complacent viewer or an adventurous one?

As you read through this chapter, you will find the selections of dramas diverse in origin, structure, and style, but despite these differences you will find they share certain common elements. Aristotle, in his analysis of drama, isolated six basic elements. The first is diction, or to use the current term "dramatic language." Dramatic language, then, is the interpretation and communication of ideas through speech, action, dance, music, and song, singly or combined. Another element is plot. This is dramatic action moving in a series of scenes from beginning to end. Character is the third element. Thought, the fourth element, consists of a drama's underlying ideas or themes. Spectacle, the fifth element, refers to a drama's production and includes every phase of staging. Melody, the last element, combines the music, song, and dance that were essential to ancient Greek theater. Today, music may be either essential or incidental, depending on the specific drama.

For a drama to be successful, its elements must be balanced. Consequently, if a drama lacks significant ideas or believable characters, its playwright or director is apt to pad a thin plot with unnecessary and contrived scenes or with lavish staging. A film or television director might resort to extremely violent or kinetic scenes or to ever more thrilling special effects. Sensationalism and spectacular effects, whether staged or filmed, are no substitute for substance. Their impact is momentary at best and they leave no imprint on their audiences. Considering today's media exposure, it is important to remember that drama is an art, not a commodity to be used and tossed aside. The art of drama invites you to think because it makes the activity so pleasurable.

The Spanish writer Miguel Cervantes (sir VAHN teez) expressed his thoughts on drama through his most famous character Don Quixote (kee-HO-tee), who advises a companion:

> . . . I would have you look kindly upon the art of the theater and, as a consequence, upon those who write the pieces and perform in them, for they all render a service of great value to the State by holding up a mirror for us at each step that we take, wherein we may observe, vividly depicted, all the varied aspects of human life; and I may add that there is nothing that shows us more clearly, by similitude, what we are and what we ought to be than do plays and players. (From *The Portables Cervantes* by Miguel de Cervantes Saaverdra, translated by Samuel Putnam, Translation copyright 1949, 1950, 1951 by Viking Penguin Inc. Used by permission of Viking Penguin, a division of Penguin Books USA Inc.)

HEROISM: EAST AND WEST

The *Ramayana* (rah MAH ya na) and *Mahabharata* (ma HAH BAR ah tah) are two ancient **epics** that have had an extraordinary influence on the drama, literature, painting, and sculpture of India and Southeast Asia. The *Mahabharata* is the older of the two epics, dating from about 1000 B.C., and it consists of more than 100,000 verses in eighteen books, making it fifteen times longer than the Bible. In 1985, director Peter Brook staged portions of the *Mahabharata* and later adapted them for television; the stage production was nine hours long and the televised production six hours.

For Westerners unfamiliar with the cultures of India and Southeast Asia, it is important to understand that the *Mahabharata* is steeped in the belief of Hinduism and in India's caste system. For this reason it would be pointless to approach dramatic characters or their actions from a Western perspective. Instead, characters and their actions must be seen in a larger, cosmic sense and in relation to every character's *swadharma*. Swadharma is a person's total background and includes, among other influences, certain innate traits inherited from previous lives.[1] The caste into which a person is born must also be considered because this affects not only the way a character will act but the reasons behind the actions. Indian drama is also unique in structure: it does not move, like most Western drama, in a linear plot from beginning to end, but instead tends to ramble. In this respect, it is still a storyteller's art. As Indian director Rustom Bharucha explains: "Always the elaboration is more important than the thrust of the narrative . . . A story lasts for as long as there is a need for it."

Two ancient epics of the Western world are the *Iliad* and *Odyssey*, written by the Greek poet Homer around the eighth century B.C. The *Iliad* describes the bravery of Trojan War heroes Achilles and Hector, and the *Odyssey* tells of another hero from the war Odysseus (Ulysses) and the adventures he encounters on his homeward journey. These two epics greatly influenced Greek arts and education. Homeric gods and humans, many of them demi-gods, provided playwrights, poets, sculptors, and painters with an almost unlimited supply of subjects. Those same subjects permeated an educational system based on noble and heroic virtues. With the onset of the European Renaissance and its emphasis on classical Greek and Latin studies, a new cycle of Homeric influence began, and it lasted for more than four hundred years.

EPIC HEROISM IN THE MAHABHARATA

Central to the stories of the *Mahabharata* are the five Pandava brothers, who are heroes, and the hundred Kaurava brothers, who are villains. The bravest Pandava brother is Arjuna, who was fathered by the Hindu God Indra, and therefore possesses magical power. Arjuna is truly a demi-god: a most fearsome warrior and skillful archer; he is also an irresistibly handsome man and a talented lover. The epic begins when Arjuna's older brother loses the Pandava's share of the kingdom to the Kauravas in a crooked dice game. This forces the Pandavas into exile for twelve years, a time when they undergo countless trials and challenges and encounter various gods, monkey-gods, yogis, and ogres. During this twelve year period, while they combat evil in its many disguises, they are forced to fend off the Kauravas who repeatedly try to kill them. Eventually a final battle between the two families is fought, the five Pandavas defeat the hundred Kauravas, and good triumphs over evil.

Eastern drama and literature are filled with tales of adventure and romance, but never tragedy. Tragedy has no part in Eastern drama and literature because it is inconceivable that a hero would fail or that a man would dare to challenge a god. Similarly, Eastern drama and literature do not address the causes, motives, repercussions, or rationales that cause behavior. The Indian scholar Balwant Gargi makes this comparison between dramas of the West and the East:

> One can still perceive the core of Sophocles and Aeschylus in Western drama where the character is torn between his inner self and outer circumstance . . . The common Indian playgoer does not care for the complex psychological character of the West. He patronises the hero who triumphs, the heroine who suffers and finally meets her lord, the struggle between Good and Evil, Truth and Falsehood . . .[2]

"ARJUNA WIWAHA" (ARJUNA'S WEDDING),
A TRADITIONAL DANCE-DRAMA FROM JAVA

"Arjuna's Wedding" is a dance-drama written originally for the palace court at Jogjakarta (fig. 6.1). Dancers who first performed it were professional entertainers who studied and lived in the palace and danced only for the pleasure of the king and his guests. Today's dancers are, of course, free from any such restrictions and are encouraged to perform worldwide. Their training at the palace school of dance at Jogjakarta is in a style of dance more than a thousand

FIGURE 6.1 • The dance-drama, "Arjuna Wiwaha." Don Hogan Charles/New York Times Pictures.

years old. To master this style, they must begin their studies at an early age when muscles are still flexible enough for the specialized movements this dance requires. In Javanese dance, hips must arch so that the torso leans slightly forward, and hands must bend far enough to curve the fingers gracefully downward and slightly backward toward the wrists. Dance tempo is languid, slow by Western standards, but meaningful in the pauses and poses that accent its rhythm. Always, the movements are interpretative, stately, and elegant. Dancers wear what was once the costume of the court: a batik patterned silk skirt, vest-like top, and a long sash fastened with a large, gold ornament. The sash has long streamers that the women periodically grasp between two fingers, raise, then release in such a way that the cloth, instead of just dropping, appears to float gently downward, almost like a leaf in the air. Dancers' crownlike head-dresses are made of thin gold and shaped into a large coil in back. The gamelon, an ensemble of various gong, chime, and percussion instruments, furnishes musical accompaniment. Vocal accompaniment by one or more singers narrates the story in a style that is not so much sung as intoned with a mix of speech and song.

The story of "Arjuna's Wedding" begins with the defeat of a demon and ends with Arjuna's marriage to the Princess Sembodro. The performance has a subtle quality difficult to describe but typical of Javanese dance, which places greater emphasis on mood than on narrative. The word *rasa*, meaning flavor, is used to describe the unique and individual quality of a dance-drama in which each and every movement is significant in its own right. No one in the audience really cares—or ever considers—that Princess Sembodro first rejected Arjuna and then agreed to marry him only after he fought a battle for her. What is most important to a Javanese audience is not the narrative of the dance but its aesthetic quality: seeing the formal beauty of the dancers' movements as they interpret Arjuna's heroics and the merging of Arjuna's and Sembodro's individual destinies into one.

GREEK THEATER

Ancient Greeks believed drama was a gift from Dionysus, the god who came to them from the east—quite possibly from India. From ritual choral dances, called dithyrambs, performed in Dionysus' honor, Greek drama gradually evolved into a structured form. Greek dramas were performed during city festivals that lasted from three to six days. On a typical festival day, audiences, numbering in the thousands, entered outdoor theaters at dawn to watch three tragedies and a short comical satyr play—before lunch. In the late afternoon, audiences returned to the theater to watch two more plays before dark. *Theatron* means "seeing place," and most scholars agree that the first theaters probably consisted of wood benches built into a hillside. Later, that same plan seems to have been followed when stone theaters replaced earlier wooden structures. Most theaters were similar in design to the outdoor structure at Epidauros, which is still standing (fig. 6.2). The circular area called the **orchestra** is where performances took place. This held a raised wooden stage built in front of a small building containing dressing rooms. All actors and members of the chorus were men who wore masks, high headdresses, and thick-soled boots that gave them additional height. The playwright Aeschylus, who directed his own plays, was the first to paint the masks. He also helped design costumes, although by today's standards these were quite simple: mostly robes not unlike ordinary Greek dress.

Existing copies of Greek plays reveal the literary structure but contain few details concerning staging and performing. What little is known of the dances that were so essential to Greek drama has been pieced together largely from three sources: written descriptions; vase paintings; and several folk dances of ancient origin, most of them from the island of Karpathos where they are still performed.

The literary structure of the dramas is quite similar. Some tragedies begin with a prologue, others with the **parodos**, which is that part of the play in which the chorus makes its entrance. The *parodos* is followed by a series of episodes or scenes, each separated by choral songs or recitations. Most plays include an **exodus** for both chorus and actors, although in *Prometheus Bound*, the concluding scene ends with the chorus standing by the hero.

A **chorus** of between twelve and fifty men was essential to Greek drama, and the role of the chorus was to interact with leading characters and with the audience by advising, questioning, reacting to events, and expressing opinions. Historians generally agree that the chorus's lines were performed with recitations, chants, and songs and that their movements were choreographed. The chorus was accompanied by woodwind and percussion instruments and occasionally a lyre.

FIGURE 6.2 • Greek theatre at Epidauros, ca. 350 B.C.
© Robert Lamm.

PROMETHEUS BOUND

BY AESCHYLUS (525–456 B.C.)

The initial performance of Aeschylus' (ES ka les) drama *Prometheus Bound* took place at a festival in the city of Athens sometime after 468 B.C. Prometheus was a Titan who had fought alongside Zeus in his battle to become supreme ruler over all Gods. After Zeus' victory, Prometheus went to him and asked if he could take fire to the humans who lived on earth without light or heat. Despite Prometheus' pleas that humans were barely surviving in a dark, cold world, Zeus refused. Prometheus, torn between his pity for human beings and his duty to Zeus, defied the order. As punishment, Zeus ordered him taken to an isolated mountain top, bound to a rock with unbreakable chains, and abandoned. Aeschylus has Prometheus relate the events of the myth early in the play, although it is not the myth that shapes the plot but the punishment itself.

The entire play takes place on the mountain top where Prometheus is chained. In the first scene, Zeus's two henchmen, Force and Violence, hold Prometheus while Hephestus, God of Metalsmiths, nails the chains to a rock. Force typifies the man who never questions an order; Hephestus, on the other hand, is someone who weighs the issues, regrets what he must do, but still performs his duty. After Force, Violence, and Hephestus leave Prometheus, the shackled Titan cries out to the universe in anguish. Alone on the mountain, he tells what led to his act of disobedience, and it is here the audience learns that with fire, he gave human beings knowledge. The prologue concludes with his desperate words: Look at me then, in chains, a god who failed, the enemy of Zeus, whom all gods hate, all that go in and out of Zeus' hall. The reason is that I loved men too well . . .[3]

The chorus, garbed as sea nymphs, enters, and its leader comforts Prometheus. "Tell us your tale" the chorus leader says, and Prometheus summarizes Zeus' rise to power while elaborating on the evils of tyranny in general. The chorus, powerless to help him, can only offer sympathy and the comfort of their presence. The chorus brings the *parodos* to its conclusion.

In the next three scenes, three characters approach the hero separately. Ocean is the first character: a stereotypical hack politician who keeps switching from persuasive tactics to pompous boasts. "New fashions have come in with this new ruler," he cajoles. "Why can't you change your own to suit?" Later, he brags, "And I am proud, yes, proud to say/ I know that Zeus will let you go/ just as a favor done to me."

The second character is a young woman named Io who has been changed into a cow by Zeus's jealous wife Hera. From dialogues between the hero and Io, the audience learns that Prometheus knows a secret prophesy. He tells Io that if Zeus should ever take another wife—a woman he refuses to name—the child of their union would be capable of taking Zeus's throne. He also prophesies that Io will have a descendant who—in future generations—will free him.

Source: Excerpts pages 286–287 from *Prometheus Bound* by Aeschylus in *World Masterpieces through the Renaissance,* vol. I, 3d ed., W. W. Norton, 1973. Reprinted from *Three Greek Plays,* translated by Edith Hamilton, 1937, W. W. Norton & Company, Inc., New York, NY.

The third character is the God Hermes, sent by Zeus to learn the identity of the mystery woman. Prometheus refuses to name her, and Hermes warns that Zeus will send three waves of evil:

the last "an eagle red with blood
. . . All day long he will tear to rags your body,
great rents within the flesh,
feasting in fury on the blackened liver.
Look for no ending to this agony."

Pausing, Hermes turns to the chorus and asks, "The thunder peals and it is merciless./ Would you too be struck down?"

The brave chorus leader is defiant: "Not to stand by a friend—there is no evil/ I count more hateful./ I spit it from my mouth."

The play concludes with Prometheus' last great monologue that ends with these final, tragic words: "O holy Mother Earth, O air and sun,/ behold me. I am wronged."

By emphasizing Prometheus' bravery, Aeschylus dignified what was, in fact, an act of civil disobedience. Aeschylus portrayed a hero who fought courageously for a leader, but when that leader turned tyrannical, was not afraid to

FIGURE 6.3 • Pieter Paul Rubens, *Prometheus Bound*, 1611–12. Oil on canvas, 95 7/8 × 82 1/2 in.
Philadelphia Museum of Art: The W. P. Wilstach Collection W'50-3-1.

defy him. The play's theme is a challenge that echos through the centuries, a plea to fight against repression. It is a theme of particular interest in light of Aeschylus' own background. His career as a playwright was continually interrupted by the Persian War. For more than twenty years he served as a warrior and was decorated for valor at the Battle of Marathon. Ten years later, he fought at Salamis, where the Greeks won the decisive naval battle that ended the war. Shortly after this last battle, Aeschylus was proclaimed a national hero.

THE COMIC HERO

DON QUIXOTE, FROM THE RENAISSANCE NOVEL *THE INGENIOUS GENTLEMAN DON QUIXOTE DE LA MANCHA* BY MIGUEL DE CERVANTES SAAVEDRA (1547–1616)

Picture Don Quixote (kee HO tee) as a none too prosperous gentleman of about fifty, tall with a skinny frame encased in an ill-fitting, outdated suit of armor, and sitting astride an even skinnier horse with the preposterous name of Rocinante. Here is a man in search of adventure, a man who wants to be a knight, a man looking to right wrongs and fight battles for a fair lady. Here is a man who has read so many adventure stories that in Cervantes's words:

> . . . his brain dried up and he went completely out of his mind. He had filled his imagination with everything that he had read . . . and as a result had come to believe that all these fictitious happenings were true: they were more real to him than anything else in the world.[4] (From *The Portable Cervantes* by Miguel de Cervantes Saavedra, translated by Samuel Putnam, Translation copyright 1949, 1950, 1951 by Viking Penguin, Inc. Used by permission of Viking Penguin, a division of Penguin Books USA Inc.)

Cervantes' comic hero fights windmills believing they are giants, he thinks a country inn is a castle, and that a lion stays in its cage rather than fight because *it* is afraid of *him!* He is robbed, beaten-up more than once, and constantly ridiculed. He cannot possibly win a fight or rescue himself, much less a damsel in distress, but he tries. He never loses hope that some day chivalry will return to a world that neither wants nor needs it. His foil is his servant Sancho Panza, a plain thinking man who joins Don Quixote only for a promised reward but remains because of loyalty. Sancho's common sense contrasts with the Don's flights of fancy and his reasoning with his master's wild imagining. Yet before the novel ends, Sancho, together with other characters, finds that life has become more colorful and far more meaningful because of Don Quixote.

THE MUSICAL:

MAN OF LA MANCHA BY DALE WASSERMAN, WITH LYRICS BY JOE DARION, MUSIC BY MITCH LEIGH

Man of La Mancha opened in New York City in the late fall of 1965 and ran on Broadway for more than two thousand performances (fig. 6.4). Its success had a special meaning for playwright Dale Wasserman, who remembers that producers and backers ". . . regarded it as too radical, too 'special' and, most crushing of all, too intellectual."[5]

When a writer adapts one art form from another—in this instance a twentieth century musical from a sixteenth century novel—considerable latitude in structure and style is to be expected. This is important to keep in mind because a novel is structured by its dialogue and narrative, but a musical is structured by the combination of dialogue, song, dance, and music. This difference notwithstanding, an adaptation can remain faithful to the original if it retains the same dominant themes. *Man of La Mancha's* most memorable song is "The Impossible Dream" and one indication of the musical's thematic integrity.

Wasserman has explained that in developing the story idea he became as fascinated by the details of Cervantes' life as by the escapades of Don Quixote.[6] Cervantes was an *hidalgo*, the Spanish term for landed gentry, and, in Cervantes' situation, a man with land but no money. Forced to go elsewhere, Cervantes became an adventurer. He joined the army but fought very little since

FIGURE 6.4 • *Man of La Mancha* with Richard Kiley as Cervantes.

Courtesy of The New York Public Library, Astor, Lennox, and Tilder Foundation.

he was almost immediately wounded and captured by pirates. Soon after returning to Spain, he protested against the tyranny of the Church and for up-
holding his moral principles was thrown into prison several times, once by the
Inquisition that subsequently excommunicated him. Professionally, Cervantes
wanted to become a successful playwright; but although he wrote more than
forty plays, they were mediocre at best. He was fifty-eight and badly in need
of money when he wrote the novel *Don Quixote*. After its publication in 1605,
he received some little recognition but financial success eluded him until the
publication of Part II of the novel ten years later. Sadly, Cervantes had only
a year to enjoy his new found prosperity. He died in 1616, the same year as
William Shakespeare.

Man of La Mancha opens on a dark, vaulted stone common room in a
Spanish prison. Soldiers enter, bringing two men. The first is a pudgy servant
carrying an old straw trunk; the second is Cervantes, a tall, thin, middle-aged
man who holds a large, wrapped package. When the soldiers exit, a group of
prisoners threaten Cervantes and his servant. To fend off the inevitable rob-
bery of his few possessions, Cervantes offers to entertain them by reciting the
tale of a certain gentleman named Don Quixote. With the help of his servant,
he opens his trunk, changes costume, applies makeup and is transformed to
Don Quixote. His servant, of course, becomes Sancho Panza, and during the
course of the play, prisoners assume a number of different roles.

In this way, the musical is structured as a play-within-a-play. Reality is the
Spanish prison with its inmates, soldiers, and masked men of the Inquisition.
Fantasy is the story of Don Quixote that unfolds with dialogue, music, song,
and dance. Many scenes from the novel are included—the Don's first adventure in the musical is his fight with the windmills—but a number of roles are
changed. The role of Aldonza, for example is expanded. She is the prostitute
who the Don sees as Dulcinea, the virtuous noble lady of his dreams.

THE BALLET:

DON QUIXOTE, WRITTEN AND CHOREOGRAPHED BY GEORGE BALLANCHINE (1904–1983) WITH MUSIC COMPOSED BY NICOLAS NABOKOV (1903–1978)

This particular ballet, written in 1965, is one of several that have been adapted
from Cervantes's book.[7] The novel's plot translates easily into a ballet libretto
(narrative) and meets other requirements as well. A number of the novel's
characters have roles that can be adapted for male dancers, ballerinas, and the
corps de ballet. In a ballet, the narrative with all its moods must be interpreted
through dance and music, since there is no dialogue or song. A full scale ballet
includes solo dances, at least one **pas de deux** (dance for two), ensemble
dances, dances with the *corps de ballet*, and **divertissements** (diversions). Although *divertissements* are a part of ballet (and some operas) they do not enact
or interpret the story as other dances must; they are exactly what their name
implies, diversions.

Don Quixote is in three acts with a prologue that takes place in the Don's study. There, the hero, surrounded by stacks of books on chivalry, has fallen asleep while reading. He dreams of rescuing a girl from a dragon, and his dream becomes a dance. When he wakens, Sancho Panza helps him change costume, and his adventures begin.

The second act includes the scene of a palace ball, a scene that is not in the novel. By adding it, choreographer George Balanchine was able to include *divertissements* and make them appear as entertainments performed for guests at the ball. One such dance is a ballet adaptation of a Spanish Gypsy Flamenco dance, and others are adaptations of Renaissance social dances.

FIGURE 6.5 • Ivan Wogy and Cynthia Gregory in *Don Quixote*.
© Linda Vartoogian.

The final scene presents the kind of somber, almost ritualistic performance that is so effective in dance. It begins with a *pavanne,* a slow, stately Renaissance dance, performed as the Don lies dying. When the *pavanne* ends, the Don's last dreams materialize in a series of short dances. He envisions hooded Inquisitors burning his books; he sees various people encountered during the course of his adventures and also the people of his village; and, for the last time, he rests his eyes on Dulcinea, the noble lady of his dreams who has appeared to him as so many different women. Slowly, as his dreams become as real as the close friends standing at his side, the ballet ends.

PORTRAITS OF EVIL

The novelist Joseph Conrad wrote that "A belief in the supernatural source of evil is not necessary; men alone are quite capable of every sort of wickedness."

The two plays summarized in the next several pages portray evil much as Conrad saw it: as a distinctly human trait. Shakespeare's arch villain Richard III may be a monster king, but the schemes he hatches are his own, and he plans them with the concentrated skill of an expert chess player. Moreover he enjoys every minute of the game. Richard is fascinating to watch, especially since he is not a one-dimensional character but a man gifted with intellect and wit—a murderer with a sense of humor! Richard III lived during a time when the Divine Right of Kings was an accepted fact. This is the belief that the right to rule comes directly from God, not from the people. People could unseat unpopular rulers, and occasionally they did, but they usually replaced them with others of royal blood.

There is no royalty in Lillian Hellman's drama *The Little Foxes.* Her characters are successful American entrepreneurs living at the turn of the nineteenth century. They are perhaps best described as "exploiters of the earth," a more contemporary term than "Divine Right." Like Shakespeare's Richard, Hellman's characters make a game of their schemes, except that their plans revolve around business. Success in business governs their lives, justifies their actions, shapes and strengthens their egos, and—in their estimation—raises them above other people.

ELIZABETHAN THEATER

If you lived in sixteenth century London and wanted to see a play you had several choices. You could attend one of three private theaters that catered largely to the aristocracy but admitted anyone with the price of a ticket or you could buy a much less expensive ticket at any of the larger public theaters. London had eight public theaters located beyond the city limits on the south

FIGURE 6.6 • A model of the interior of the Globe Theatre. The model is based on research of John Cranford Adams, former President of Hofstra University. Courtesy of Hofstra University.

side of the Thames River, in an area where you would also find cock-fighting and bear-baiting pits and brothels. Theaters had names like The Rose, The Fortune, and The Globe, where Shakespeare's actors performed (fig. 6.6). All advertised their plays with handbills and on performance days hoisted flags that could be seen from across the river.

Theater buildings were slightly different in size and overall shape, but most were large, three-storied wooden structures with roofed galleries that enclosed three sides of an open space called the yard. At the far end of the yard stood the roofed stage. Tickets were priced according to accommodations that could vary from standing-room only in the yard to benches and private boxes in the galleries. From all accounts, the theaters were comfortable, attractively decorated, and even quite sumptuous. Stage scenery was simple but adequate, but costumes were lavish. Since authenticity was not a consideration, costumes followed prevailing fashions except for ghosts or fantasy characters. Music, song, and dance were incidental to most plays, but were included, nevertheless, because audiences expected more than acting and dialogue. Trumpet fanfares heralded every play's performance and established a tradition that continues for most Shakespearean productions even today.

Other customs would probably seem quite strange to you. You would, for example, find all female roles played by young men since women were not allowed on the English stage. You would find that all performances were matinees since theaters were required by law to close before dark. You would find the audiences a cross-section of society that included aristocratic ladies and gentlemen, many wearing masks; university students; guild members; shopkeepers; and laborers and peasants. The noise and commotion would probably shock you. Elizabethan audiences were known to be quite rowdy during performances, and vendors hawking fruit, wine, ale, and beer added to the din.

THE ROYAL VILLAIN:

RICHARD III, BY WILLIAM SHAKESPEARE (1564–1616)

When the play begins, Richard's older brother, Edward, is king but is seriously ill. Since Clarence, the middle brother, is next in line for the throne, Richard hatches a scheme to pit Edward against Clarence. The scheme works: Clarence is murdered and Edward conveniently dies. To strengthen his position, Richard decides to marry the very rich Lady Anne, widow of a prince he murdered several months earlier. In Act I, Scene II, Richard approaches the Lady Anne as she follows the funeral procession of her father-in-law who was also murdered by Richard. Sword in hand, Richard orders the procession to halt. Appalled by his callousness, Lady Anne turns first to the guards and monks in the funeral cortege and then to Richard, crying out:

> O, gentlemen, see, see! dead Henry's wounds
> Open their congeal'd mouths and bleed afresh!
> Blush, blush, thou lump of foul deformity;
> For 'tis thy presence that exhales this blood
> From cold and empty veins, where no blood dwells;
> Thy deed, inhuman and unnatural,
> Provokes this deluge most unnatural.
> O God, which this blood madest, revenge his death!
> O earth, which this blood drink'st revenge his death!
> Either heaven with lightning strike the murderer dead,
> Or earth, gape open wide and eat him quick,
> As thou dost swallow up this good king's blood,
> Which his hell-govern'd arm hath butchered!

Lady Anne voices a medieval superstition that a victim's wounds bleed anew in the presence of the murderer. Calling on God, she curses Richard, calling him the butcher of both her husband and father-in-law. In her fury she curses any woman he might take as wife. Ironically, Lady Anne curses herself, for Richard has decided to marry *her*. This he accomplishes by alternately cajoling, flattering, threatening, and professing his love for her. In a scene that continues to perplex audiences and Shakespearean scholars alike, Lady Anne acquiesces. After she accepts his ring, Richard stands alone on stage and muses gleefully to the audience:

> Was ever woman in this humor woo'd?
> Was ever woman in this humor won?
> I'll have her; but I will not keep her long.

Richard is crowned king, but his triumph brings no peace. To remove every possible threat to his throne he orders the murder of his two nephews, mere children already imprisoned in the Tower of London. Lady Anne also dies of unknown causes, leaving Richard free to marry his niece. As one heinous crime follows another, news of Richard's reign of terror reaches the Earl of Richmond in France. He sets sail for England, determined to fight Richard. Their battle takes place, and with its outcome the play concludes.

Richard epitomizes an evil that is neither amoral nor psychopathic. Richard knows right from wrong but he chooses what is morally wrong because he enjoys, actually relishes, every second of the crimes he commits. He admits as much, unabashedly, to the audience in a number of soliloquies. Unlike Franz Becker in the film M (p. 137), a psychotic who cannot help what he does, Richard never loses control. What, then, is the cause of such deviant behavior? Shakespeare makes no excuse for Richard's actions, but he does offer a possible explanation—or rather he allows Richard to explain in his soliloquy in the first scene of Act One. Richard, standing before the audience, describes his appearance:

> I, that am curtail'd of this fair proportion,
> Cheated of feature by dissembling nature,
> Deformed, unfinish'd, sent before my time,
> Into this breathing world, scarce half made up,
> And that so lamely and unfashionable
> That dogs bark at me as I halt by them;
> Why, I in this weak piping time of peace,
> Have no delight to pass away the time,
> Unless to spy my shadow in the sun
> And descant on mine own deformity:
> And therefore, since I cannot prove a lover,
> To entertain these fair sell-spoken days,
> I am determined to prove a villain
> And hate the idle pleasures of these days.

The man who stands before the audience is a prince, a brave soldier, an excellent swordsman, a man with a brilliant mind, but a man so deformed "That dogs bark at me as I halt by them." The audience is left to decide if Richard's words explain his obsession with evil and his lust for power. His words would seem to rationalize his actions, but do they excuse them?

Some actors playing Richard have emphasized his deformity by portraying him as hunchbacked, palsied, limping, or with a withered arm and hand. Other actors have opted to downplay his deformity by limiting it to a stooped shoulder, a nervous twitch, or facial tic (fig. 6.7a,b). Actors have also interpreted his personality in various ways; some have played the role with a feral, nervous cunning, others with wit and malice.

What of the real King Richard III? History records no villainy of any sort either before or during his reign, and his portraits reveal no physical deformity

FIGURE 6.7a • Stacy Keach as King Richard in *Richard III*.
Courtesy of the Shakespeare Theatre, Washington, D.C. © Joan Marcus.

whatsoever. He did marry Lady Anne and she was a widow, but their marriage was a love match of long duration. The only evidence of deception seems to have occurred with Clarence, the middle brother who is assassinated early in the play. The real Clarence tried to prevent Richard's marriage to Lady Anne, and it is possible his actions were motivated by jealousy since Lady Anne had inherited enormous wealth and property. The disappearance of Richard's two young nephews from the Tower of London is based on fact, but no one knows what actually happened to them or who was responsible.

FIGURE 6.7b • Sir Lawrence Olivier as Richard III.

THE BOURGEOIS VILLAIN:

THE LITTLE FOXES BY LILLIAN HELLMAN (1906–1984)

This play's locale is a small southern town in the year 1900. Its title is from "Song of Solomon," 2:15: "Take us the foxes, the little foxes, that spoil the vines, for our vines have tender grapes." The play's characters are two middle-aged brothers named Ben and Oscar Hubbard and their sister, Regina Giddens, an attractive, intelligent, and strong-willed woman of about forty. As owners of Hubbard and Son's, an assortment of businesses started by their grandfather, Ben and Oscar literally own the town where they live. Ben is a confirmed bachelor and the smarter of the two brothers. Oscar is married to Birdie, a kindly but pitiful woman who lives mostly in the past and who peppers her conversations with talk of the once great plantation that had been her childhood home. Birdie and Oscar have a son, Leo, a dissolute and rather dim-witted young man who works in the bank owned by Regina's husband Horace Giddens. The Giddens's seventeen-year-old daughter Alexandria (Zan) is a pleasant girl closely attached to both parents. Other characters are Addie and Cal, the Giddens's two black servants and Mr. Marshall, a Chicago financier who appears only briefly in the first scene but whose business venture is the catalyst for the play's action. Marshall has agreed to build a cotton mill in the town—with the stipulation that Ben, Oscar and Horace will each invest $75,000.

When the play opens, Regina Giddens is giving a farewell dinner party for Mr. Marshall to celebrate the proposed venture (fig. 6.8). After he leaves, she informs her brothers that since they need Giddens's money to retain controlling interest in the mill she will see that they get it—but only if she and Horace get forty percent of the profits instead of a third. Regina has, it seems, dreams of beginning a new and very rich life in Chicago. Ben, barely able to disguise admiration for his sister's spirit, says, "You're holding us up, and that's not pretty, Regina, not pretty but we need you." He reminds her, however, that since Horace has been hospitalized in Baltimore for the past five months and has not responded to their letters, they need a firm commitment. Regina assures them that *she* will get Horace to come home.

In Act II Horace returns. He cannot walk unaided, he is medicated and must keep a bottle of medicine nearby in the event of a heart attack. Once they see the seriousness of Horace's condition, Regina and her brothers waste no time in discussing the business of the mill. A physically drained but still mentally alert Horace asks Ben some rather pointed questions, and Ben's answers reveal heretofore undisclosed details about the mill venture. Ben boasts of the bargain he made with the governor for free water power, "You'd think the governor of a great state would make his price a little higher." He also reveals the assurances he made to Mr. Marshall that mill wages will be half the wages of Northern mill workers. Horace, barely able to hide his anger, responds, "Sure, and they'll take less than that when you get around to playing them [black and white workers] off against each other. You can save a little money that way, Ben. And make them hate each other just a little more than

FIGURE 6.8 • Original cast of *The Little Foxes* that starred Tallulah Bankhead as Regina.

Billy Rose Theatre Collection, The New York Library for the Performing Arts, Astor, Lenox, and Tilden Foundations.

they do now." Ben merely laughs, then gloats, "Marshall said to me, 'What about strikes?' I say to him 'What's a strike? I never heard of one. Come South, Marshall. We got good folks and we don't stand for any fancy fooling.' " Horace cannot listen to any more. He tells Ben flatly that he is not interested in *any* more deals with the Hubbards. At this point, Regina explodes. Horace, nearly faint from exhaustion now, retreats to his bedroom. Regina follows him upstairs, shouting at him and arguing nonstop.

Meanwhile, Leo, who works in his uncle Horace's bank, has told his father and his uncle Ben that Horace has $88,000 in bonds in a safety deposit box that he seldom opens. Ben and Oscar seize the opportunity. Spitefully, Ben tells Regina they no longer need her money! A few days later, Horace learns of the theft. He confides to Regina, then astonishes her by saying he will not prosecute her brothers and nephew since he intends to make out a new will leaving the stolen bonds to Regina—and everything else to their daughter Zan. Regina's disdain for her husband flares into the hatred that has kindled for so many years. In a scene remarkable for its cruelty, she tells Horace how much she detests him. On and on she spews her venom until Horace, gasping for breath, reaches for his medicine bottle. It falls to the floor and breaks. When he begs her to get a second bottle upstairs in his room, Regina hesitates.

This is the play's climax: all dramatic action has led up to this moment, and the resolution of that action—the play's **dénouement** (day noo mahn)—depends on what happens in this scene. The audience, at this point, knows that Regina hesitates because she is mentally weighing her plans against Horace's life or death. The audience knows what Regina is thinking, but it does not know what she will do.

Hellman's play is a complex web of relationships. Regina and her brothers—the trio of foxes—are shrewd, tough, mean-spirited and compulsively ambitious. To them, life is a business, a game they enjoy playing against outsiders and each other. Ben admires Regina for holding out for forty percent: her win, his loss. Regina, too, enjoys the game. Near the end of the play, when Ben says to her, "You get farther with a smile, Regina, I'm a soft man for a woman's smile," she answers with a sly warning, "I'm smiling, Ben, I'm smiling because you are quite safe *while* Horace lives . . ." Near the play's end, Regina makes an offhand remark to Ben that causes the audience to examine her actions from a slightly different perspective. She quips, "Ah, Ben, if papa had only left me his money."

Other characters and their relationships provide colorful contrasts: the strong Regina against the weak Birdie; the smart, conniving Ben against the obtuse and abusive Oscar; the naive yet bright and sincere Zan against her dull and spineless cousin Leo, and the efficient and commanding Addie against the more docile Cal. Every one of these characters is essential. The roles of Zan and Addie, although minor, perform a specific function. One of Hellman's biographers, Katherine Ledderer, refers to Zan and Addie's dialogue throughout the play as "choral," clearly equating their roles with that of a Greek Chorus.[8] One of Addie's comments is a direct reference to the moral issues the play addresses:

Yeah, they got mighty well off cheating niggers. Well, there are people who eat the earth and eat all the people on it like in the Bible with the locusts. Then there are people who stand around and watch them eat it. Sometimes I think it ain't right to stand and watch them do it.

Thirty-four years after the initial production of *The Little Foxes* in 1939, Lillian Hellman wrote in her book *Pentimento* that the characters in the play were fictional but based, nonetheless, on members of her own family. Her relatives were prosperous Southerners who had moved North for greater prosperity, and as Hellman describes them, they were people obsessed with the gamesmanship in making money. Hellman admits that the play's favorable reviews actually depressed her because she felt audiences and critics had missed the point, so to speak: ". . . I had meant the audience to recognize some part of themselves in the money-dominated Hubbard's; I had not meant people to think of them as villains to whom they had no connection."*

If audiences and critics in 1939 missed that point they did not hear Ben's revealing and prophetic remark to Regina:

The century's turning, the world is open, open for people like you and me ready for us, waiting for us after all, this is just the beginning. There are hundreds of Hubbard's sitting in rooms like this through the country. All their names aren't Hubbard, but they are all Hubbard's and they will own this country someday. We'll get along.

COMIC PORTRAITS

Comedy in Western drama has been shaped by farce, satire, and commedia dell'arte (comedy of professional players). Characters in a **farce** are superficial and usually stereotypical, and the humor in a farce arises from plot complications that are contrived, ridiculous, and often based on mixed-up identities. Acting is boisterous and involves some type of broad physical activity: actors might hide under beds or in closets, chase each other around the stage; or perform **slapstick** routines. Farce was popular among ancient Romans, and its place in current television situation comedies would seem to prove its longevity.

Satire ridicules or exposes human shortcomings and foolishness. Its humor is more verbal than physical for it tends to criticize with wit. It, too, is an ancient form. The Greek dramatist Aristophanes (air i STOF uh neez) wrote a number of satirical dramas. One, *Lysistrata*, is a pacifist play in which the women of Athens become so tired of war they agree, as a last resort, to abstain from sex until government leaders sign a peace treaty. Some of the play's scenes include elements of farce, but overall, the play is a satire on governments more eager to make war than peace.

Commedia dell'arte began in Italy as farce, but it evolved into a distinctly unique form after the mid-sixteenth century. It became popular very quickly and spread from its native Italy across most of Europe. *Commedia*

---

*Source: Lillian Hellman, *Pentimento*, Little, Brown and Company, Boston, MA.

dell'arte actors worked without written scripts, preferring instead to improvise both dialogue and action around a brief plot outline discussed beforehand. They could work in this manner because each actor always played the same stock character in every play. One such character was Pantalone, an old man, usually unkempt, often miserly, and always lecherous. Other stock characters were a pair of young lovers and *zanni*, a pair of servants, one shrewd and the other stupid. Artecchino, for example, was originally the name of a servant who wore a costume covered with patches but who evolved into the more familiar Harlequin with his diamond-patterned costume and sad face. *Commedia dell'arte* actors made whatever role they played uniquely their own by devising specific *lazzi* (actions) to suit it. Lazzi could include verbal puns, exaggerated mannerisms and gestures, acrobatic routines, juggling, and clown tricks.

MOLIÈRE AND HIS AUDIENCE

Molière (mole-ee-air) (1622–1673) and Shakespeare are considered two of the greatest playwrights in the history of drama: Shakespeare acclaimed for his tragedies and Molière for his comedies. Although Molière lived a full century after Shakespeare, like the English bard, he was both an actor and playwright and had a long and prosperous career.

Molière's true name was Jean-Baptiste Poquelin. His father was a prosperous upholsterer and furniture maker in Paris, but it was his grandfather who nurtured his love of theater by taking him to see the French and Italian comedies that were performed regularly in the city. Molière was educated at the College of Clermont and later studied for the law. At nineteen he fell in love with a twenty-one-year-old actress named Madeleine Béjart. Three years later he quit the law, changed his name, and together with Madeleine, now his mistress, and several members of her acting family, started a troupe called the *Illustre Théâtre*. The venture failed, and Molière was jailed for debt until his father paid his bills and obtained his release. Afterward, Molière left Paris with Madeleine and her family, joined a traveling troupe of actors, and for thirteen years toured the French provinces.[9]

These were the years when he perfected his art. In addition to acting, he became the troupe's director and producer. Although he performed in tragedies and later wrote several—with disastrous results—eventually both his acting and writing evolved into a new and different style of comedy. Along the way, however, both farce and *commedia del'arte* were major influences on his work. Both forms of comedy were extremely popular in France and were performed regularly by Molière's troupe. When the troupe finally returned to Paris their performance of the farce *Le Docteur amoureax* (The Doctor in Love) caught the attention of King Louis XIV. The following year, when they performed Molière's own play *Les Précieuses ridicules* (The Precious Damsels) they won not only the King's favor but the public's praise.

With this, his third play, Molière turned drama in a new direction by creating a comedy of character and manners that exposed the frailties and follies of human nature. Molière's characters have weaknesses so obsessive, behavior so deviant that their actions affect everyone and everything around them. Their own faults turn them into laughable caricatures. Molière's biographer, Gertrud Mander, writes:

> Molière understood the comical drama of human life as arising from conflict in social and personal relationships. This approach was in opposition to the traditional view of comedy, which called for the execution of mere surprises in plot by superficially delineated characters.[10]

Molière's audiences, like Shakespeare's, consisted of aristocrats, bourgeoisie, and peasants, and he made them all laugh at themselves. Everyone in his audiences knew *someone* who behaved like the characters in his plays. *The Precious Damsels,* for example, was written at a time when ladies of the court considered it fashionable to speak in a pretentious and highly affected manner. The play is about two young bourgeois women who assume what they consider to be courtly manners. In their search for suitable husbands, they are both snobbish and foolish; and the men they fancy are about as "real" as the men in modern day romance novels. This play was a tremendous success, but there were other plays that brought censure instead of applause. *Tartuffe*, a comedy that exposes religious hypocrisy, was written at a time when overstated public displays of piety had become fashionable. Its plot concerns a sanctimonious minister with a misplaced fervor for money and other men's wives. French clergy considered the play an attack on all religion and banned its performance. It was finally reinstated after several rewrites and the King's approval, but the clergy's animosity toward Molière remained until his death, denying him even a burial service.

A COMEDY OF CHARACTER AND MANNERS:

THE MISER BY MOLIÈRE

The Miser is the story of Harpagon, a wealthy, sixty-year-old widower who loves money. When the play begins, Harpagon has arranged to marry his daughter, Élise, to Anselm, a man his own age, only because Anselm will marry the girl without receiving a dowry. What Harpagon does not know is that Élise loves Valère, his valet. Harpagon also has a son Cléante, who rebels against his parsimonious father by becoming a spendthrift. Unfortunately, his debts have sent him to an anonymous and unscrupulous moneylender who, as the audience learns later, is his own father. Harpagon, meanwhile, has decided to take a wife for himself and is negotiating with the matchmaker Frosine for a beautiful and very young woman named Mariane. Mariane, however, is in love with Cléante, who loves her, too.

FIGURE 6.9 • *The Miser.*
Courtesy, The Guthrie Theatre, Minneapolis/St. Paul.

The play takes place in Harpagon's large, expensive house where paint is peeling off walls, where old ugly furniture is in disrepair, and where horses in the stable are bony and ill-fed. Because Harpagon refuses to spend money for a wig, the actor playing the role is usually made up with thin wisps of lank grey hair that hang down around his ears. Usually he is dressed in threadbare breeches with a slovenly shirt that might have once been white. Everything sags including his socks. When Harpagon asks the matchmaker Frosine whether the beautiful, young Mariane might not prefer a younger man, she assures him that youth could never compete with this "magnificence of old age" (fig. 6.9). Hypocrisy? Of course. The entire play moves along on wheels of lies and deception, scheming and cheating. Duplicity is the only way to live with, work for, or do business with Harpagon. The man assumes that because money is so important to him, it is equally important to everyone; therefore everyone wants to steal from him. He calls his strongbox "beloved," and fondles it lovingly. His most intimate, private moments are spent with his strongbox, never with people. When the box turns up missing, he goes absolutely berserk.

Molière, who loved to do stand-up comedy routines with audiences, played Harpagon in the original production, and in a scene the playwright obviously wrote with himself in mind, Harpagon stands alone on stage haranguing the audience. First, he accuses other characters of the theft, then he mistakes his own hand in his pocket for a thief's. After this bit of farce, he mounts a verbal attack on the audience, railing at them for stealing his box. Finally exhausted by his tantrum, he falls down, presumably dying; but, of course, he soon recovers and goes off to search for his "beloved."

From the first to the last scene, Harpagon's character never changes. When he learns that his son Cléante is in love with Mariane, he is jealous and never once paternal; and when he sees that Mariane loves Cléante he is petulant, deciding finally to give her up only because it is cheaper than paying for a wedding!

A MODERN-DAY COMEDY OF CHARACTER AND MANNERS:

SPEED THE PLOW BY DAVID MAMET (1947–   )

David Mamet, following in the tradition of Molière, writes comedies of modern-day character and manners. One of his early plays, *Sexual Perversity in Chicago*, first performed in 1976, satirizes a sexually liberated generation. He followed this play with *American Buffalo*, the story of small-time crooks operating out of a Chicago junk yard. His next drama, the film *House of Games*, makes a none-too-subtle comparison between a psychiatrist who writes a "best seller" and a gang of con men. In Mamet's play *Glengarry Glen Ross*, the con men are real-estate salesmen peddling Florida swampland, and in *Speed the Plow*, they are hustling Hollywood movie executives.

Mamet's characters are usually unsavory and their language vulgar, but their counterparts in life do exist. Mamet is a master at writing the empty phrase and pretentious comment. His characters talk *past* each other while expounding like experts on absolutely nothing. They excel at mediocrity. Mamet gives them dialogue that is fast paced, idiomatic, and riddled with glib remarks and clichés. In the words of the British drama critic Robert Cushman: "Nobody alive writes better American."

Mamet's comedy is rarely farcical. Plots are usually based on problems brought about by the characters' own shortcomings. Characters are often so busy trying to dupe others they are easily outwitted by people like themselves. This kind of interaction creates the thematic substance of Mamet's plays, for these are people who fail to connect. They may pretend to connect; they may want to form relationships that have some depth of feeling, but they are just too shallow.

Mamet's satire is apparent in the play's title taken from a fifteenth century saying "God, speed the plow," meaning grant success to this endeavor. What is this endeavor? A twenty-four hour option on a movie script about prison buddies, a movie exactly like the ones that showed a profit last year, and a movie that a bankable star wants to make. It can't lose. Charlie Fox, an independent producer, is selling it to his old friend Bobby Gould, who is now Head of Production for a major studio. Bobby loves the deal but can't greenlight it until Ross, the head of the studio, gets back from New York the next morning. That cuts the time on Charlie's twenty-four hour option very close, but he agrees to wait rather than take it to another studio.

Both men are in their early forties and dressed in Rodeo Drive suits and jewelry. Their dialogue is filled with banal comments and platitudes plus one revealing statement in which they both readily admit to having no qualms about "whoring" for money. Periodically, Charlie slips into fantasies about the wealth this film will bring him, and Bobby fishes for compliments by whining about the decisions he is forced to make and the people who only want to *use* him. He continually whines about the scripts that clutter his desk, waiting to be read. One in particular is his nemesis: a "courtesy read" requested by Ross. It is, of course, a book with absolutely no potential for film, a novel with the ponderous title *The Bridge; or, Radiation and the Half-Life of Society. A Study of Decay.* At one point, Charley picks it up and reads aloud, causing both men to laugh at its pretentious, quasi-scientific gibberish.

When the men ask for coffee it is served by Karen, a temporary replacement for Bobby's secretary. Karen is cute, very cute, but finding the coffee machine was difficult for her and making Bobby's luncheon reservation was impossible. Before Charlie leaves, he bets Bobby five-hundred dollars that he can't get her in bed. When Karen steps back into Bobby's office to talk about his luncheon reservation, she describes herself with a word that she repeats not only here but throughout the entire second act. The word is "naive." Bobby, while expounding on "art" and "artsy," keeps grumbling that people are always using a "hook" to get him to do something for them. What he does for Karen is ask her to read the radiation book and report back to him at his apartment that evening.

She loves it! She tells Bobby what a wonderful movie it would make and how much *she* would like to work with *him* when he produces it. She reads excerpts aloud, then proceeds to discuss—somewhat disjointedly but in the best New Age jargon—such profundities in the book as *change, fear, signs, God,* and *power,* especially "power," a word she keeps repeating along with "naive." Bobby is both befuddled and intrigued, because while Karen's dialogue is philosophic, her body language is not. The seduction scene moves into reverse.

In Act Three the next morning, Charlie learns the awful truth: that Bobby is going to film the radiation book. Charlie wheedles, implores, threatens, and when words fail, knocks Bobby down and pummels him. It is ten minutes before the scheduled meeting with Ross, and in desperation Charlie asks Karen to come into the office. He then proceeds to unmask this very cute, very seductive, and very naive secretary—or is she naive? Mamet leaves some doubt.

By the play's end, the buddy movie is reinstated, Bobby and Charlie's friendship is restored, and off they go to their meeting with Ross. Already they are picturing how their names will appear in the film credits.

PERSPECTIVES ON LOVE: EAST AND WEST

"All mankind love a lover." Neither fact nor fiction corroborates this optimistic statement by the poet and essayist Ralph Waldo Emerson. About the same time England's Queen Elizabeth I executed the man she loved, Shakespeare's star-crossed lovers Romeo and Juliet met their deaths on the stage. In France a century later, a middle-aged Molière married the much younger sister of Madeleine, his mistress for many years; and the younger woman proceeded to make the playwright's life absolutely miserable.

Love, nevertheless, remains a popular and consistent theme world wide. The course of love, however, reveals that manners, customs, and codes affecting it are inconsistent and determined far less by emotions than by variables of time and society. Reading *Rain on the Hsiao-Hsiang* you may find it difficult to empathize, much less sympathize, with the heroine who returns to her husband. In modern America, her decision would be controversial to say the least, but this heroine lived in thirteenth century China where, as her husband reminds her, "the husband is the wife's heaven."[11]

CHINESE THEATER IN THE YUAN DYNASTY (1279–1368)

China had private and public theaters a full two centuries before Europe. China also had wandering troupes of male and female actors. Private theaters were a part of the court and therefore restricted to nobility, but public theaters existed in all large cities. Like the Elizabethan theaters that were still far in the future, Chinese theaters, flying flags and banners, were located in districts specifically set aside for entertainment. Stages were roofed and in some buildings the galleries on either side. Stage scenery was sparse and actors' make-up subdued, but costumes were as lavish as expenses allowed.

Chinese drama was structured by a combination of song, dance, and dialogue. The style of acting was more formal than realistic and included pantomime and acrobatics. Both dialogue and songs were in verse. Small ensembles of musicians played cymbals, wooden clappers, drum, lute, and a zitherlike instrument. Most plays were written in four acts, but occasionally a prologue or an additional short act called a "wedge" was added. The dramatic climax occurred in the last act and was followed by a winding down—the **denouement**—of the action. Dramatic roles were based on stock characters, and leading roles always featured singers.

The Yuan dynasty began with Kublai Khan, conquerer of China, strong leader, and generous patron of the arts. Among the artists welcomed at his court was the woman painter Kuan Tao-Shen (see fig. 2.43). Playwrights were especially favored at court, and during this short-lived dynasty, more than 700 plays were written and performed.

In Yuan dramas, the plots and characters are based on myth, legend, and history. Oriental scholar J. I. Crump, who translated *Rain on the Hsiao-Hsiang*, furnishes this information about the play's background:

> As with so many Yuan dramas this one is an amalgam of history and legend. There was a Chang T'ien-chueh exiled in Southern Sung times, but the tribulations that he and his daughter undergo here come partly from item #14 in the *Ch'ing-shih* (a collection of literary language fiction edited by Feng Menglung [ca. 1620] which revolves around some verse written on the wall of a posthouse by a young woman) and the composer's imagination. The story still remains popular, and there is an act in Peking opera of today called 'At the Lin-chiang Posthouse' which is based on this Yuan drama.[12]

RAIN ON THE HSIAO-HSIANG,

ATTRIBUTED TO YANG HSIEN-CHIH

When the play begins, Chang T'ien-Chueh, a widower and a minister of the state, is traveling with his eighteen-year-old daughter Ts'ui-Luan. The journey has been long, and since it is an official trip he is anxious to complete it. While they wait for a boat to cross the River Huai, he is asked to make sacrifice to the Spirit of the Huai. This he refuses to do, replying that a high government official like himself does not bother with such practices. Soon after they sail, high winds and waves wreck the ship. The father is rescued, but his daughter is missing. He searches but cannot find her. Sadly he continues his journey, but not before offering rewards to anyone finding the girl.

Luckily, Ts'ui-Luan is rescued by a kindly fisherman who takes her to his home. Because the village where he lives is remote, word of the search parties never reaches him. Ts'ui-Luan, in the meantime, believes her father has drowned, but her grief is partially softened by the affection she feels for the old fisherman. The fisherman can only assume that Ts'ui-Luan is now an orphan and, concerned for her welfare, introduces her to his nephew Ts'ui T'ung and suggests they marry. Ts'ui T'ung is a handsome and intelligent young man, and she agrees to the match. They are betrothed before he leaves the village to take examinations for government employment in a distant city.

In the city, Ts'ui T'ung meets and favorably impresses an official, who sends a delegate to inquire if the young man is married. Slyly Ts'ui T'ung answers the delegate's question with a question, "If I am married, what then? Or what if I'm not married?" The delegate replies that if he is married he will be offered a government post, but if he is not married, he will be offered both the post and the high official's daughter. Ts'ui T'ung marries the daughter.

Three years pass and Ts'ui-Luan and the old fisherman hear nothing from Ts'ui T'ung. The fisherman urges the young woman to go to the city in search of her husband. After arriving there she is directed to Ts'ui T'ung's house, where she announces herself as his wife. Ts'ui T'ung is more angry than surprised. In front of his second wife, he denounces her, calls her nothing but a slave in the house of his uncle and also a thief. He has her arrested, put in chains, and beaten. He orders her sent away to a penal colony and suggests to her guard that it would be better if she never arrives.

Fortunately, the guard takes pity on the bleeding, bruised woman. In a scene where they travel across a dismal, rain-drenched countryside, she sings a short, plaintive song:

> The feelings of Heaven must be drawn by the heart
> strings of
> man
> For here
> Upon my face the many tracks of tears that
> overflowed my
> eyes.
> (she speaks)
> Oh, heavens, heavens.
> (then sings)
> And down them
> Run teardrops as numerous as the drops of this
> autumn
> rain.

Guard and prisoner stop at a posthouse where, as the audience already knows, one of the travelers is Ts'ui-Luan's father. Expectantly, the audience watches as father and daughter almost miss each other but are finally reunited. Within minutes the father's joy turns to rage when he sees what has happened to his beautiful daughter. He orders her husband arrested.

In the play's final scene, the kindly fisherman begs Ts'ui-Luan to save his nephew, her husband, from execution. At first she refuses, then reconsiders for two very logical reasons. The first stems from her gratitude and love for the old fisherman, but the second is based on the realities of Chinese society. Quite simply, she realizes that after this tragedy, no one else will marry her—she has lost face—consequently she is better off with the husband she has than none at all!

The second wife, who has the stock role of "bad woman," gives the play's ending a surprising twist. After accepting her punishment to serve as Ts'ui-Luan's servant, she reminds the heroine, "If I must be your maid, then maid I will be—but let me warn you, a maid can go anywhere in a home a wife can, so do not imagine you will have a husband all to yourself!" Translator J. I. Crump includes this wry comment about the dialogue: "Here, in the marsh-mallow and marzipan of the conventional happy ending, one suddenly comes upon a razor blade!" [13]

Hardly a happy ending by today's standards, but the play reflects prevailing religious and social beliefs. The low position held by women in Chinese society did not negate love. The moral virtue of filial love—in this instance the love of two fathers—is a theme intended to balance or at least compensate for one husband's cruelty. It is, however, Chang T'ien-Chueh's excessive pride in his position and his refusal to sacrifice to the river god that brings down the wrath of a Taoist god. Ts'ui T'ung makes a similar mistake when he marries the official's daughter and remarks offhandedly, "Besides, it's better to cheat the gods a little than to let slip an opportunity."

Taoism and Confucianism were tremendous influences on Chinese thought and society. From the second century B.C. until the twentieth century, Chinese Civil Service examinations—like the ones Ts'ui T'ung takes in the play—were based on the teachings of Confucius. Confucianism also lent support to the rigid, stratified society that figures so prominently in the play. In the last scene, for example, the second wife's punishment is reduced because her father is a high official, yet she *must* accept some punishment because Ts'ui-Luan's father holds an even higher rank.

JAPANESE KABUKI THEATER

Japanese society was more feudalistic and stratified than China's. Because the noh theater, Japan's most ancient form of drama, was restricted to the samurai class, kabuki, meaning "song-dance-acting," emerged as popular drama early in the seventeenth century. Although kabuki originated with a woman temple dancer named Okuni, within twenty-five years the government issued an edict forbidding women to appear on stage. This ban gave rise to one of kabuki's most unique features, namely the **omnagatas**: male actors who specialize in performing women's roles.

A number of other features distinguish kabuki. Unlike the Chinese theater that relied on only a few simple props, kabuki scenery was—and still is—spectacular. Backdrops and sets are designed with great skill and ingenuity. A revolving stage has been in use for almost 300 years, and the **hanamichi** (flower-walk) is older still. The *hanamichi* is a long ramp leading from the stage to the rear of the theater (fig. 6.10). Its use for certain entrances and exits moves action away from the stage and into the audience proper—always with a highly dramatic effect. Make-up and costumes are elaborate and often fantastic. Certain villains paint their faces and arms with thick red lines meant to represent engorged veins (fig. 6.11). Actors' wigs are handmade and many costumes are silk and brocade, some with exquisite embroidery. In the past, such expensive costumes were allowed only in the noh theater, because class status determined what fabrics and colors could be worn. The rules were strict and so rigidly enforced, more than one kabuki actor was jailed for wearing costumes considered too luxurious.[14]

Until recently a ticket to kabuki bought an entire day's entertainment because a typical production included from three to five different plays. In past centuries, members of the audience might watch their favorite plays and then between plays or during long intermissions, leave the theater to visit nearby

FIGURE 6.10 • (Opposite) Kabuki stage with *hanamichi*.
Reproduced by Courtesy of the Trustees of the British Museum.

FIGURE 6.11 • (Opposite) Performers from The Grand Kabuki of Japan.
© Jack Vartoogian.

tea houses, bath houses, or other establishments of interest. Kabuki theaters were built in that section of cities referred to as the "pleasure quarter," a location not all that different from the public theater district in sixteenth century London.

Today, three categories of Kabuki plays are performed. Dance dramas that originated in the older noh theater make up the first category and are exactly what their name implies. Historical plays, the second category, describe the exploits and intrigues of warriors and nobles and are usually tragic. Domestic dramas, that can be tragic or comic, constitute a third category and largely concern problems encountered by commoners.

A MESSENGER OF LOVE IN YAMATO

BY MONZAEMON CHIKAMATSU (1653–1724)

Chikamatsu, considered one of Japan's greatest playwrights, wrote for both the kabuki and puppet theaters. What is perhaps most remarkable about his domestic dramas is the depth of his characterizations. His play *Koi Bikyaku Yamato Orai* (A Messenger of Love in Yamato) is based on the true story of a courier named Chubei who fell in love with a geisha and embezzled money to free her from bondage.

The play is in two acts and begins in the city of Osaka. An ensemble of wind, string, and percussion instruments "announces" the play's beginning just before the striped curtain is pulled to one side. On stage-right (from the audience's view, this is on the left) stands an open-walled geisha house. Umegawa, a beautiful geisha, sits demurely on the floor while Chubei, the young man who loves her and wants to free her from geisha servitude, talks to Jiemon, the proprietor of the house. Chubei, who works as a courier, does not have enough money to buy her freedom, but he does persuade Jiemon to wait before selling her to someone else. Since it was not considered proper in Japanese society for a man and woman to show affection in public, the actors playing Umegawa and Chubei must communicate their love with furtive and tender glances, a feat they accomplish brilliantly.

Kabuki acting seems highly exaggerated if judged by contemporary Western standards, but the style is intentionally formalistic rather than realistic. Dialogue is half-spoken, half-sung in a rhythmic intonation, and frequently lines of dialogue are punctuated by sounds of woodwind or percussion instruments. Actors' movements are choreographed like dances. When Umegawa walks across the stage, she glides with the short, mincing steps of Japanese women in ancient times. When she moves, her gown flows and swirls with every motion, and her hands flutter gracefully in the air. In a recent production of the play by The Grand Kabuki, the role of Umegawa was played by Tomotaro Nakamura, a young actor who is not, in the strictest sense, an omnagata since he performs both male and female roles. His illusion of femininity, however, was flawless. The actor playing Hachiemon, a rich man and Chubei's rival for Umegawa, was equally effective. He strutted around the stage and gestured with motions that left no doubt of his self-importance. When Hachiemon devised a scheme to eliminate Chubei, he postured boldly in front of the audience, sneered, and then stepped sideways with twisting, snakelike motions.

Hachiemon's scheme is to trick Chubei into breaking the seal on a courier packet containing gold. When his plot succeeds he hurries away to notify the authorities. To break a courier seal—even accidentally—was a crime punishable by death. Poor Chubei, realizing that nothing can change his fate, decides he might as well use the gold to save Umegawa. He tells her what he has done, and the young couple decide that with luck they may have a few days together; afterward, they will commit suicide. They tell no one their secret; and in a touching scene, Jicmon and the geishas gaily see them off on what they believe is a honeymoon journey.

When the curtain is pushed aside at the beginning of act two, the painted backdrop brings applause. It has the effect of a Japanese woodcut magnified many times: a scene of snow covered trees backed by distant mountains. High in the mountains, is a village where the couple have come to say good-bye to Chubei's father. Fate, however, is unkind, for the old man has already heard of his son's crime. He confides to Umegawa that he loves his son but will never be able to see him because of the dishonor. Umegawa brings

FIGURE 6.12 • *Kanegamisaki [The Cape of the Temple Bell]*. Tamasaburo solo performance. Japan Society, NYC
© Linda Vartoogian.

father and son together by placing a blindfold over the old man's eyes. Again, fate intervenes: the moment father and son clasp hands, the authorities appear. Now there is no escape. Chubei is sentenced to death. Slowly, snow begins to fall, and the audience is left with a Buddhist-like image of nature covering all traces of the human tragedy they have just witnessed.

OPERATIC THEATER

Opera, in its own way, is as spectacular as kabuki, although its dramatic and musical structure and its performing style are totally different. Think of opera as pure musical drama written to celebrate the beauty of the human voice. Operatic arias and ensemble pieces require virtuoso skills, and operatic choruses provide a multicolored background of male and female voices ranging from bass to soprano. Add to this a full orchestra and spectacular staging and costumes, and you have an exciting and important dramatic form.

Opera originated with the Camerata of Florence, a small group of Italian Renaissance Humanists who met regularly to study the literature, drama, and art of ancient Greece. Reading ancient manuscripts, they learned that music and song were essential to Greek drama. Descriptions in the manuscripts were vague, but this group of dedicated men decided to write and produce works they believed were similar to the ancient Greek dramas. Essentially, the Camerata combined choreographed movements with intoned dialogue and musical accompaniment. At first the plays were a novelty, but in time they developed into a completely new form. Through the years, as composers and librettists continued to write for this new musical-drama, early vocal intonation developed into **recitative**, which is the sung dialogue; solo songs became longer and more complex, developing into **arias**; and musical ensembles became full sized orchestras.

LA TRAVIATA (THE LOST ONE)

BY GUISEPPI VERDI (1815–1901)

La Traviata is a tale of the tragic romance between Violetta Valéry, a French courtesan, and Alfredo Germont, the son of a prosperous French family. Like *A Messenger of Love in Yamato*, it is based on a true love affair between the nineteenth century French writer, the younger Alexandre Dumas, and a courtesan named Marie Duplessis. Dumas broke off the relationship shortly before he left France for an extended trip with his father. He could not, however, forget Marie. He wrote to her admitting his mistake, but she died before he could return to Paris. Dumas wrote his novel *La Dame aux camélias* (Lady of the Camelias) shortly afterward, and later adapted it for the stage. This play so intrigued Italian composer Guiseppi Verdi (VER-dee) that he adapted it for opera.

The entire first act is staged in Violetta's home. Here, crystal chandeliers, silver candelabra, oriental rugs, gilded furniture, and expensive bric-a-brac provide an opulent background for the courtesan and her friends. Violetta is having a dinner party, and one of her guests introduces her to the very handsome Alfredo. When Alfredo is able to speak with her alone, he mentions his concern over her recent illness and confesses that he has loved her since the first day he saw her. "One happy, never-forgotten day," he sings. Violetta is flattered and obviously attracted, but much too cynical to believe him. Later, when the guests have gone, she reflects on his words. She sings the aria "Ah, perhaps it is he," that is a soliloquy sharing her innermost thoughts with the audience. She admits finding her own emotions perplexing and disturbing because she has never experienced love. With an abrupt shift in mood, she sings "Folly!" and fills a glass with champagne. "I must always be free," she sings, reminding herself of the kind of life she enjoys. Alfredo's voice, soft and distant, intrudes, repeating his love for her, but she counters cynically, "I must always be free."

The second act opens in Violetta's country house where she and Alfredo now live together. Her former bravado to the contrary, she and Alfredo are very much in love. Sadly, their idyl is destroyed when Alfredo's father visits Violetta and asks her to end the affair. His family's good name—including Alfredo's—is suffering, he tells her. When she realizes that her reputation could harm Alfredo, she returns to Paris, leaving him a farewell note.

The second scene in act two takes place at an elegant ball held in the house of Flora, another courtesan and Violetta's friend. This stage set is more opulent than the first. Violetta arrives with the Baron Douphol, the man who had been her "protector" when she met Alfredo. Soon, Alfredo arrives at the party, angry and jealous because he believes Violetta has jilted him for the baron. When he sees Violetta and the baron together, he insults her in front of everyone. This scene is remarkable for its extravagant dramatic and musical contrasts.

The third act takes place in Violetta's bedroom, where she lies dying. She reads a letter from Alfredo's father informing her that Alfredo has learned the truth and is returning to Paris. "Farewell to dreams of the past," she sings, remembering their short, wonderful time together. When Alfredo arrives, she gives him a locket with her picture and dies in his arms.

La Traviata is a romantic opera in every sense of the word. It is a tragic tale of idealized, romantic love, and it was written in the romantic style of the nineteenth century. This style is found not only in music and drama but in literature and the visual arts as well. It is a style marked by exuberance, idealism, imagination, and passion. Works of art in the romantic style, whether describing love or war, are beautifully, profusely sensuous, thus appealing directly to the emotions. This is why Verdi's music is so "right." His music soars to emotional heights and plummets to despondent and tragic depths. His music communicates, projects, intensifies all the visual imagery on stage. After you see this opera, it is almost impossible to think of Violetta or Alfredo and not remember the music of their story.

APPALACHIAN SPRING,

DANCE DRAMA BY MARTHA GRAHAM (1895–1991), MUSIC BY AARON COPLAND (1900–1990)

There is romance in the dance drama *Appalachian Spring* but nothing of the romantic style. The story is simple: a young pioneer couple are about to be married and begin their new life on a small farm. The theme is mythic in the sense that it embodies the excitement and joy, the fears and uncertainties felt by any young couple on their wedding day. Both story and theme unfold with the dance. This is modern dance, a twentieth century art form that began as a protest against the romantic style's excesses and classical ballet's rigid conventions.

Martha Graham, who was one of the innovators of modern dance, believed that dance gestures and movements originate with whatever idea or emotion the dancer experiences. Her concepts are easily perceived in *Appalachian Spring*. This dance drama was first performed in 1944, and it was a collaborative triumph for Graham and two other Americans: the composer Aaron Copland (kope land), who wrote the musical score, and the sculptor Isamu Noguchi (no GOO chi), (p. 78) who designed the set. The set—with no attempt at realistic depiction—suggests a farmhouse (fig. 6.13). It is mostly open-walled with prominent angled beams that cast long shadows. On a small porch is a rocking chair, simple and abstract in shape; and next to one of the walls a plain wooden bench. The entire set is designed so that the audience is able to see the dancers at all times.

Aaron Copland's musical score begins with sustained chords and a clarinet solo, and its mood is as soft and gentle as the morning in the country that it suggests. Slowly, a group of people walk on stage. A Revivalist preacher leads

FIGURE 6.13 • *Appalachian Spring,* 1944. Erick Hawkins and Martha Graham and Company.
© Arnold Eagle.

and is followed by the young couple he will marry, then a single pioneer woman, and an ensemble of four younger women who represent the Revivalist's congregation.

When this little group is positioned on stage, the drama commences with a series of solo dances that alternate with duets and ensembles. With each new dance, characters reveal individual personalities. The Revivalist, for example, stands back at first, slightly removed from other dancers and watching them. When it is time for him to preach, he dances a fire and brimstone sermon. Making wild and furious gestures with his arms, he takes wide leaps from crouched positions and repeats the leaps several times. When his four women followers join in, the dance becomes more sprightly. The music is lively country fiddle, square dance music.

The bride performs two solos. In the faster one, she moves among the wedding guests pausing in front of each person. Her movements are anxious and hesitant, almost as if she is asking these people soon to be her neighbors for their friendship and support. Later, when the bride dances with her husband, all hesitancy disappears. Their duet is joyful and confident. For this particular dance, Aaron Copland composed a series of variations on an old Shaker hymn called "Simple Gifts." The music is fitting and memorable. In the last scene, the music becomes hushed, instruments muted. Now the guests have gone, and the young couple stand together at the entrance to their home, as if looking toward the future they will share together.

VICTIMS AND SURVIVORS

In life, the true heroes, villains, and lovers are not likely to be kings or courtesans but quite ordinary people who struggle daily against the whims and tricks of fate. Russian playwright Anton Chekov (CHEH-kauf) believed that genuine tragedy is a wearing away, a slow rusting out of life itself. This, according to Chekov, is the tragedy experienced by people from every class of society: people who bumble along as best they can, occasionally tripping over their own uncertainties. These are the people you meet in his plays.

Chekov, together with playwrights Henrik Ibsen and George Bernard Shaw, brought realism to twentieth century drama. All three playwrights wrote about the problems encountered by ordinary people, much as kabuki playwright Monzaemon Chikamatsu had done two centuries earlier. There, however, any similarity ends because the three Western playwrights and their successors developed themes of strong social comment. Chekov's *The Cherry Orchard* describes the strata of Russian society in pre-Revolution times. Ibsen's play *A Doll's House*, written in 1879, concerns a woman who must break away from society's imposed role of wife and mother to find her own identity. Shaw's comic play *Major Barbara*, written in 1905, examines the concept of "corrupt" money from opposite points of view, one held by an idealistic Salvation Army worker and the other by a munitions manufacturer.

TWENTIETH CENTURY DRAMATIC STYLES

To enhance the image of life, realist playwrights eliminated the soliloquies and asides that require actors to address their audiences directly. Except for Ibsen's earliest plays, writers ceased using verse and wrote instead in plain speech that included colloquialisms and idioms. These changes in the literary content of plays required corresponding changes in the acting. As a result, directors and actors worked together with playwrights to bring a new perspective to the art of interpretative performance.

Realism, however, was only one of many dramatic styles that included symbolism, expressionism, constructivism, **absurdism,** and Epic Theater. Of these and other styles, the two that have had the widest and most long lasting influence are realism and absurdism. Absurdism has its origins in existentialism, a philosophy concerned with the search for meaning in what it considers an irrational and alienated world. First defined by Danish philosopher Soren Kierkegaard and later expanded by other philosophers, existentialism's basic premise is one of commitment to life. This means that a person develops a sense of self solely by his or her own choices and actions. Commitment infers that responsibility for any action rests solely on the individual and is not shared by society or family or any events that might be construed as fate.

Existential influences are apparent in the themes and structure of absurdist dramas. Alienation, futility, social disorder, and universal chaos are common themes. Characters are often symbolic or representative of a particular social class, profession, or personality type. Dialogue may be disoriented, disruptive, and inconsistent with the action; or it may include parables, allegories, and metaphors. Time and place in absurdist dramas are often unspecified: locale could be a nonspecific room or a public place such as a beach or a park, or it could be completely anonymous and unidentifiable. Although absurdist playwrights represent unique and highly individual styles, uniformly they present a world that is illogical, contradictory, uncertain, and—in a word—absurd.

PASSIVE VOICES:

THE CHERRY ORCHARD BY ANTON CHEKOV (1860–1904)

Realist playwright Anton Chekov wrote about Russia at the turn of the century: a Russia in transition with its old values and traditions already buffeted by strong winds of social change. He died before the old social order was swept away by Revolution, but he anticipated the change. Chekov was born a serf. When he was nine, his grandfather purchased freedom for the entire family with savings accumulated from years of hard work and trading. The young Chekov worked his way through school, graduated from medical school, and then became a writer.

The Cherry Orchard is his last play. It takes place the same year it was written, in 1904, on a large family estate in the Russian countryside. The estate's owner, Madame Ranevsky, whose given name is Lyubov, is an attractive, capricious, indecisive widow, and one of two major characters. The other is Lopahin, a businessman and former serf. Surrounding them are a host of supporting characters.

In the first act, Lyubov arrives home with her seventeen-year-old daughter Anya and an entourage of servants. Lyubov has lived abroad for many years, and this visit, while sentimental, is nevertheless occasioned by two traumatic events: her lover in Paris has just jilted and swindled her, and her extravagances have put the entire estate in financial jeopardy. Lopahin provides the only sensible solution when he suggests that she sell the cherry orchard, divide it into lots, and lease them for summer villas. He even offers her a loan. Lyubov, however, sees the long neglected cherry orchard as a thing of beauty filled with childhood memories. Also, the thought of summer people living nearby is—in her words—so "vulgar" she finds it difficult to make a decision.

When the first act ends she is undecided; when the second act ends she is still undecided. During the third act, she dines and dances with family and friends on the day the estate is auctioned off. Lopahin buys it. In the fourth act, most of the furniture in the big house is gone; Lyubov is packed and ready to return to her lover—who has had a change of heart; her daughter Anya is returning to school; and the play ends with poor old Firs, the family's eighty-seven-year-old valet forgotten and left inside the empty house.

Chekov's plot is neither complex nor suspenseful. The complexity in this drama—and it is complex—is in characters' interactions. These are people who do not so much *act* as *react* to life. Their conversations are filled with trivialities and are likely to take erratic detours. In one scene, Lopahin suggests selling the cherry orchard, but his sensible comments are interrupted by a dotty old family friend who asks Lyubov if she eats frogs when she is in Paris. Lyubov replies with a giggle that she eats crocodiles. Lopahin tries without success to get the conversation back on track, but it continues to wander, as directionless as the characters' thoughts.

Every scene is filled with stage business that adds another layer of complexity to the play. One character drops a bouquet; a second breaks a teacup; a third runs around looking for his galoshes. Even Lopahin, the most dependable, falls asleep over a book he is reading to help stay awake and, as a result, misses the train he was staying awake to meet. By the last act, the audience realizes Lopahin has missed something far more important than a train when his absorption with business causes him to overlook the woman who loves him.

Chekov's characters represent Russia's pre-Revolution, multi-layered society, and the cherry orchard is a symbol of the topmost layer. Lopahin, the hard-headed businessman who epitomizes the middle layer, sees the cherry orchard as nothing more than a profitable venture—until he buys it. Then he reveals a side to his character that even he may not have been aware of. Laughing, singing, and dancing, he shouts to everyone that his grandfather and his father should rise from their graves to see *him*, Lopahin, the boy who went barefoot in the winters, the serf who grew up on the estate, *now* its owner. He is ecstatic, but he forgets Trofimov's warning. Trofimov, an idealistic student and socialist, warns any and all who will listen that social change requires a corresponding change in attitude. Trofimov criticizes Lopahin's middle class, saying its members have none of the virtues of the aristocracy and all of their faults. He calls them crass and totally insensitive to the poor.

Who are the poor as defined by Chekov? People like Firs, a serf only recently freed and a very old man for whom the past seems more real than the present. Chekov's poor are laborers, servants, clerks, governesses: people who depend on the aristocracy for their support, meager as it is. Chekov's poor are workers, extremely class conscious and highly suspicious of anyone different from themselves like Lyubov's adopted daughter, who by association with the aristocracy no longer fits into any social class.

Chekov's picture of aristocrats is colorfully painted with words and actions. Like the cherry orchard, these Russian nobles have a charming, fragile beauty, but time and neglect have made them not only unproductive but a luxury society can no longer afford. Prophesying the fury of a Revolution that would bring about their demise, Chekov ends his play with the sounds of an ax cutting down the orchard.

REACHING THROUGH THE BARS:

THE ZOO STORY BY EDWARD ALBEE (1928–)

The Zoo Story is an absurdist drama about two men who meet in Central Park on a Sunday afternoon. First, the audience meets Peter, who sits alone on a park bench, reading a book. He looks about forty, and from the style of his clothes and eye-glasses, appears to be an executive of some sort. Jerry enters and walks directly toward Peter's bench. Jerry is somewhat younger than Peter; his clothes are rumpled and unkempt but otherwise quite ordinary. He stands directly in front of Peter and announces loudly that he has been to the zoo. Peter glances up from his book, then returns to it in an attempt to ignore the intrusive stranger, but Jerry persists.

This play is about contrasts. Peter, who is an executive in a publishing firm, lives in a nearby apartment with his wife, two daughters, two cats, and two parakeets. Jerry, who may or may not have a job, lives alone in a rooming house run by an alcoholic landlady with amorous intentions and a feisty dog. Jerry does most of the talking, but Peter's comments, although merely short answers to Jerry's questions, are extremely revealing. Very quickly, the audience understands that Peter's life is circumspect and very safe. Anything out of the ordinary is, as he admits, to read about, not to experience.

The play is in one act and, except for the last ten minutes, its action is compressed into dialogue. Peter never moves from the bench, and Jerry stands during most of the play. Occasionally Jerry takes a few steps, gestures erratically and kicks a few stones, but he actually moves about very little. Mostly he talks: about a childhood lacking warm family relationships; about his rooming house and its rootless, disconnected tenants; about his possessions that include, among other things, picture frames without pictures and a strongbox without a lock. Jerry tells how he is forced to avoid his thoroughly repugnant landlady; yet, at the same time, he reveals a desperate need to make some kind of connection, to form some kind of bond—if only with the landlady's dog.

Jerry's tragicomic story of the dog reveals the violence bottled up inside him, ready to explode when pressures of rejection reach a certain point. Peter adds to the pressure. No matter what Jerry says, no matter how bizarre the people he describes or how eccentric his behavior, Peter remains aloof. Peter *is* curious but it is obvious that he finds Jerry merely an afternoon's diversion. Peter is like people who experience the world through television: totally passive, he is remote, and alienated from life.

Violence erupts in the last ten minutes of the play, and what occurs is surprising because it contradicts the kind of behavior the audience has come to expect from Peter. From the first scene to the last, Jerry belittles whatever Peter has to say about himself or his family. Repeatedly, Jerry insults Peter, calling him among other things a "vegetable." Yet Peter barely reacts. If Jerry's intention is to force a confrontation, he fails. Not until those last ten minutes—and for only the most absurd reason—does Peter finally *do* something. Then, in a few seconds, violence blurs the line between victim and survivor.

THE COST OF SURVIVAL:

FENCES BY AUGUST WILSON (1946–)

Troy Maxon is a survivor. He is tough, resilient, hard. Yet there is humor in him and in the tall tales he spins for his friend and co-worker Jim Bono on Friday evenings when they sit on the front porch steps sharing a bottle. The time is 1957, the place any big city. The men are African-Americans, and they earn their Friday paychecks working as garbage collectors. Near the porch is a pile of lumber bought for a fence that never gets built (fig. 6.14). The fence was Troy's wife Rose's idea intended, Bono says, to keep people in, a way for Rose to hold on to the people she loves. Rose is a strong character, a stalwart woman in her forties. Her little family consists of Troy and their eighteen-year-old son, Cory. At one time, Troy's brother Gabriel lived with them, and he still visits nearly every day. Gabriel is a gentle but confused man who is mentally disabled from a head injury incurred in the war. Another visitor is Lyons, Troy's son from a first marriage, who drops by most Fridays for a loan.

Wilson's plot, like Chekov's, stems from the interaction of its characters. There is no single incident or event that determines the play's outcome. Wilson purposely eliminates suspense by providing the audience with broad hints of forthcoming action. That Troy, after eighteen years of marriage, is probably having an affair is alluded to by Bono in the first few minutes of the play. What the audience expects to happen to Troy and Rose's relationship does happen. The first act also prepares the audience for Cory's eventual break with his father. In the first scene, Troy tells Rose and Bono—in no uncertain terms—that he will not allow his son to play football, promises of a college scholarship notwithstanding.

This is realism that sustains your interest through ambivalence: what you think will happen and what you want to happen are at odds. As a dramatic technique, it works because Wilson's characters are, without exception, likeable people. Even Lyons, the weakest character, is understandable. True, he shows up on Fridays for a loan from Troy, but the lecture he gets along with the money is, at least, *some* attention from a father who was never around when he grew up. Cory, as the son of a second marriage, did have Troy around, but

FIGURE 6.14 • *Fences* by August Wilson, starring James Earl Jones. Courtesy Wm. B. Carter.

father and son are not close. When Cory asks his father if he likes him, Troy doesn't understand the word "like"; what Troy understands is the word "responsibility." This is a man who prides himself on surviving a sharecropper background and a prison term; this is a baseball player who was denied admittance to the major leagues because of his race; this is a man who, despite being illiterate, managed to get a job and a house and hang onto them both. For Troy, a home of his own, an eighteen year marriage, and a Friday paycheck represent stability and security. All this information is communicated by the play's text, but what its subtext tells the audience is that Troy is fifty-three years old and he needs something more.

August Wilson's play is not based on anything as simple as one man's midlife crisis. Wilson's portraits are penetrating psychological studies of people relating to each other and to society as a whole. Troy dominates his family, yet the more Rose and Cory try to understand him, the less they know him. For Troy, survival is paramount, and it means persevering—not only financially but emotionally—in a society that does not want him.

As a playwright, Wilson is committed to portraying the cultural milieu of his fellow African-Americans. *Fences* is the third in a series of plays that describes life among African-Americans living in different decades. *Jitney*, Wilson's first play in the series, takes place in the 1970s; *Ma Rainey's Black Bottom* in the 1920s; *Joe Turner's Come and Gone* in the teens; *Piano Lesson* in the 1930s; and *Two Trains Running* in the 1960s.

DRAMATIC ARTS LANGUAGE

Drama communicates through speech, acting, dance, and song. At one time these interpretative arts were never separated because drama's origins are in ritual: in the age-old celebrations that marked important passages through life, and in the reenactments of significant events. When ancient rites of worship and initiation merged with the myths and legends of storytellers, drama truly became a performer's art.

READING PLAYS

Because plays are written to be performed, the value of reading them is sometimes questioned, but reading offers a number of advantages. Since most professional performances take place in major cities or on university campuses, and then only for a limited time, reading a play may be the only means of experiencing it. When reading a play, *you* set the pace, taking time to reread or reconsider a scene or a line of dialogue. There is an added benefit, too: because scripts include few character descriptions or stage directions, you are compelled to be imaginative as well as analytical in your assessment. These are skills rarely used in combination.

POWERFUL WORDS, BEAUTIFUL SPEECH

Words have a double existence. Because they are read silently but spoken aloud, only live or recorded performances of drama reveal their full power. Shakespeare's plays, for example, are true masterpieces of language. Elizabethan English, so foreign to the modern ear, is rich with images and rhythms, and when composed by Shakespeare into a pattern of blank verse, the words are sonorous and beautiful to hear. Listen to this speech from *Richard III* in which Tyrrel tells how the murder of the two children in the Tower affected even the assassins who killed the young princes.

Richard III.
Courtesy of the Shakespeare Theatre, Washington, D.C. Photograph © Joan Marcus.

> Dighton and Forrest, whom I did suborn
> To do this ruthless piece of butchery,
> Although they were flesh'd villains, bloody dogs,
> Melting with tenderness and kind compassion
> Wept like two children in their deaths' sad stories.
> 'Lo, thus' quoth Dighton, 'lay those tender babes:'
> 'Thus, thus,' quoth Forrest, 'girdling one another Within their innocent
>   alabaster arms:
> Their lips were four red roses on a stalk,
> Which in their summer beauty kiss'd each other.
> A book of prayers on their pillow lay;
> Which once,' quoth Forrest, 'almost changed my mind;
> But O! the devil'—there the villain stopp'd:
> Whilst Dighton thus told on: 'We smothered
> The most replenished sweet work of nature,
> That from the prime creation e'er she framed.'

These are the words, the text of speech, but speech includes a **subtext** also. Subtext is the intent of words: the motives and reasons behind them. The most innocuous sentence can have any number of meanings depending on the way it is spoken. Consider Richard's words when he encounters his brother Clarence who is being escorted, under guard, to the Tower.

> Well, your imprisonment shall not be long;
> I will deliver you, or else lie for you:
> Meantime, have patience.

"Deliver" is a most significant word in this instance because Richard is behind the plot that sends his brother to the dreaded Tower. When Clarence exits, Richard offers this farewell:

> Go, tread the path that thou shalt ne'er return,
> Simple, plain Clarence! I do love thee so,
> That I will shortly send thy soul to heaven,
> If heaven will take the present at our hands.

COMPARISONS BETWEEN STAGE AND SCREEN

Stage performances have a spontaneity and rapport that film and television lack. To compensate, film and television establish an intimacy impossible to achieve on stage by moving audiences—vicariously with cameras—up to and sometimes directly into the action itself. A close-up camera shot puts audiences only inches away from an actor. For example, in the film version of *Richard III*, when Richard bids farewell to his brother Clarence, the film audience is positioned at Richard's shoulder.

Interior of the Tyrone Guthrie Theatre, Minneapolis/St. Paul. Sir Tyrone Guthrie's 1963 production of Chekhov's *The Three Sisters*.
Courtesy of the Guthrie Theatre, Minneapolis/ St. Paul.

FIGURE 6.15 • Glyndebourne building and grounds.
Photo courtesy of the Glyndebourne Festival Opera.

When *La Traviata* was produced at the 1987 Glyndebourne Festival in England under the direction of Peter Hall, one performance was videotaped. Three years earlier, this same opera had been made into a film by the stage and film director Franco Zeffirelli. Since both are available on videotape, they make an interesting comparison.

Attending a live performance at the Glyndebourne Festival is a singularly unique experience (fig. 6.15). The excellence of these summer productions is known worldwide. To reach Glyndebourne you must travel about fifty miles from London, into the English countryside of Sussex Downs. Every opera performance has a dinner intermission, and on warm summer evenings, most people picnic on the lawn. The theater is on the grounds of a large manor house owned by Sir George Christie, whose father built the theater fifty years ago.

Glyndebourne's setting does not appear in the tape of *La Traviata*. Neither the audience who watched this particular performance nor any part of the theater is visible. The orchestra appears for a few brief minutes before the credits appear on screen accompanied by the opera's overture. Edited along with the credits are images of camellias, candles, and other objects that are significant to the opera. In contrast, Zeffirelli's film *La Traviata* begins in absolute silence, and its credits roll across a background of Paris street scenes. The overture begins with a scene that Zeffirelli created and added to the opera. When the overture ends, Zeffirelli begins the opera as a flashback.

The filmmaker made additional changes to the opera, shortening some scenes and lengthening others. For example, Zeffirelli divided the first scene in Act II at Violetta's country house into a series of short scenes showing Violetta and Alfredo boating, riding in a pony cart, and walking, hand in hand, through the woods.

This visual authenticity is impossible to achieve on stage, but director Peter Hall's Glyndebourne production is spectacular in its own right. In Act II, Flora's party—a climactic scene—Hall emphasized two concepts essential to the opera's dramatic action: the licentiousness of courtesan life and the omnipresence of death (fig. 6.16). Guests at the party, enacting a mock bullfight, dance wantonly and drunkenly with Gypsy entertainers. But among the laughing, frolicking crowd stand others who are silent, their faces hidden by white death masks. A masked Alfredo stands among them.

Zeffirelli's interpretation of the scene is more lighthearted and has no fateful reminder of death. The dances, less frenzied, are superbly performed by members of the Bolshoi Ballet. It is important to remember, however, that these dances were filmed with as many takes and retakes as needed.

When comparing two different productions, the most crucial element is, of course, the performers. What do they bring to the role? Opera singers must act *with* the voice, a most difficult art. Violetta's role is particularly demanding because it requires a singer capable of performing passages composed for three different soprano voices: coloratura, lyric, and dramatic. Marie McLaughlin sings the role in the Glyndebourne production, and her interpretation is one of a sophisticated woman with great strength of character. Teresa Stratos, who plays Violetta in the film, gives a more fiery, emotional interpretation of the character. Alfredo, a role written for tenor voice, is interpreted by Walter MacNeil in the Glyndebourne production as a sincere and somewhat naive young man. Placido Domingo, in the film, is a more assertive and reckless Alfredo.

FIGURE 6.16 • Scene from Flora's party, *La Traviata*, 1988, Glyndebourne Festival.

Photo courtesy of the Glyndebourne Festival Opera. © Guy Gravett.

In the film, singers were never required to perform any one scene or song from beginning to end. This means, of course, that the demand on their voices was lessened considerably. This is an important consideration because the Glyndebourne production—like any stage production—commences from beginning to end. In addition, the film includes a number of scenes in which Violetta and Alfredo are not actually singing; their songs were recorded later and added to the soundtrack.

ACTING

Unlike television and film, there can be no retakes in a stage production, and there are no editors to cut mistakes or to put together a scene from the best of the retakes. When *Speed the Plow* opened in New York in 1988, its three-person cast was made up of Joe Mantegna and Ron Silver, both experienced stage actors, and Madonna, who is not. Without exception, drama reviewers referred to Madonna's performance as wooden. Her screen persona did not carry over to the stage, and as a result her poorly defined Karen weakened the play as a whole. Three drama reviewers felt the playwright shared the blame in not creating a believable character. In their opinion it didn't seem plausible that a young woman actually persuaded a cynical, middle-aged Hollywood producer to change his mind about a business decision.[15] In subsequent productions of the play in the United States, Canada, and Great Britain, experienced stage actresses proved them wrong.

Some drama scholars maintain that Shakespeare and Molière were masterful playwrights precisely because they were actors. Shakespeare shared some of his thoughts about acting in *Hamlet*, Act III, Scene II and *A Midsummer's Night Dream*, Act I, Scene II. Molière's biographer, Gertrud Mander, writes that today's audiences enjoy Molière's plays for the same reasons their original audiences did:

> They knew—and we learned—that from head to toe he [Molière] was a man of the theater who never wrote a single word that was not conceived of as being either spoken on a stage or translatable into mime, no scene which could not be rounded off into a theatrical whole, and no play which could achieve its ultimate effectiveness without being performed on a stage.[16]

Theories and Styles of Acting on Stage and Screen

One of theater's great dramatic coaches was Konstantin Stanislavsky (1863–1938), the Russian actor and director. Stanislavsky is known for his innovative work with the Moscow Art Theater and particularly for his collaboration with Anton Chekov on *The Cherry Orchard*. Stanislavsky developed what was later called **the Method**, a style of acting that appears completely natural but results from intense training. His ideas were adopted in the United States by Lee Strasberg, founder of the Actors Studio in New York. In essence, Stanislavsky emphasized three qualities necessary for a creative performance: concentration, communication, and preparation. To develop these qualities he felt it was necessary for actors to delve into their own past, searching for the emotion that would be similar to what they must feel in a particular role. Whatever occurred in their lives to trigger that emotion could be recalled and reexperienced. "Truth" as he described it comes from delving into one's own subconscious to search for the play's subtext. He also stressed the importance of ensemble acting and criticized the practice of dividing a cast into stars and subordinates.

There are perhaps as many theories of acting as there are styles. Actors in Great Britain study and train to achieve a more "external" approach that stresses the importance of observing people in daily life. Actors literally put together a character by combining the dress, movements and speech patterns, and little gestures and habits they observe in others. Training is rigorous and emphasizes concentration of a different type. In the British theater, concentration literally means "putting on a role," but never forgetting Sir Laurence Olivier's advice that "You always take off the part with your makeup."

In his book *On Acting*, Sir Laurence describes his preparation for the film role of *Richard III* (fig. 6.17a and b):

> I'd played Richard III so often on stage, I'd let ham fat grow on my performance. This I had to rid myself of before the cameras got me. So for two weeks I hid myself away and studied the text and my inflections anew, hacked off the extra flesh and the broad gestures I need on stage to reach the back row of the upper circle some fifty yards away, made myself lean and austere in my expressions, and changed the phrasing, because Richard would be flirting with the camera—sometimes only inches from his eyes—and would lay his head on the camera's bosom if he could. He is the classical actor's favorite bravura part, but he must be kept credible, and the bravura must be carefully marshalled. On the stage his hideous wooing of Lady Anne works brilliantly, but if it's too sudden on the screen the unaccustomed audience would cry, 'Hold it. We don't believe this!' So I cut the scene in two, let time pass and gave Richard two glorious climaxes: 'I'll have her, but I will not keep her long' and 'Was ever woman in this humour woo'd?/ Was ever women in this humor won?'
>
> I took Richard's misshapen body and his sardonic smile, but I wanted to convince the audience of the mind behind the mask. A demonic mind, a witty mind. But there's something of the flirting, calculating witch about him, so I kept the long black curls to insinuate this femininity. I made his nose and hump smaller than for the stage, but the nose was big enough to have the effect of concentrating the focus on the eyes . . .
>
> When an actor gets his eyes right on film, he's reached a peak in his professional life. Imagine my joy when Richard is trying to make Buckingham agree to the killing of the Princes in the Tower and I got just the right sort of hatred in his eyes on 'Cousin, thou wast not wont to be so dull./ Shall I be plain? I wish the bastards dead . . .'" (From Sir Laurence Olivier, *On Acting*. Copyright © 1986 by Wheelshare Ltd. Reprinted by permission of Simon & Schuster.)

Kabuki acting represents a style totally different from any type of Western acting. When a Kabuki actor prepares for a role he begins by studying the styles of his predecessors and then proceeds to create a performance that is uniquely his own but one based on tradition and experience. Kabuki places great importance on tradition, and some Kabuki families go back seventeen genera-

FIGURE 6.17a • Laurence Olivier without makeup standing next to Ralph Richardson as Lord Buckingham and John Gielgud as Clarence standing to the left in the film production of *Richard III*.
© The Hulton-Deutsch Collection.

FIGURE 6.17b • Lawrence Olivier being made up for his film role in *Richard III*.
© The Hulton-Deutsch Collection.

tions. Foremost, Kabuki acting is formalized. Its choreographed movements and intoned speech were discussed earlier in the chapter, but another stage technique is unique to Kabuki. Called *mie,* it is a combined gesture and expression performed at a climactic moment of the play. It begins when the actor takes a highly dramatic pose and pauses. While staring directly at the audience, he slowly assumes an intense expression—and then crosses his eyes.

DANCE

The two most influential forms of professional dance are ballet and modern dance. Ballet originated with elaborate entertainments of music, song, and dance performed at fifteenth century Italian courts. When the Italian Princess Catherine de Médici married King Henry II of France, she brought these musical dance-dramas with her. Several generations later, the French King Louis XIV instituted changes in court dance dramas that culminated in the founding of a school for professional dancers and musicians. Louis was an avid dancer. He was also an admirer and supporter of Molière, and in his attempts to improve the quality of amateur court productions, he commissioned Molière to write several comic ballets in collaboration with the composer Jean Baptiste Lully. He also hired professional dancing masters and set designers, sparing no expense since he was more than likely the star of his own productions. Louis, who had the title of "Sun King," was especially fond of dancing the role of Apollo.

Eventually, professionals replaced amateurs, and ballet developed into the dance performed today; nevertheless a few of its court origins remain. When dancers bow to their audiences with a graceful flourish, bending low to the ground, they perform what was once a royal curtsy, and when a ballerina's arms curve downward, they seldom touch her body but instead come to rest where—in centuries past—they would have touched a wide skirted gown. Some of ballet's intricate footwork also reveals its origins in the social dances of French and Italian courts.

The footwork, movements, and positions that make up ballet's vocabulary result from a ninety-degree turnout of the legs (fig. 6.18a and b). This is where ballet's grace and elevation begin. **Ballerinas** dance on *pointe,* a difficult and sometimes painful position requiring shoes with added toe support. Male dancers perform *demi-pointe,* rising only on the ball of the foot. Study and training in ballet begin early and involve mastering a series of traditional positions and movements. A few that are easily recognized are the *grand jeté* (fig. 6.19), and the *cabriole* (fig. 6.20).

Modern dance, as mentioned earlier, is a child of the twentieth century, and a rebellious child at that. Its pioneer was Isadora Duncan, a woman whose philosophy of freedom carried over into her life. Isadora believed that just as dancers must free themselves from the restrictions of the past, so, too, must

FIGURE 6.18a • Fifth position, arms low (en bas).
© Jack Vartoogian.

FIGURE 6.18b • Fifth position, on toe (sur les pointes), arms high (en houte).
© Jack Vartoogian.

FIGURE 6.19 • Grand jete—Natalia
Makarova rehearsing *Don Quixote*.
© Linda Vartoogian.

FIGURE 6.20 • Cabriole—Baryshnikov
in Eliot Feld's *Variations on America*.
© Linda Vartoogian.

women free themselves from restrictions of society (fig. 6.21). Unfortunately no films exist of Isadora dancing, only written descriptions. Other dancers shared Duncan's beliefs but expanded modern dance by adding techniques and styles uniquely their own. For the most part, these were dance pioneers who rebelled against what they saw as the restrictions of ballet. For inspiration, they turned to dances from the East and to ancient ritual and folk dances. As a result, modern dance evolved as an amalgamation of positions, steps, and movements (fig. 6.22a and b).

The strong belief in freedom of expression that gave birth to modern dance exists today. Every dance company has a style and flair of its own, yet within each company, certain individual dancers forge strongly personal styles that force them to break away and experiment anew by forming their own dance companies. Martha Graham was one of those dancers; Alvin Ailey was another (fig. 6.23).

FIGURE 6.21 • Edward Steichen, *Isadora Duncan at the Portal of the Parthenon,* 1921. Gelatin-silver print, 19 5/8 × 15 1/4".

Collection, The Museum of Modern Art, New York. Gift of the photographer. Reprinted with the permission of Joanna T. Steichen.

FIGURE 6.22a • Movements in modern dance with Twyla Tharp and Richard Colton in *Baker's Dozen*.
© Jack Vartoogian.

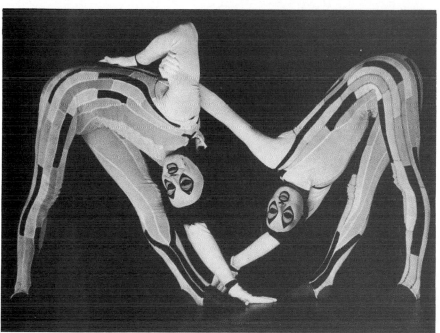

FIGURE 6.22b • Modern dance, Nikolais Dance Theatre.
© Jack Vartoogian.

FIGURE 6.23 • *Revelations*, Alvin Ailey and company.
Photo: © Jack Mitchell.

NOTES

[1]Rustom Bharucha, "Peter Brook's *Mahabharata*: A View from India," Theater, Vol XIX, Fall/Winter 1987, (New Haven, CN: Yale School of Drama/Yale Repertory Theater, 1987–88), pp. 6–11.

[2]Balwant Gargi, *Theater in India,* (New York: Theater Arts Books, 1962), p. 25.

[3]Aeschylus, *Prometheus Bound* in *World Masterpieces through the Renaissance.* Vol 1., 3d ed., (New York: W. W. Norton, 1973).

[4]Miguel Cervantes, *The Ingenious Gentleman Don Quixote de la Mancha,* Part I, trans. Samuel Putnam, (N.Y. The Viking Press, Inc., 1949) in *World Masterpieces through the Renaissance.*

[5]Dale Wasserman in *Great Musicals of the American Theater,* Vol. 2, ed. Stanley Richards, (Radnor, PA: Chilton Book Co., 1976), p. 367.

[6]Wasserman, pp. 367–68.

[7]For the complete description and history of this ballet and an earlier one, see George Balanchine and Francis Mason, *Balanchine's Complete Stories of the Great Ballets.* (New York: Doubleday & Co., Inc., rev. ed. 1977), pp. 176–83.

[8]Katherine Ledderer, *Lillian Hellman,* (Boston: Twayne Publishers, 1979), p. 41.

[9]See Gertrud Mander, *Molière,* trans. Diana Stone Peters. (N.Y.: Frederick Ungar Publishing Co., 1973). See also Karl Mantzius, *A History of Theatrical, Art,* Vol. IV *Molière and His Times: The Theater in France in the 17th Century,* trans. Louise von Cossel. (Gloucester, MS: Peter Smith, 1970).

[10]Mander, p. 26

[11]*Rain on the Hsiao-Hsiang,* trans. J. I. Crump, in J. I. Crump, *Chinese Theater in the Days of Kublai Khan,* (Tucson, AZ: The University of Arizona Press, 1980), p. 302.

[12]Crump, p. 246.

[13]Crump, p. 195.

[14]For an informative discussion of government regulations of theater see A. C. Scott *The Theatre in Asia,* (N.Y.: Macmillan Publishing Co., Inc., 1972), pp. 200–204.

[15]See Moira Hodgson, "Speed the Plow," *The Nation,* June 18, 1988. See also Jonathan Lieberson, "The Prophet of Broadway," *The New York Review,* July 21, 1988, and John Simon, "Word Power," *New York,* May 16, 1988.

[16]Mander, p. 19.

GLOSSARY

A

absurdist drama A drama that emphasizes the absurdity of life; often depicts conformity and meaningless activity as part of the human condition.

apse In church architecture, a semicircular recess, usually in the east wall.

aria A difficult operatic solo performed with musical accompaniment.

B

baldachin A canopy. The dome of Hagia Sophia is an example of the baldachin principle in which the dome appears to hang like a canopy above four arches.

ballerina The principal female dancer in a ballet company.

baritone In vocal music, the middle range of male voice.

barrel vault A series of continuous arches.

bass In vocal music, the lowest range of male voice.

birds-eye view A camera shot taken from directly overhead.

Buddhism A religion founded by Buddha (Siddhartha Gautama) in India during the sixth century B.C. Based on an Eightfold Noble Path, Buddhism aims toward the achievement of nirvana as a final salvation.

C

calotype Invented by Henry Fox Talbot about 1840, this was the first successful negative-positive process; the exposed image was made on sensitized paper and prints were developed from this negative.

camera-obscura Ancestor of the camera, this was originally a dark room in which outside images were projected onto a wall through a pinpoint light source. This evolved into a portable box with a lens and viewing screen.

canon A musical composition in which the melodic theme is presented, then repeated by laying it upon itself giving the illusion of many voices and harmonies.

cantilever A method of balance in which a projecting structure is supported only at one end.

capital In architecture, the top part of a column.

casting The process of forming sculpture by the use of a mold.

catharsis Used by Aristotle in his definition of tragedy to refer to the purging of emotions experienced by audiences.

chiaroscuro The technique of using light and dark tonal values to create the illusion of three dimensions on a two-dimensional surface.

choir That area of a church reserved for choir members and clergy and located between the altar and nave proper.

chorus In ancient Greek drama a group of men who sang, danced, and commented on the dramatic action. Also, singers or dancers performing as a group.

climax That part of a traditionally structured film or play in which the rising dramatic action peaks or the conflict nears the point of resolution.

close-up A camera shot of some object or detail about the size of an actor's head.

collodion This is a photographic process in which a solution of guncotton dissolved in alcohol and ether is applied to glass plate negatives.

commedia dell'arte The name means "comedy of professional players" and refers to a dramatic form originating in Italy during the sixteenth century and characterized by stock characters and improvised dialogue and action.

composition The organization of elements in a work of art.

Confucianism A philosophy founded by Confucious (Kung Fu-tse) in the sixth century B.C. and based on a system of ethics, a theory of government, and a set of social and personal goals.

cornice A projecting ornamental molding along the top of a wall; in Classical Style architecture, the projecting top section of the entablature.

corps de ballet The chorus of a ballet company.

crossing In a church, the interception of the transcepts and the nave.

cut An abrupt transition from one camera shot to another.

D

daguerreotype   Invented by Louis Jacques Mandé Daguerre in 1839, this photographic process forms an image on a metal plate that is then sensitized and developed.

danseur   A male ballet dancer.

dénouement   A French word meaning to "untie" or "loosen." In a traditionally structured drama it is the resolution of dramatic action that follows the climax.

divertissements   Dances in a ballet that are diversions, meaning they are not essential to the narrative or dramatic action.

documentary   A nonfiction film of real people and events.

E

editing   The process of joining camera shots into scenes and sequences and mixing and adding sounds onto the film soundtrack. See montage.

elements   The components or essential parts of a work of art.

ensemble   A small group of performers, usually from two to ten in number.

epic   A poem, story, novel, or film of unusual length and often heroic in nature.

exodus   The final exit of the chorus in an ancient Greek drama.

extreme close-up   A camera shot of minute details, for example an actor's mouth or eyes.

extreme long-shot   A camera shot taken from a great distance and giving a panoramic view.

F

falsetto   A technique used by a male singer to extend the upper vocal range.

farce   A type of comedy characterized by stereotypical characters, broad humor, and contrived or ridiculous plot complications.

flying buttress   A half-arch supporting a wall and transmitting the thrust of a vault to the ground.

frieze   In architecture, a decorated horizontal band.

fresco   Painting on plaster. With *buon* or true fresco, the pigments are applied directly to wet plaster; with *secco*, pigments are applied to dry plaster.

fugue   A musical composition beginning with a theme that is then repeated and altered in various ways, including augmentation, diminution, and inversion.

G

gamelan   An instrumental ensemble found mainly in Bali and Java.

gargoyle   In Gothic architecture, a waterspout carved in a grotesque shape.

genre   A term used to classify films having similar subjects or character types; for example, westerns, thrillers, and horror films.

glissando   A smooth sliding between pitches.

griot   The African counterpart to the European minstrel, a griot performs songs of a social, historical, and sometimes personal nature.

groin vault   A vault formed by the intersection of two barrel vaults.

H

harmony   Two or more pitches sounded simultaneously.

hemiola   A rhythmic grouping of six notes between 2 groups of 3 or 3 groups of 2.

Hinduism   A religion originating with the Aryan people who first settled in India. Hinduism is pantheistic, and Brahma, Shiva, and Vishnu are its major deities.

Humanism   A Renaissance philosophy based on the belief that people are free to make their own choices and chart their own destinies within the guidelines of their religion.

I

irony   Dramatic action that is the reverse of what would be expected; also dialogue in which the literal meaning is the opposite of what would be intended.

L

legend   A story, often of a heroic nature, that cannot be verified.

M

mastabas　Early Egyptian tombs; blocklike structures first made of brick and then made of stone.

match-cut　A cut between two scenes or subjects in which the second subject is similar in shape to the first or else appears in approximately the same area of the screen.

melody　A group of musical tones sounded in some progression that makes a meaningful whole.

medium shot　A camera shot that shows an actor from waist to head or the equivalent part of an object or scene.

metope　In Greek architecture, the area between roof joists that is often decorated with sculpture.

method　A style of acting that appears completely natural but results from intense training.

mie　A pose taken by a Kabuki actor in which he stares directly at the audience while crossing his eyes.

minstrel　A generic term for itinerant musicians of Europe during the Middle Ages.

modeling　In sculpture, shaping a form with a pliable material such as clay or wax.

montage　The term is applied to individual camera shots edited to intensify a scene's drama by showing condensed or lapsed time. In Europe this is a generalized term applied to all film editing.

mosaic　Small pieces of glass (tesserae), stone, or tile embedded in plaster.

motif　A recurring subject, idea, or design.

mudra　In India, symbolic hand positions.

myth　A story of unknown origin that attempts to explain some mystery of nature or human behavior.

N

nave　That part of a church between the main entrance and the choir; the longer section of the cross in a cruciform plan.

narthex　In a church, the enclosed passage between the main entrance and the nave.

Neo-Platonism　A Renaissance philosophy holding that talent is a gift from God and those people so gifted will strive for the perfection defined by Plato.

nirvana　In Buddhism, the final state in which all desires and passions are extinguished, leaving the soul free.

O

oculus　Open hole in a dome's center that provides light.

oil paint　A medium in which pigments are mixed with poppy or linseed oil.

omnagata　A kabuki actor who specializes in performing women's roles.

opera　An elaborate drama that is sung with musical accompaniment.

oratorio　An elaborate choral work often having a religious theme.

orchestra　In an ancient Greek theater, the circular open dancing area.

P

parodos　That part of an ancient Greek play where the chorus makes its entrance.

parallel editing　Editing that alternates between different scenes to show action occurring simultaneously.

pas de deux　In ballet, a dance for two.

pediment　The triangular space formed by a pitched roof.

pendentive　Concave, triangular-shaped masonry between a dome and the corners formed by its four supporting arches.

plainsong　Vocal music of the Middle Ages having a single melodic line; also called Gregorian Chant.

plot　The plan or progression of a dramatic work that includes the interaction of characters and incidents. See story line.

polyrhythm　Two or more rhythms performed simultaneously.

print　A work of art that is designed and duplicated a number of times by the artist or under the artist's supervision; woodcuts, etchings, and silkscreens are examples of prints. Also in photography, the positive picture or image obtained from a negative.

R

recitative Operatic speech that is sung in a rhythmically free vocal style.

relief A sculpture that is carved against a background and therefore viewed from the sides and front, unlike sculpture in-the-round.

rib One portion of an arch used to support a vault.

S

satire A type of humor that ridicules or exposes human shortcomings and foolishness.

scene A unit of dramatic action occurring at a single time or location.

sequence In film, a unit of related scenes and often having a definite beginning and end; similar to an act in a play or a chapter in a book.

serdab A hidden chamber in an Egyptian tomb used to hold a statue of the deceased.

slapstick A type of comedy involving boisterous or violent physical activity.

soliloquy A speech usually delivered by an actor alone on stage and often revealing a character's innermost thoughts or emotions.

sonata A musical composition usually consisting of three or four sections called movements.

soprano The highest range of female voice; designated as soprano, mezzo-soprano, and alto-soprano.

squinch A triangular, concave section of masonry between a dome and its square or polygonal base.

story line The plan or progression of a dramatic work that includes the interaction of characters and incidents. See plot.

stupa A large mound-shaped Buddhist shrine.

style A distinct manner or mode of expression or design.

stylobate In Greek architecture, the platform or top step.

subtext Implies a meaning or intent that is not stated openly.

suspension system Used in bridge engineering and architecture, this system suspends or hangs a bridge or roof from steel cables attached to support piers.

symphony A large multi-movement work for orchestra.

T

Taoism A religion founded in the sixth century B.C. by Lao-tzu, whose teachings are based on the *Tao Te Ching,* a book describing the Tao or "way."

tenor The highest range of male voice.

theme and variation A musical form in which a melodic theme is presented and then varied in a number of ways.

timbre Tone color; the quality of tone for a particular instrument or voice.

torana One of the four portals or gateways in the stone fence surrounding a stupa.

transept In church architecture, one of the arms crossing the nave in a cruciform plan.

truss Any wood or metal frame shaped by triangles.

U

urna The small tuft of hair, often depicted as a dot, in the center of Buddha's forehead.

ushnisha The protuberance on top of Buddha's head that signifies wisdom.

V

vibrato Slight fluctuation in a musical pitch.

W

watercolor A medium in which pigments, usually mixed with a gum binder, are thinned and applied with water.

Y

yakshi In India, a female fertility symbol.

SUGGESTED READINGS

A Century of Photographs: 1846–1946, Selected from the Collection of the Library of Congress. Compiled by Renata V. Shaw. Washington, D.C.: Library of Congress, 1980.

Akeret, Robert U. *Photoanalysis.* New York: Peter H. Wyden, Inc., 1973.

Alfred Stieglitz. Millerton, New York: Aperture, 1976.

Andrews, Wayne. *Architecture in America.* New York: Atheneum Publishers, 1977.

Ansel Adams: An Autobiography. Boston: Little, Brown and Co., 1985.

Anselm Kiefer. Exhibition Catalogue. Biennale Venedig l980: Deutscher Pavillon, Frankfurt, Bundesrepublik Deutschland.

Anton, Ferdinand and Frederick J. Dockstader. *Pre-Columbian Art and Later Indian Tribal Arts.* New York: Harry N. Abrams, Inc., n.d.

Attenborough, David. *The Tribal Eye.* New York: W. W. Norton & Co., Inc., 1976.

Baines, John and Malek Jaromir. *Atlas of Ancient Egypt.* New York: Facts on File Publications, 1958.

Balanchine, George and Francis Mason. *Balanchine's Complete Stories of the Great Ballets.* New York: Doubleday & Co., Inc., 1977.

Barnouw, Erik. *Documentary: A History of the Non-Fiction Film.* London: Oxford University Press, 1974.

Barthes, Roland. *Image, Music, Text.* New York: Hill and Wang, 1977.

Batterberry, Michael and Ariane Ruskin, eds. *Primitive Art.* New York: McGraw-Hill Book Co., 1973.

Bazin, André, *Jean Renoir*, Translated by W. W. Halsey and William H. Simon. New York: Simon and Schuster, 1973.

Bebey, Francis, Translated by Josephine Bennet. *African Music: A People's Art.* Westport, CN: Lawrence Hill & Co., 1975.

Bernard, Bruce, ed. *Vincent by Himself.* Boston: Little, Brown and Co., 1985.

Bolten, J. and H. Bolten Rempt. *Rembrandt*, Translated by Danielle Adkinson. Danbury, CT: Master Works Press, 1976.

Boulanger, Robert. *Egyptian Painting and the Ancient East.* New York: Funk & Wagnalls, 1965.

Bowers, Faubion. *Theatre in the East: A Survey of Asian Dance and Drama.* New York: Thomas Nelson & Sons, 1956.

Brandon, James R. *Brandon's Guide to Theater in Asia.* Honolulu: The University Press of Hawaii, 1976.

Brandon, James R. *Theatre in Southeast Asia.* Cambridge, MA: Harvard University Press, 1967.

Brockett, Oscar G. *History of the Theatre.* Boston: Allyn and Bacon, Inc., 1977.

Buckman, Peter. *Let's Dance.* London: Paddington Press, Ltd., 1978.

Bullard, E. John. *Mary Cassatt: Oils and Pastels.* New York: Watson Guptill Publications, 1972.

Burdick, Jacques. *Theater.* New York: Newsweek Books, 1974.

Cameron, John B. and Wm. B. Becker. *Photography's Beginnings: A Visual History.* Albuquerque, NM: University of New Mexico Press, 1989.

Cameron, Kenneth M. and Theodore J. C. Hoffman. *A Guide to Theatre Study*, 2d ed. New York: Macmillan Publishing Co., Inc., 1974.

Chase, Gilbert. *America's Music.* New York: McGraw-Hill Book Co., Inc., 1955.

Chernoff, John Miller. *African Rhythm and African Sensibility.* Chicago: The University of Chicago Press, 1979.

Childe Hassam. Exhibition Catalogue. Tucson, AZ: University of Arizona Museum of Art, 1972.

Chinese and Japanese Music-Dramas. Edited by J. I. Crump and William P. Malm. Ann Arbor, MI: Center for Chinese Studies, The University of Michigan, 1975.

Chissell, Joan. *Clara Schumann: A Dedicated Spirit.* New York: Taplinger Publishing Co., 1983.

Clark, Kenneth. *Landscape into Art.* Rev. ed. New York: Harper & Row, Publishers, 1976.

Complete Letters of Vincent Van Gogh. 3 vols. Boston: New York Graphic Society Books/Little, Brown and Co., 1958.

Coper, Jerry. *How to Listen to Jazz.* New Albany, IN: 1990.

Cottress, Leonard. *The Lost Pharoahs.* Westport, CN: Greenwood Press, 1951.

Covarrubias, Miguel. *Indian Art of Mexico and Central America.* New York: Alfred A. Knopf, 1957.

Crowther, Bosley. *The Great Films: Fifty Golden Years of Motion Pictures.* New York: G. P. Putnam's Sons, 1967.

Davis, J. G. *Temples, Churches and Mosques.* New York: The Pilgrim Press, 1982.

Davis, Phil. *Photography*. Dubuque, IA: Wm. C. Brown Publishers, 1990.

de la Croix, Horst, and Richard G. Tansy. *Gardner's Art through the Ages*. 6th ed. New York: Harcourt Brace Jovanovich, Inc., 1975.

de Micheli, Mario. *Siqueiros*. New York: Harry N. Abrams, Inc., 1968.

Diamonstein, Barbaralee. *American Architecture Now II*. New York: Rizzoli, 1985.

Dunstan, Bernard. *Painting Methods of the Impressionists*. New York: Watson-Guptill Publications, 1983.

Elsaesser, Thomas. *New German Cinema: A History*. New Brunswick, NJ: Rutgers University Press, 1989.

Emmerich, Andre. *Art before Columbus*. New York: Simon and Schuster, 1963.

Eugéne Atget. Millerton, New York: Aperture, Inc., 1980.

Ewen, David. *Opera*. New York: Franklin Watts, Inc., 1972.

Expressions: New Art from Germany. Exhibition Catalogue. Prestel-Verlag Munich & The St. Louis Art Museum, 1983.

Eyo, Ekpo and Frank Willett. *Treasures of Ancient Nigeria*. New York: Alfred A. Knopf, 1980.

Frank, Elizabeth. *Jackson Pollock*. New York: Abbeville Press, 1983.

Gargi, Balwant. *Theatre in India*. New York: Theatre Arts Books, 1962.

Gassan, Arnold. *Exploring Black & White Photography*. Dubuque, IA: Wm. C. Brown Publishers, 1989.

Gauss, Kathleen McCarthy. *New American Photography*. Los Angeles: Los Angeles County Museum of Art, 1985.

Geist, Sidney. *Brancusi: A Study of the Sculpture*. New York: Grossman Publishers, 1968.

Geist, Sidney. *Brancusi: The Sculpture and Drawings*. New York: Harry N. Abrams, Inc., 1975.

Goldron, Romain. *Ancient and Oriental Music*. New York: H. S. Stuttman Co., Inc. 1968.

Graham, Ronnie. *Stern's Guide to Contemporary African Music*. London: Zwan Publications, 1988.

Heyden, Doris and Paul Gendrop. *Pre-Columbian Architecture of Mesoamerica*. Translated by Judith Stanton. New York: Harry N. Abrams, Inc., 1973.

Hughes, Spike. *Famous Verdi Operas*. Philadelphia: Chilton Book Co., 1986.

Hunter, Sam. *Isamu Noguchi*. New York: Abbeville Press, Inc., 1986.

Hürlimann, Martin and Jean Bony. *French Cathedrals*. New York: The Viking Press, 1967.

Isaacson, Joel. *Observation and Reflection: Claude Monet*. New York: E. P. Dutton, 1978.

Jencks, Charles. *Architecture Today*. New York: Harry N. Abrams, Inc., 1988.

Kah-Ge-Ga-Gah-Bah (G. Copway), Chief of the Ojibway Nation. *The Traditional History and Characteristic Sketches of the Ojibway Nation*. London: Charles Gilpin, 1850. Reprint, Toronto: Coles Publishing Co., 1972.

Keys, Roger S. and Keiko Mizushima. *The Theatrical World of Osaka Prints*. Philadelphia: Philadelphia Museum of Art, 1973.

Kohrs, Karl Ed. *The New Milton Cross' Complete Stories of the Great Operas*. Garden City, New York: Doubleday & Co., Inc. 1960.

Kultermann, Udo. *New Directions in African Architecture*. New York: George Braziller. 1969.

Lederer, Katherine. *Lillian Hellman*. Boston: Twayne Publishers, 1979.

Lee, D. N. and H. C. Woodhouse. *Art on the Rocks of Southern Africa*. New York: Charles Scribner's & Sons, 1970.

Lindenberger, Herbert. *Opera: The Extravagant Art*. Ithaca, New York: Cornell University Press, 1984.

Lyle, Cynthia. *Dancers on Dancing*. New York: Drake Publishers, Inc., 1977.

Mander, Gertud. Translated by Diana Stone Peters. *Molière*. New York: Frederick Ungar Pub. Co., 1973.

Mantzius, Karl. Translated by Louise von Cossel. *A History of Theatrical Art* vol 4. Gloucester, MS: Peter Smith, 1970.

Masakatsu, Gunji. *Kabuki*. Tokyo: Kodansha International, (distr. Harper & Row), 1985.

Mathews, Nancy Mowll. *Mary Cassatt*. New York: Harry N. Abrams, Inc., 1978.

Meltzer, Milton. *Dorothea Lange: A Photographer's Life*. New York: Farrar, Straus, Giroux, 1978.

Mies van der Rohe. New York: Simon and Schuster, 1970.

Moody, Richard. *Lillian Hellman Playwright*. New York: Pegasus, 1972.

Munsterberg, Hugo. *Art of India and Southeast Asia*. New York: Harry N. Abrams, Inc., 1970.

Münz, Ludwig. *Rembrandt*. New York: Harry N. Abrams, Inc., 1984.

The Musée d'Orsay, Paris. Translated by Jane Brenton. New York: Harry N. Abrams, Inc., Publishers, 1987.

Noguchi & Rickey & Smith. Exhibition Catalogue. Bloomington, IN: Indiana University Art Museum Publication, 1970.

Olivier, Laurence. *On Acting*. New York: Simon and Schuster, 1986.

Pal, Pratapaditya, Janice Leoshko, Joseph M. Dye, and Stephen Markel. *Romance of the Taj Mahal.* Los Angeles: Los Angeles County Museum of Art and Thames and Hudson, 1989.

Panofsky, Erwin. *The Life and Art of Albrecht Durer.* 4th ed. Princeton, NJ: Princeton University Press, 1955.

Parker, Fred R. *Manuel Alvarez Bravo.* Pasadena, CA: Pasadena Art Museum, 1971.

Parsons, Michael J. *How We Understand Art.* Cambridge, England: Cambridge University Press, 1987.

Payzant, Geoggrey and Glenn Gould. *Music & Mind.* Toronto: Van Nostrand Reinhold Ltd., 1978.

Pickvance, Ronald. *Van Gogh in Saint-Rémy and Auvers.* New York: Metropolitan Museum of Art, 1986.

Prawer, S. S. *Caligari's Children: The Film as Tale of Terror.* Oxford: Oxford University Press, 1980.

Revelaciones: The Art of Manuel Alvarez Bravo. San Diego, CA: Museum of Photographic Arts, 1990.

Reich, Nancy B. *Clara Schumann: The Artist and the Woman.* Ithaca, NY: Cornell University Press, 1985.

Richard Meier Architect: 1964–1984. New York: Rizzoli, 1984.

Richards, Stanley, ed. *Great Musicals of the American Theatre,* vol. 2. Radnor, PA: Chilton Book Co., 1976.

Robertson, Donald. *Pre-Columbian Architecture.* New York: George Braziller, 1963.

Roland, Benjamin. *The Art and Architecture of India.* Baltimore: Penguin Books, 1953.

Romare Bearden: Origins and Progressions. Detroit: Detroit Institute of Arts, 1986.

Romare Bearden: The Prevelence of Ritual. New York: The Museum of Modern Art, 1971.

Rosci, Marco. *Leonardo.* Translated by John Gilbert. Danbury, CT: MasterWorks Press, 1984.

Sachs, Curt. *The History of Musical Instruments.* New York: W. W. Norton & Co., 1940.

Sachs, Curt. *The Rise of Music in the Ancient World, East and West.* New York: W. W. Norton & Co., 1943.

Sachs, Harvey. *Virtuoso.* New York: Thames and Hudson, 1982.

Safadi, Yasin Hamid. *Islamic Calligraphy.* Boulder, CO: Shambala, 1979.

Scharf, Aaron. *Pioneers of Photography.* New York: Harry N. Abrams, Inc., 1976.

Scott, A. C. *The Theatre in Asia.* New York: Macmillan, 1978.

Scruggs, Jan, C. and Joel L. Swerdlow. *To Heal A Nation: The Vietnam Veterans Memorial.* New York: Harper & Row, Pub., 1985.

Scully, Vincent, Jr. *Modern Architecture.* New York: George Braziller, 1967.

Seltzer, Daniel, ed. *The Modern Theatre.* Boston: Little, Brown and Co., 1967.

Sendrey, Alfred. *Music in the Social and Religious Life of Antiquity.* Cranbury, NJ: Associated University Presses, Inc., 1974.

Siegel, Marcia B. *The Shapes of Change: Images of American Dance.* Boston: Houghton Mifflin Co., 1979.

Silva, Fred. *Focus on The Birth of a Nation.* Englewood Cliffs, NJ: Prentice-Hall, Inc., 1971.

Sontag, Susan. *On Photography.* New York: Farrar, Straus and Giroux, 1977.

Steichen, Edward. *A Life in Photography.* New York: Bonanza Books, 1984.

Surjodiningrat, R. M. Wasisto. *Gamelan Dance and Wayang in Jogjakarta.* Jogjakarta: Gadjah Mada University Press, 1971.

Suzuki, Hiroyuki, Reyner Banham, and Katsuhiro Kobayashi. *Contemporary Architecture of Japan 1958–1984.* New York: Rizzoli, 1985.

Temko, Allan. *Notre Dame of Paris.* New York: The Viking Press, 1955.

Terry, Walter. *How to Look at Dance.* New York: William Morrow and Co., Inc., 1982.

von Hagen, Victor Wolfgang. *The Ancient Sun Kingdoms of the Americas.* Cleveland: The World Publishing Co., 1961.

Wager, Walter, ed. *The Playwrights Speak.* New York: Delacorte Press, 1967.

Walton, Guy. *Louis XIV's Versailles.* Chicago: The University of Chicago Press, 1986.

Ward, Geoffrey C. with Rick Burns and Ken Burns. *The Civil War: An Illustrated History.* NY: Alfred A. Knopf, Inc., 1990.

Weaver, Mike, ed. *British Photography in the Nineteenth Century.* Cambridge: Cambridge University Press, 1989.

Weaver, Mike. *The Photographic Art: Pictorial Traditions in Britain and America.* New York: Harper & Row, Publishers, 1986.

Willett, Frank. *African Art.* New York: Praeger Publishers, 1971.

Wright, Frank. *A Testament.* New York: Bramhall House, 1957.

INDEX

*Boldface terms/numbers here reflect boldface terms in the text.

345